OUR HEARTS
ARE AS ONE *fire*

OUR HEARTS
ARE AS ONE *fire*

AN OJIBWAY-ANISHINABE
VISION FOR THE FUTURE

JERRY FONTAINE

UBCPress · Vancouver · Toronto

29 28 27 26 25 24 23 22 21 20   5 4 3 2 1

Printed in Canada on FSC-certified ancient-forest-free paper (100% post-consumer recycled) that is processed chlorine- and acid-free.

LIBRARY AND ARCHIVES CANADA CATALOGUING IN PUBLICATION

Title: Our hearts are as one fire : an Ojibway-Anishinabe vision for the future / Jerry Fontaine.
Names: Fontaine, Jerry, 1955- author.

Description: Includes bibliographical references and index.

Identifiers:
Canadiana (print) 20200235753 | Canadiana (ebook) 20200243039 | ISBN 9780774862882 (softcover) | ISBN 9780774862875 (hardcover) | ISBN 9780774862899 (PDF) | ISBN 9780774862905 (EPUB) | ISBN 9780774862912 (Kindle)

Subjects: LCSH: Leadership. | LCSH: Indigenous peoples – Canada – Politics and government. | LCSH: Political leadership. | LCSH: Politics and culture. | LCSH: Social structure.

Classification: LCC HM1261 .F66 2020 | DDC 303.3/4—dc23

Canadä

UBC Press gratefully acknowledges the financial support for our publishing program of the Government of Canada (through the Canada Book Fund), the Canada Council for the Arts, and the British Columbia Arts Council.

This book has been published with the help of a grant from the Canadian Federation for the Humanities and Social Sciences, through the Awards to Scholarly Publications Program, using funds provided by the Social Sciences and Humanities Research Council of Canada.

Cover illustrations: Steve Pego | The crane is representative of ogimawiwin (*leadership*) and the seven eagle feathers represent seven grandfathers; the floral design on the banner reminds us that we all belong to Mother Earth. In the Circle of Life, blue is for the men, red for the women, and silver for the leaders that have left this world. The pipe represents communication with the spirit world.

UBC Press
The University of British Columbia
2029 West Mall
Vancouver, BC V6T 1Z2
www.ubcpress.ca

To the Special Circle

CONTENTS

FOREWORD

I COULD NEVER understand why Jerry Fontaine wanted me to write the foreword for his book, but I've learned that, as with most things, Jerry follows his own path, a path that has been guided by the spirit of three great leaders – Obwandiac, Tecumtha and Shingwauk. Maybe it's because I've been privy to Jerry's very personal journey for almost twenty years, a journey of uncompromising commitment, not only in studying and telling the history of these three great men and the Three Fires Confederacy, but in upholding their legacy. It is that journey that has culminated in the writing of *Our Hearts Are as One Fire*. Whatever the reason, I am honoured that he asked me to contribute to his efforts.

Jerry Fontaine, makwaa ogimaa, is unique in many ways: he speaks Anishinabemowin, is an inter-generational survivor of residential school, was an elected *Indian Act* chief, has been an advisor to indigenous communities and industry, and has obtained an MBA, an MA and a PhD. These are all significant achievements, especially when one considers that he was told time and again that he would amount to nothing. Jerry received guidance from his parents, leaders, traditional mentors and elders and understands that the past is intricately connected to the future – his actions in life illustrate this. As an *Indian Act* chief, his leadership style often applied the traditional approach to governance that this book explores, letting the citizens of Sagkeeng drive the direction of the community and conduct business as a sovereign nation – even going so far as to arrest INAC officials for breach of fiduciary duty, and provincial Sherrifs and the RCMP for trespassing. As a university instructor, he has gained a reputation as an innovator through his use of language, storytelling and ceremony in his classes, rather than textbooks. His classes, set up in clans, make decisions as a collective, in keeping with the way decisions were made by the Three Fires Confederacy.

It was this background, together with the single-mindedness – tied to tradition – with which he tackles all aspects of his life and informed the particular methodology that Jerry applied to both his research and his writing. He followed Ojibway-Anishinabe protocol, used ceremony to conduct his research and wrote from an Ojibway-Anishinabe perspective, rather than a western one, offering insight into their thinking, their positions and their decision making. This approach led him to direct descendants of Obwandiac, Tecumtha and Shingwauk, who, through the generations, have continued to speak of their ancestors and truth (the oral history). Jerry passed tobacco to those folks and they knew, through his following of traditional protocols, that they could trust him with their history. Through the stories they then shared with Jerry, he came to understand more fully how the land, language, ceremony, spirituality and clan system are all so very connected; that language is the doorway to the Ojibway-Anishinabe worldview. In turn, Jerry is sharing this understanding with the readers of this volume, and beyond.

I have come to believe that Jerry has a strong spiritual connection with Obwandiac, Tecumtha and Shingwauk. Certainly, his understanding of their approach to leadership, and their vision, has guided his every move, be it as *Indian Act* chief, an educator or a member of the great Anishinabek nation and, by extension, the Three Fires Confederacy. And I have often heard him muse on how – by gaining an understanding of the past, and traditional ways of leadership that are inclusive of all citizens – a contemporary leader could bring together the Anishinaabek of Manitou Aki (North America) to realize decolonization, separation and sovereignty, through truth, spirituality, the connectedness of language and land, and the authenticity that following these processes brings.

Our Hearts Are as One Fire is not only a lesson in history but also a reflection of Jerry's life, which has, in large part, been devoted to the vision of these great leaders, and the sovereignty and traditional way of life and commitment to the land that they fought so hard to protect. The truth is, there would be no treaties without Pontiac; no Canada without Tecumtha and Shingwauk. Jerry's worldview is based on all of this, and he reminds us, through his words and his use of Ojibwaymowin, that, at the root of it all, we are all human beings.

There can be no reconciliation without truth, so this is an extremely important and very timely work. Why? As the courts continue to reaffirm indigenous rights, as some governments, industries, NGOs and leaders make "reconciliation" a priority, and as indigenous people take a more aggressive role with regard to sovereignty and its obligations, it is critical that we understand the true history of this land and the importance of the great visionaries and leaders who are contemplated in this work.

LEE ANNE CAMERON,
kń sukinaqnxtət tkəłmilxʷ ła nkmapəlqs
(AN OKANAGAN WOMAN FROM HEAD OF THE LAKE)

AH-DI-SO-KAY ANISHINABEG

Storytellers

OVER THE LAST several years, I have had many discussions and visits with Bawdwaywidun Banaise (*Lac Courte Oreilles, Wisconsin*) and Charlie Nelson (*Roseau River, Manitoba*); Chief Lyle Sayers (*Garden River, Ontario*) and Darrell Boissoneau (Garden River, Ontario); Betty-Lou and Lana Grawbarger, Doreen Lesage and Dan Pine Jr. (Garden River, Ontario); Elmer Courchene, Rene Spence and Fabian Morrisseau (Sagkeeng, Manitoba); Tobasonakwut Kinew and Fred Kelly (Onegaming, Ontario); Patricia and Norman Shawnoo (*Kettle and Stony Point*, Ontario); William Johnson (*Mount Pleasant, Michigan*); Beatrice Menase'Kwe Jackson (Sault Ste. Marie Tribe of Chippewa Indians, Michigan); Steve Pego and Ben Hinman (Mount Pleasant, Michigan); and Jake Swamp (Akwesasne, *New York*) and other kitchi anishinabeg (*elders*) concerning the traditional and contemporary essence of leadership and governance. These discussions have focused on traditions, teachings, ceremonies and oral history specific to Obwandiac, Tecumtha, Shingwauk and the N'swi-ish-ko-day-kawn Anishinabeg O'dish-ko-day-kawn (*Our Hearts Are as One Fire*), known in English as the *Three Fires Confederacy*.

Mii i'i-way ojibway-anishinabe i-zhi-chi-gay-win. Zhigo mii'iw eta-go o-way neen-gi-kayn-dahn zhigo ni-gi-noon-dah-wah . . . Ahaaw sa. Weweni. Mii i'iw. (This is the Ojibway-Anishinabe way and as much as I know and have heard. This is all.)

MAAITAA

Prologue

**Makwa ogimaa n'di-zhi-ni-kawz, makwa n' doodem
zhigo ojibway-anishinabe niin sagkeeng doon-ji**
(My name is bear chief, I'm bear clan and an Ojibway-
speaking human being from "Where the River Widens.")

I WAS BORN an Ojibway-speaking anishinabe (*human being*), the
son of an Ojibway-Anishinabe man and an Ojibway-Anishinabe
woman, and grandchild of Ojibway-Anishinabe men and
women. And, of course, I'll die as one. I was told at a very
young age, kay-go-wah-ni-kayn andi-wayn-ji-ahn (*don't ever
forget where you come from*).

The journey I share in this book is sacred and ceremonial
in nature. Everything I've been shown and taught throughout
this journey has been done within the context of ceremony and

>>>>>>>>>

*English translations appear in the text or in endnotes the first time an
Ojibwaymowin term is used. An extensive glossary is included at the end
of the book.*

teachings, which embody the spiritual relationship between all living things and the universe. In this regard, everything shared within the context of this story is about our beginning and origin. So I begin with ah-se-ma-ke-wahd (*a tobacco offering*), calling upon the spirits and stories of Obwandiac, Tecumtha and Shingwauk. During the passing of tobacco and calling of the spirits, I ask to remain true to their visions and stories and give thanks to the ah-di-so-kahn-i-ni-ni-wahg/kwe-wahg (*sacred storytellers*) for sharing the ah-di-so-kah-nahg (*sacred stories*) and their di-bah-ji-mo-wi-nan (*stories of personal experience*), which help guide and teach us.

I'm sitting with Darrell Boissoneau of the nah-may doodem (*Sturgeon clan*), outside the lodge at his home in Ketegaunseebee (Garden River, Ontario). Darrell and I first met as *Indian Act chiefs* during the Assembly of First Nations national chief election in 1991.

We're talking about the ceremony that we'll begin shortly. Everything said about the ceremony is spoken quietly and in a thoughtful manner. This is a serious thing and we have to do it right and respectfully.

............**❝**............

We're sharing these stories this fine, warm evening – it's still spring on the calendar but it feels like summer here. We're inside a lodge that we constructed. This lodge was constructed by many people who came over to help build it . . . nephews and friends and so on. It was initiated by our sweat lodge chief, James Roach. So this is where we are this evening. This is where we come to teach, where we come to learn, where we come to share, where we come to feast, where we come to do sweat lodge and bring families of the community together. What is important is that we started off in the sacred ceremony.

First of all, tobacco was passed, then the pipe was lit, and it was lifted. These are important anishinabe protocols that you must follow because in the past this is how we began our ceremony and conducted ourselves. Unfortunately, we've forgotten that this is an important step when you want to share stories. Many anthropologists, researchers and other people who want to acquire the knowledge of our people come in without using this part of the research, the protocol of sharing. They forget the offering of gifts and the expression and importance of these ceremonies so that we can share them in a respectful and truthful way. So I think that starting off in this way is a good way.

Starting off in such a sacred and important way is again giving recognition to how we did things and that we will continue to do this in the future. It tells us how we're different and how we do things differently from western society. This acknowledges and validates our own methods of research, our epistemology, our pedagogy, because this is where our truth resides – within these lodges and the stories shared – from lifting the pipe and all the sacred symbols that belong to our people. Being inside this lodge is honourable and we'll be guided by our ancestors and the spirits that you asked to be with us this evening, so that at all times we will speak the truth.[1]

.... 𝄢 ....

OUR HEARTS
ARE AS ONE *fire*

Nitam igo

INTRODUCTION

OUR HEARTS ARE *as One Fire: An Ojibway-Anishinabe Vision for the Future* describes the impacts of Obwandiac (Ojibway and Ota'wa-Anishinabe),[1] Tecumtha (Shawnee-Anishinabe)[2] and Shingwauk (Ojibway-Anishinabe)[3] – their leadership and gift of vision – and of the N'swi-ish-ko-day-kawn Anishinabeg O'dish-ko-day-kawn (*Our Hearts Are as One Fire*), known in English as the *Three Fires Confederacy*, on the Ojibway, Ota'wa and Ishkodawatomi-Anishinabe world. The use of the literal and metaphoric o-dah-bah-ji-gahn (*sacred bundle*), within which my pipe, medicines, knowledge of ceremonies, songs, teachings, and sacred, moral and personal stories lie, and ah-zhi-kay-ni-mo-nahd-a-di-sid bay-mah-di-sid[4] to help us learn and understand is uniquely Ojibway, Ota'wa and Ishkodawatomi-Anishinabe. *Our Hearts Are as One Fire* is an attempt to share the spiritual journey of these three men through the eyes of their family, traditional storytellers and an Ojibway-Anishinabe person.

Our truth, gah-wi-zi-mah-ji-say-muh-guhk (*stories of origin*) and ah-di-so-kah-nahg ground the Ojibway, Ota'wa and Ishkodawatomi-Anishinabe identity and intimate relationship with the land. This is what Obwandiac, Tecumtha and

3

Shingwauk sought to protect. Incredibly, we still struggle with this even today! Their struggles reflected their strength of vision and their commitment to protecting the Ojibway, Ota'wa and Ishkodawatomi-Anishinabe way of life; Manitou Aki (*Creator's Land*); and the notion of naa'wi aki (*the middle ground*), which John Borrows describes as an "established body of intercultural law" with entrenched political, economic and military relationships between Anishinabe and *Euro-American* nations.[5] For Obwandiac, Tecumtha and Shingwauk, the middle ground was both a physical and spiritual place. It represented – and still does to some extent – a separation between cultures and nations. This separation is reflected throughout the collective history in the *Two Row Wampum*,[6] as the Anima-wi-ti-go-ing,[7] A-shig-a-ning[8] or the *indian nation*. Intimate accounts of experiences at different moments in the lives of Obwandiac, Tecumtha and Shingwauk were nurtured by unwritten messages and ah-way-chi-gay-wi-nan (*moral stories*), which acknowledged their commitment and responsibility to the Ojibway-, Ota'wa-, and Ishkodawatomi-Anishinabeg. To their minds, separation meant reconciliation.

I have drawn heavily from Ojibway-Anishinabe gi-ki-do-gah-gi-bi-i-zhi-say-ma-guhk[9] or gah-gi-gi-do-win (*oral history*),[10] the ah-di-so-kah-nahg and di-bah-ji-mo-wi-nan, three layers of knowing that help us understand the significance of o-gi-ma-wi-win (*to be esteemed*), o-gi-ma-win (*governance*), i-na-ko-ni-gay-win (*social order*) and di-bayn-di-zi-win (*to own one's self; to be self-determining and self-governing*). Ojibway, Ota'wa and Ishkodawatomi-Anishinabe nah-nah-gah-dah-wayn-ji-gay-win[11] and i-nah-di-zi-win[12] are really about the Ojibway-Anishinabe story in thought and application.

Our Hearts Are as One Fire explores and speaks to the Ojibway, Ota'wa and Ishkodawatomi-Anishinabe belief and de-bwe-win-da-mo-win (*faith*) in the principles of o-gi-ma-wi-win. It also tells us that generations ago, the honour and respect shown to Ojibway, Ota'wa and Ishkodawatomi-Anishinabe leadership reflected the ideals of Ojibway, Ota'wa

and Ishkodawatomi-Anishinabe societies. The families of the
Anishinabeg have been respectful of the legacies of Obwandiac,
Tecumtha and Shingwauk, which have been long-lived.

It's also fundamentally important to discuss Obwandiac,
Tecumtha and Shingwauk's impact within the N'swi-ish-ko-day-
kawn Anishinabeg O'dish-ko-day-kawn and the role the confederacy would have in shaping the *United States* and *Canada*. In
fact, at the height of its power and influence, the confederacy
had no parallel.

Ojibway, Ota'wa and Ishkodawatomi-Anishinabe i-zhi-tah-
win (*customary*), ah-ni-kay-o-gi-mah-kah-nah-wahd (*hereditary*)
and o-gi-chi-dahg (*strong heart*) leadership had a definitive role
within the structure of Ojibway, Ota'wa and Ishkodawatomi-
Anishinabe society. In fact, any discussion today concerning
Ojibway, Ota'wa and Ishkodawatomi-Anishinabe sovereignty
has to take into consideration the clearly defined parameters of
leadership and governance. Obwandiac, Tecumtha and Shingwauk reflected leadership in its most organic form, because
they held no formal authority or power as such but were still
able to unite the Ojibway, Ota'wa and Ishkodawatomi-
Anishinabeg and allied nations in brilliant and effective alliances that challenged the colonial powers of the day.

I've heard elders reflect that we sometimes get the power of
knowing from the spirit that comes to us in stories and dreams.
Not surprisingly, I have come to recognize and understand this
in using Ojibway-Anishinabe–grounded i-zhi-chi-gay-win/
ah-zhi-kay-ni-mo-nahd-a-di-sid bay-mah-di-sid to seek knowledge and answers. These ways have been used by our people
since the beginning of time to learn things and find answers
to complex issues. In this regard, o-dah-bah-ji-gahn[13] helps us
understand the significance of Anishinabe manitou kay-wi-nan
(*ceremonies*), n' zhwa-sho-gi-ki-nah-mah-gay-wi-nan (*the seven
teachings*) and miskew ah-zha-way-chi-win (*the act of flowing;
blood memory*).[14] We listen to and are touched by the stories
of Obwandiac, Tecumtha and Shingwauk and that of the

N'swi-ish-ko-day-kawn Anishinabeg O'dish-ko-day-kawn from a place that is both refreshing and spiritually grounded.

My understanding of the world comes from this Ojibway-Anishinabe perspective, and I write and share everything from this unique place. This is not meant to disrespect anyone; rather, it is about honesty in acknowledging my place and that of my parents and grandparents. I imagine the same should be true for those who are Ojibway-French-Anishinabe, Ojibway-English-Anishinabe and Ojibway-German-Anishinabe and who wished to acknowledge their father and mother and so on.

The memories of Obwandiac, Tecumtha and Shingwauk and of the N'swi-ish-ko-day-kawn Anishinabeg O'dish-ko-day-kawn are preserved and acknowledged throughout Ojibway, Ota'wa and Ishkodawatomi-Anishinabe communities and within our miskew ah-zha-way-chi-win, ah-di-so-kah-nahg (*sacred narratives*), ah-way-chi-gay-wi-nan and manitou kay-wi-nan. Together with our own di-bah-ji-mo-wi-nan, they form important parts of this story's metaphorical and literal o-dah-bah-ji-gahn.

They speak to Ojibway, Ota'wa and Ishkodawatomi-Anishinabe truth and reinforce the accuracy of our stories, which is important from my point of view because academic discourse is often prone to long-winded monologue and rhetoric, making it difficult to listen to. Therefore, this conversation is meant to be direct, with specific focus on nah-nah-gah-dah-wayn-ji-gay-win, i-nah-di-zi-win and a-zhi-kay-ni-mo-nahd-a-di-sid bay-mah-di-sid/Ojibway-Anishinabe i-zhi-chi-gay-win – all of which connects us with a world that is grounded in the spirit of the land itself.

We've always understood that our Ojibway-Anishinabe gah-wi-zi-mah-ji-say-muh-guhk and ah-di-so-kah-nahg define our identity and intimate relationship with the land in its purest form. This is what Obwandiac, Tecumtha and Shingwauk sought to protect.

Our Hearts Are as One Fire seeks to bring some clarity to Obwandiac, Tecumtha and Shingwauk's understanding of

Neolin's (Lunaapewa-Anishinabe) and Lau-lau-we-see-kau's (Shawnee-Anishinabe) understanding of and spiritual visions regarding colonization and loss of culture and territory. I have to make it perfectly clear that this story is not an exercise intended to provide definitive answers regarding Ojibway, Ota'wa and Ishkodawatomi-Anishinabe virtues specifically as they relate to leadership and governance. Rather, it seeks to explore the idea of leadership as expressed from the perspective of Obwandiac, Tecumtha and Shingwauk's responsibilities and influence. In sharing their stories, we explore the ideas of Ojibway, Ota'wa and Ishkodawatomi-Anishinabe o-gi-ma-wi-win, o-gi-ma-win and the N'swi-ish-ko-day-kawn Anishinabeg O'dish-ko-day-kawn.

Our Hearts Are as One Fire also attempts to provide an appreciation for Obwandiac, Tecumtha and Shingwauk's understanding of their worlds as shared through their visions and beliefs. In some instances, when we speak of ceremony, the written word can often remain mute, depending on who is reading and writing. Chickasaw-Cheyenne-Anishinabe legal scholar Sakej Henderson, for example, points out that the original philosophers and thinkers of this land believed unequivocally that their stories were an intrinsic part of the universe.

It's important to keep in mind that how we came to think this way about our reality and our way of being and how we use these ways of knowing, thinking, doing, ceremony and spirituality to find answers can help all of us understand the subtle underpinnings of what is shared and written. The focus of *Our Hearts Are as One Fire* is therefore both ceremonial and academic, creating a strange dichotomy.

The personal and collective stories of Obwandiac, Tecumtha, Shingwauk and the N'swi-ish-ko-day-kawn Anishinabeg O'dish-ko-day-kawn concentrate on their resistance to Euro-American colonial hegemony and explore the complex relationships each had with the world around them. These relationships were often different from the one-dimensional blood-thirsty, stoic and noble-savage stereotype used to portray Ojibway, Ota'wa and Ishkodawatomi-Anishinabeg in the literature and throughout history. This story, on the other hand, describes the multilayered and multidimensional spiritual, intellectual, emotional and political relationships Ojibway, Ota'wa and Ishkodawatomi-Anishinabeg had with the world around them.

Ojibway-Anishinabe spiritual leader and philosopher Bawdwaywidun Banaise (Eddie Benton-Banai), from Lac Courte Oreilles, Wisconsin, tells us that "a long time ago, may-wi-zhuh our people, the original first peoples of this part of the world were organized in many different ways" and that the N'swi-ish-ko-day-kawn Anishinabeg O'dish-ko-day-kawn was established at the time of chi-bi-mo-day-win (*migration*), when the earth was young. In time it came to represent a political, economic, military and spiritual alliance that asserted sovereignty over a broad expanse of territory. The history of the N'swi-ish-ko-day-kawn Anishinabeg O'dish-ko-day-kawn goes back to the prophecy of the seven fires. Each fire represents a period of time marked by the occurrence of significant events such as dreams, celestial happenings and prophesied experiences.

In terms of responsibility within the N'swi-ish-ko-day-kawn Anishinabeg O'dish-ko-day-kawn, the Ishkodawatomi-Anishinabeg (*youngest brother*) were given the responsibility for safekeeping the *sacred fire*, the symbol of independence and sovereignty. The Ota'wa-Anishinabeg (*middle brother*) were responsible for preserving the sacred bundles and providing for the economic well-being of the confederacy. Lastly, the Ojibway-Anishinabeg (*eldest brother*) would look after the spiritual knowledge of the three nations, and record their history and their sacred and moral stories.

The N'swi-ish-ko-day-kawn Anishinabeg O'dish-ko-day-kawn's leadership, governance structure and use of the doodem (*clan*) was effective from a political, economic and military perspective because it defined nation responsibility, territorial control and protection from other nations.

A NOTE ABOUT LANGUAGE

In applying this Ojibway-Anishinabe approach and pedagogy, I have used Ojibwaymowin concepts and words throughout the text. Ojibwaymowin is an important aspect of the Ojibway-Anishinabe gah-ki-do-gah-gi-bi-i-zhi-say-ma-guhk, kayn-dah-so-win (*ways of knowing*) and ah-zhi-di-bah-ji-mo-wi-nan (*traditions*) that have been passed from father to son, from mother to daughter, and from one generation to the next. The Ojibwaymowin words are written phonetically. I've also taken the liberty of italicizing the first appearance of Anglicized words for Anishinabe place names and English word translations, since Ojibwaymowin is my first language. Again, this is not meant to offend anyone; rather, it's simply how I view the world. I make no apologies for this.

I use the word "Anishinabe" to describe other *indigenous* peoples and nations throughout this discussion because I have serious difficulties with western-imposed terms such as "*aboriginal*" and "indigenous." In reality they have no meaning or substance for me. I imagine I could be accused of the same thing for using the term "Anishinabe"; however, I have to be clear that I use the term out of respect for humankind. Having said this, I have no problem with the Mohawk-Anishinabeg describing me as Ojibway-Onkwehonwe, or the Okanagan-Anishinabeg doing the same with Ojibway-Sylix, the M'kmaq-Anishinabeg referring to me as an Ojibway-Ji'nm, or the Cree-Anishinabeg calling me Ojibway-Ininew. The point of all this is to move away from prescribed western words/classifications that have sought to minimize our being and invalidate our existence as Anishinabeg and human beings.

>>>>>>>>>

English translations appear in the text or in endnotes the first time an Ojibwaymowin term is used. An extensive glossary is included at the end of the book.

The use of Ojibwaymowin throughout this discussion provides some context for traditional concepts of Ojibway-Anishinabe leadership, governance, ceremony and ethos, as the Ojibway-Anishinabe language speaks to our family, life and spirit. I appreciate those Ojibwaymowin teachers and speakers who support the standardization of writing, spelling and applying the principles of the double-vowel system. However, I have made a conscious effort to ignore this approach and the old-world Latin linguistic structures because of the linguistic colonization of our stories and memories that has taken place.

Gerald Vizenor, an Ojibway-Anishinabe scholar, tells us that the "anishinabe past was a visual memory and oratorical gesture of dreams and songs and tales incised as pictomyths on birch bark scrolls."[15] I have therefore also made a conscious decision to ignore the rules of those who invented the written language, who invented the "indian, renamed the tribes, allotted the land and divided ancestry by geometric degrees."[16] In my mind and spirit, Ojibwaymowin is the land and heart. It's also difficult to apply English words and meanings to ah-zhi-di-bah-ji-mo-wi-nan, manitou kay-wi-nan, ah-di-so-kah-nahg, di-bah-ji-mo-wi-nan and the manitou wi-win (*coming to an understanding of the mystery*), because they are deeply spiritual at their core.

Our description of Ojibwaymowin as a kind and caring language is also helpful, since this is the language of ceremony, which has the natural ability to gift our dreams and visions with clarity and truth. Ojibwaymowin spiritually connects us because we feel it; we watch, listen and learn. Accordingly, I write and spell in Ojibwaymowin as I hear and feel it because it's my mother and grandmothers whom I hear.

It was also important for me to reference seasons and dates weweni (*in a more truthful way*), mindful that Ojibway, Ota'wa, Ishkodawatomi, Menominee, Sac-Fox, Myaamia[17] and Bwa-a-nuk[18] Anishinabe nations would gather at Tchingabeng (*Cross Village*) to sound their voices and bring out the o-dah-bah-ji-gahn

for significant community and nation business from after the
first thunder in April until the last thunder in mid-October. All
important business was done in this way.[19]

Once decisions were reached, the opwaagan (*pipe*) was
smoked and a visual record was made to remind everyone that
the diplomatic and societal protocols were acknowledged and
respected by the protocols of biin-di-go-dah-di-win (*to enter
each other's lodges*) and bezhig onaagan gaye bezhig emikwaan
(*one dish with one spoon*) – principles that governed how we
treated each other.

Since the window for doing business was short (April–
October),[20] seasons were very important. Treaties and other
significant agreements would be negotiated and signed in June,
July, August or September. (I'm therefore not sure what to
make of treaties negotiated and signed during the winter
months.)

I've decided to write this way because of attempts to
erase our history and change our stories. If you visit Ojibway-
Anishinabe sacred sites you won't see plaques or anything
indicating why a particular site or name was important to
us, as its importance is often reflected in the description of
the place.

When you try to kill a language and replace it with another,
you kill part of the truth and story. Can you imagine a world
whose languages have been killed? That world becomes less
articulate and beautiful. Using Ojibwaymowin is fundamentally important to reclaiming our voice and visions, because
it's a way of talking with the universe.

This story echoes the generational experience of Ojibway,
Ota'wa and Ishkodawatomi-Anishinabeg and our relationship
with the land. Obwandiac, Tecumtha and Shingwauk's leadership in challenging Euro-American colonial hegemony gave
context to the idea of the middle ground, which was firmly
rooted within this relationship.

THE CONTRIBUTIONS OF BAWDWAYWIDUN BANAISE

Bawdwaywidun Banaise (Edward Benton-Banai) took on the responsibility of sharing elements of this story, as he considered it important in helping Ojibway, Ota'wa and Ishkodawatomi-Anishinabeg understand the interrelationships of space, land and territory.[21] In one sense, it's this concept of space, land and territory that anchors the stories and collective memories found in this narrative.

A pivotal moment in *American* history occurred on July 28, 1968, when a group of Anishinabeg started a movement to address the issues of equal rights, self-determination, improved living conditions, and protection and implementation of treaty rights. Spirituality and traditions soon became the rallying points of the American Indian Movement (AIM).

The movement and its notion of Red Power saw self-determination as both a means to an end and a means for taking control of *indian* lives in indian communities. At the forefront of the movement were spiritual leaders like Bawdwaywidun Banaise. There are some who believe that the movement actually began when Bawdwaywidun talked to Stillwater Prison inmates, urging them to "break the cycle of indians being sent to prison, not getting training, being released, and then going back to prison."[22] To do this, he believed that indians had to establish a political agenda founded on "spiritualism"[23] – the one common thread that bound us to the land, our ancestors and each other.

The movement argued that police brutality, poor housing, unemployment, and poor education opportunities and facilities in *Minneapolis* had to be addressed and given municipal, state and national priority. Bawdwaywidun Banaise was one of the few who was able to create a narrative about this systemic violence and racism. He patrolled the city's streets to protect indian people from police brutality; he insisted that government prosecute those who killed indians; he demanded respect for indian peoples' rights, customs and land. This commitment to purpose and action was not lost on the Ojibway, Ota'wa and Ishkodawatomi-Anishinabeg.

I've had opportunities over the last several years to speak to Bawdwaywidun about the creation of the American Indian Movement and many other issues. Some of our discussions focused on the following questions: How did the United States and its historical social, political and economic narrative shape the movement's vision during the 1960s and 1970s? What were the critical events that moved people like him to start the movement? What were the movement's specific objectives when it was created? What can we learn from the movement's strategy of focusing on hope, self-determination and sovereignty? I refer to his responses to these questions throughout *Our Hearts Are as One Fire*.

Throughout this journey, Bawdwaywidun helped me understand who we are, how we came to these places and how we came to accept this way of life, which was "preserved in many different places like the pieces of a jigsaw puzzle that has been scattered from the Atlantic to the Pacific."[24] I also came to appreciate the way in which our di-bah-ji-mo-wi-nan and ah-di-so-kah-nahg helped define how we see ourselves. To my mind, Obwandiac, Tecumtha and Shingwauk spoke and sought to protect all of this.

Mii i'i-way ojibway-anishinabe i-zhi-chi-gay-win.
Zhigo mii'iw eta-go o-way neen-gi-kayn-dahn zhigo
ni-gi-noon-dah-wah ... Ahaaw sa. Weweni.

1

Gah-o-mah-
mah-wahn-dah-wi-zid
gah-ki-nah-gay-goo
ji-gi-kayn-dah-so aki

A PROPHET IS SOMEONE WHO HAS
A COMPLETED VIEW OF THE WORLD;
HE/SHE IMAGINES A WORLD THAT
DOESN'T EXIST, SEES THINGS AS THEY
ARE AND ASKS WHY, OR HE/SHE MIGHT
DREAM THINGS THAT NEVER WERE
AND SAY WHY NOT

Ni-biin-daa-koo-ji-ge gaye ni' o-nah-ko-nah
ah-di-so-kah-nahg zhigo di-bah-ji-mo-wi-nan
g'dah mi-kwe-ni-mah-nahn obwandiacbun (nigig),
tecumthabun (mizhibizhi), miinwaa shingwaukbun
(I pass tobacco and ceremonially call upon the sacred
narratives, stories of personal experience and spirit
of Obwandiac, Tecumtha and Shingwauk.)
Meegwetch.

I BEGIN THIS part of the story by calling upon the sacred stories
and spirit of Obwandiac, Tecumtha and Shingwauk. I ask that
I be truthful and respectful to their stories and I offer my
tobacco.

Mii i'i-way ojibway-anishinabe i-zhi-chi-gay-win.
Zhigo mii'iw eta-go o-way neen-gi-kayn-dahn zhigo
ni-gi-noon-dah-wah ... Ahaaw sa. Weweni.

When I was elected to my first term as *Indian Act* chief at
Sagkeeng, an Ojibway-Anishinabe community, in 1987, my
father pointed out that I would probably be expected to take
on many responsibilities different from the ones prescribed by
the *Indian Act* because this was the nature of the colonial beast.
The challenge, he warned, would be to determine the fine line
between being an advocate for the people and being effective
opposition to the policies of the federal and provincial levels
of government.

At the outset, I struggled to adjust to this new role because
of the political and social dysfunction that was entrenched in
the community. I came to realize very early that the *Indian Act*
didn't do us any favours. This was in stark contrast to the world
we once knew, one that produced leaders who were respectful

and understood the importance of balance and harmony within the clan, community and nation. Ojibway, Ota'wa and Ishkodawatomi-Anishinabe society allowed for and encouraged this. It couldn't function any other way.

In the past, factional strife over any issue was a rarity; matters of the clan, community and nation were always discussed and decided in assembly by consensus. During these debates, o-gi-ma-wi-win were expected to listen and act in accordance with the decisions reached and in external matters were expected to be respectful and fair-minded and to have the ability to maintain a balance between competing interests.

OGIMAWIWIN | LEADERSHIP

In every respect, Obwandiac, Tecumtha and Shingwauk's leadership styles came to define the true meaning of "leadership" within an Ojibway, Ota'wa and Ishkodawatomi-Anishinabe construct. It should be noted that there is an obvious distinction between leadership and the notion of power within the Ojibway, Ota'wa and Ishkodawatomi-Anishinabe world; leadership was certainly not about power.

For the most part, Ojibway, Ota'wa and Ishkodawatomi-Anishinabe leadership have always been guided by the gift of spirituality and vision. I think this would be true of most Anishinabe societies as well. Comparatively, Tecumtha's vision of a sovereign Ojibway, Ota'wa and Ishkodawatomi-Anishinabe state centred on a confederacy of Ojibway, Ota'wa and Ishkodawatomi-Anishinabe nations was the outcome of at least two generations of activism and resistance. Tecumtha was therefore able to reach back into the past and draw on networks of international relations that stretched from the east coast to the most southerly parts of Manitou Aki, the west coast and the far north – economic, political, social and military relationships that had been vibrant and sustained since the beginning of time.

The question of leadership became more important to me during my tenure as *Indian Act* chief because of the political divide that existed. This political separation was complicated by the lack of mutual accountability, and it seemed that the damage was almost irreparable. It struck me very early on that my political survival depended on mitigating some of these problems.

SAGKEENG | WHERE THE RIVER WIDENS

Sagkeeng doon-ji (*I'm from Where the River Widens*). This is the place where my parents[1] and many from my family were born and are buried. It's an incredibly beautiful and spiritual place, yet it can be one of the most difficult places to live. Sagkeeng is an Ojibway-Anishinabe community situated at the mouth of *Lake Winnipeg,* where the *Winnipeg River* empties into it, and is one of the largest Ojibway-Anishinabe communities in Manitou Abi (Manitoba), with a population of approximately 8,500 citizens. Sagkeeng is also a signatory to Treaty 1, signed on August 3, 1871.

The separation of the community by the Winnipeg River into north and south shore has created many problems financially, politically and socially for Sagkeeng. It's certainly made for interesting political dynamics, given that many of the community's services and organizations are geographically situated on the south shore. Consequently, the community has had to continually address issues of north shore disconnect and separation for as long as I can remember.

Sagkeeng has always been an interesting study in contrasts. However, to my mind these contrasts are what keep the community focused on its vision for the future, one of political, social and economic sovereignty, along with improved social conditions, higher levels of employment and greater self-determination.

In March 1987, Sagkeeng was in receivership and in the midst of serious turmoil. There were issues with Indian and Northern Affairs Canada (INAC), the *Indian Act chief and council*–appointed school board, co-management and so on. It was an incredibly volatile place. As the newly elected *Indian Act* chief and council, we felt that we had thunder and lightning in our hands and were ready to make change. However, we were quickly brought back to earth. On our very first day in office, we were given our first dose of reality. There was no joyous welcome or ceremony. It was mid-March and winter was being stubborn about leaving. The day was cold, damp and grey. Inside and outside the band (administrative) office, people were starting to gather.

In its arrogance or incompetence, INAC was either late or simply not coming to distribute the monthly welfare disbursements. After a few telephone calls, we found out that INAC wouldn't be coming that day. Problems with the requisitions, we were told. People became frustrated, quarrelsome and angry. Many shouted, "Why did we elect you bastards? What are my kids going to eat? You're all fucking useless!" This was certainly not how I had envisioned my first day in elected office.

However, with the help of my father and a local store-owner, we were able to assist some people with food and basic necessities. I promised myself that day that INAC would never put Sagkeeng in this situation again. The federal government, it seems, has the audacity to play with peoples' lives because this is how oppression and colonization work. It sees no harm in this!

I quickly came to the realization that two of the problems facing Anishinabeg were the *Indian Act* itself and the bureaucracy created to administer its policies. Everything disturbing about this federal piece of legislation manifests itself in the psyche of its bureaucracy and the people chosen to manage the misery it engenders. In reality, there is little that *Indian Act* leadership can do. You can kick at the *indian affairs* bureaucracy and all it does is grunt. Political dysfunction, jealousy and hatred! The *Indian Act* gave most of us a *Canadian* dystopian fantasy of who and what indians were to be by distorting our political, societal and familial reality and our notion of community.

In the contemporary world of the *Indian Act*, the position of chief is often seen as one part leader, two parts despot and the rest politician. The very thought of the position is often distorted and despised. Shingwauk's grandchildren,[2] Doreen Lesage, Dan Pine Jr., Betty Lou and Lana Grawbarger, who still live in the Ojibway-Anishinabe community of Ketegaunseebee, make an interesting observation regarding the *Indian Act* and its political impact on Shingwauk's two sons, Ogista and Buh-guj-je-ne-ne, both of whom were vying for the position of *Indian Act* chief in 1867. In their eyes, this began the fragmentation of power between traditional o-gi-ma-wi-win vis-à-vis *Indian Act*–elected leadership in many of our communities.

Of course, we continue to struggle to find balance between the *Indian Act* and its influence over leadership and community matters. Doreen, Dan, Betty Lou and Lana explain that as Shingwauk lay dying he passed his medals and title to Buh-kwun-je-ne-ne, the meaning of which is still uncertain to them.

Leadership – and all the responsibilities that go with it – is an intoxicating thing and, in some instances, very ambiguous; it has different meanings to different people. For me personally, having the opportunity to discuss this from the perspective of Obwandiac, Tecumtha and Shingwauk was exciting. I felt that it was important to talk about Ojibway, Ota'wa and Ishkodawatomi-Anishinabe leadership with these men in mind.

As well, their influence and impact on Manitou Aki and our world is still felt today. They came to represent the true meaning of Ojibway, Ota'wa and Ishkodawatomi-Anishinabe leadership. Their resolve and passion were indicative of this. Within the Ojibway, Ota'wa and Ishkodawatomi-Anishinabe universe, Obwandiac (Ota'wa-Anishinabe), Tecumtha (Shawnee-Anishinabe) and Shingwauk (Ojibway-Anishinabe) were the brilliant stars. Their spiritual guides and medicine people, Neolin (Lunaapewa-Anishinabe) and Lau-lau-we-see-kau (Shawnee-Anishinabe), were the sun and moon.

WAYESHKAD | IN THE BEGINNING

It was understood that individual leaders could never enter into or make treaties, agree to peace or make war in isolation from the clan, community or nation. It's interesting to note that that type of abuse of authority and/or political power was never an issue. In one of our many discussions, Bawdwaywidun Banaise pointed out that Ojibway, Ota'wa and Ishkodawatomi-Anishinabe o-gi-ma-wi-win in times past had the benefit of a well-structured clan and governing system to guide them because it was fundamental to everything in Ojibway, Ota'wa and Ishkodawatomi-Anishinabe society in terms of leadership and societal responsibilities. The clans[3] also ensured a responsible and knowing society that valued mutual respect and order, which were fundamental to N'swi-ish-ko-day-kawn Anishinabeg O'dish-ko-day-kawn values and teachings.

More importantly, Ojibway, Ota'wa and Ishkodawatomi-Anishinabe leadership held no formal authority or power, as they personified both parent and protector ideals. They were expected to be fair-minded and generous in their relationships with all people and communities. In political and external matters of the nation they were also expected to have the ability to maintain a balance of power among o-gi-chi-dahg (*strong heart protectors*) and ni-gahn-no-say-wi-ni-ni-wahg (*leaders, military leaders, war leaders*).

Ota'wa-Anishinabe philosopher and elder Pine Shomin (Mack-a-da-ming-giss-was), a peace and war leader from Anima-wi-ti-go-ing (*Cross Village*) in A-shig-a-ning,[4] makes this distinction when describing the difference in responsibilities between peace and war leaders:

> **Ni-biin-daa-koo-ji-ge gaye ni' o-nah-ko-nah**
> **ah-di-so-kah-nahg zhigo di-bah-ji-mo-wi-nan g'dah**
> **mi-kwe-ni-mah-nahn obwandiacbun, tecumthabun,**
> **miinwaa shingwaukbun ... Meegwetch.**

.............**66**............

A very long time ago there was darkness, and in this darkness, there were good and bad spirits. There was an old
Anishinaayba named A-nim-aki (Thunder) who started to
gather the Good Spirits to fight the Bad Spirits. He then
explained to me that "War Chief" does not mean that I should
take up a gun or rifle or hatchet. What it means is that I
should try as hard as possible to do good things to counter
the bad. "This," he said, "is what Peace and War Chief means
to us in our way of life."[5]

.............**99**............

**Mii i'i-way ojibway-anishinabe i-zhi-chi-gay-win.
Zhigo mii'iw eta-go o-way neen-gi-kayn-dahn zhigo
ni-gi-noon-dah-wah ... Ahaaw sa. Weweni.**

An-o-gon-sit (*war leader*) responsibilities were to avoid confrontation and war if at all possible, and his or her responsibilities were actually pretty clearly defined and absolute.

IKWEISM | WOMEN LEADERSHIP[6]
Gender wasn't a factor at all in determining who could serve in
leadership positions. Women's councils had input on important
decisions, such as whether to go to war or whether a village
should be moved or not. Following the War of 1812, for
example, it was O-zha-gash-ko-de-wi-kwe, the wife of John
Johnston and daughter of Wa-bo-jig (a La Pointe Ojibway-
Anishinabe leader) who advised the N'swi-ish-ko-day-kawn
Anishinabeg O'dish-ko-day-kawn leadership during peace
negotiations. Men's and women's councils would often consult

with each other about issues such as the sanctioning of small war parties. However, when the issue of war was of national concern, a more formal assembly framework would be used to debate the advantages and/or inconveniences. As well, the Grandmother's Council within the Midewigun (*Grand Medicine Lodge*) was, and remains, responsible for specific teachings. They were expected to keep balance within the Midewigun and were entrusted with the responsibility of determining the economic needs of the community. And still today, they carry on their responsibilities. At one of their meetings at Peshawbestown (Michigan), for instance, the Grandmother's Council reminded everyone that the clan system is about remembering and respecting all of our families, because everyone is related and comes from this earth. Inasmuch as we've come to understand many things within this vast wah-wi-yah-kah-mig (*universe*), it's important to acknowledge that everything we are is rooted in this land. As well, the Grandmother's Council still has the responsibility for defining our *indianness*/Anishinabeness (*humanity*) and our obligations to each other, our community and our nations. The only thing they ask is that we always honour the animals that stood up and shared their skills and knowledge with us.

BAWAAJIGAN GAYE ONWAACHIGEWIN |
VISION AND PROPHECY

We also come to know from the stories passed to us that certain leaders possessed special gifts. Obwandiac, Tecumtha and Shingwauk, for example, were known for their gifts of kindness, generosity, humility and spiritual power.

The families of Obwandiac, Tecumtha and Shingwauk cannot emphasize enough the importance of keeping oral histories, as they help us understand the depth and subtle nuance of our existence in relation to the big picture. They spoke of Obwandiac's medicine bundle, of Tecumtha's oratorical skills and of Shingwauk's return to Ketegaunseebee following

Tecumṭha's death. Shingwauk's family described a moment when he removed his breastplate and five musket balls fell to the ground.

Another story that fascinated me was one shared by Rufina Marie-Laws and her mother (Mescalero Apache-Anishinabeg) during my visit to the Mescalero Apache-Anishinabe reservation in *New Mexico*. Their story describes an incident involving their grandfather Goyathla (*One Who Yawns; Geronimo*) and the use of his medicine powers to avoid being captured by the United States cavalry. Rufina and her mother were smiling as they described how Geronimo was able to slow the coming of the morning's light to help his people avoid being captured.

Vine Deloria Jr. shares a similar story regarding Geronimo and how he was able to make his people disappear from view as members of the United States cavalry approached. In this story, Geronimo climbed to the top of a hill and began ceremony. As his people came out from hiding, they were surprised to see only cattle grazing where only a few moments earlier the cavalry had been.

In another story, Don Daniels, an elder from Long Plain (Manitoba) describes his own personal journeys to other parts of the world and accepts these experiences as fact. Despite never having travelled to other parts of the world by conventional means, he was able to describe intimate geographical and cultural details, which would have been impossible for anyone who had never physically visited those specific places.

Other stories similarly describe the extent of Shingwauk's medicine power during his first encounter with Europeans in one of his travels east. In one story, Shingwauk was able to make the fog settle at the mouth of the *St. Lawrence River* so that an encroaching ship was not able to anchor. It was something that couldn't be explained, but it acknowledged Shingwauk's spiritual, medicine and shape-shifting powers and the possibility of his ability to travel in time.

I share these stories because they openly question our reality and truth as we perceive it and the world as we know, see, taste, feel and experience it. Further, these stories reflect the spiritual bond that medicine people have with the natural order of the universe, which is revealing in and of itself. Moreover, within the context of this discussion they help us explore the idea of leadership through a spiritual and metaphysical lens, which I find proactive because of its endless possibilities.

ANOOJ OGIMAWIWIN | TYPES OF LEADERSHIP

There is also a more literal understanding of leadership that helps us reflect on the practical application of leadership. To reiterate, we know that leadership was expected to be generous and fair-minded. Their judgment was considered important in most civil and political matters. It was also understood that many of these civil leaders would have proven themselves in battle as o-gi-chi-dahg. This will be discussed in greater detail in the following chapters, which focus on Obwandiac, Tecumtha and Shingwauk specifically.

It's also important to note that other leadership positions existed throughout the communities and nations. These would include the ga-ki-gi-do-wi-ni-ni (*spokesperson*) and di-bah-ko-ni-gay-wi-ni-ni (*judge*), who were expected to take a lead role whenever disputes arose within a clan or community. There were also the oshkabewisahg (*ceremonial helpers*) and mi-shi-no-way-wahg (*economic assistants*) to the o-gi-ma-wi-win, who had well-defined roles such as the distribution of food, gifts and supplies.

In times of armed conflict, the o-gi-chi-dahg or ni-gahn-no-say-wi-ni-ni-wahg would take on greater responsibilities in the extended clans and communities. As well, the organization and structure of Anishinabe society allowed for a seamless transition from war to civil leader and for other types of leadership positions.

In many communities today there is an effort to renew the roles and responsibilities of ah-di-so-kahn-i-ni-ni-wahg/ kwe-wahg (*sacred storytellers*), o-gi-chi-dahg, jeeskahn i-ni-ni-wahg (*shaking tent men*), mi-shi-no-way-wahg, opwaaganan gay-nay-wayn-ni-mahd (*pipe carriers*) and medicine people. In this way, history is not the past but the present. We carry our history and it remains with us.

Following the defeat of Phil Fontaine during the Assembly of First Nations' national chief election in 1991, a number of young Ojibway-Anishinabe custom leaders and *Indian Act* chiefs were determined to change how things were done at the regional and national levels. Darrell Boissoneau was one of the shining lights and visionaries who began talking of the N'swi-ish-ko-day-kawn Anishinabeg O'dish-ko-day-kawn. One of the first contemporary gatherings was held at Kete-gaunseebee, in August 1991, during Darrell's term as *Indian Act* chief there.[7] This gathering became a defining moment for me personally. It came to represent everything that I've become, and bringing the N'swi-ish-ko-day-kawn Anishinabeg O'dish-ko-day-kawn fully back to life has become one of my life's missions.

As Darrell and I are having coffee one morning, we talk about the divisions throughout *indian country*. He remembers the Pine family story of Shingwauk's sons Ogista (who was Methodist) and Buh-guj-je-ne-ne (Anglican) both vying for the position of *Indian Act* chief in the 1867 election. Darrell points out that within the Ojibway-Anishinabe clan system, it would have been Tagosh (Catholic), the eldest son, who took on the role and responsibility as ah-ni-kay-o-gi-mah-kah-ni-wid. However, because of the *Indian Act* and its absurdity, Ogista and Buh-guj-je-ne-ne had to run against each other in an election process that still wreaks havoc and is often responsible for community and family divisions in the majority of our communities.

From the perspective of Ojibway, Ota'wa and Ishkodawatomi-Anishinabe society, leadership was expected to value everyone's privilege and worth. In this regard, debates concerning issues of national concern were almost always decided by consensus rather than by majority vote. It was also expected that the clans and elders', men's, women's and youth councils would be involved in all discussions and decisions reached. As a result, once decisions were made, factional strife over any issue was a rarity and the resulting actions were almost always carried out without pause.

For the Ojibway, Ota'wa and Ishkodawatomi-Anishinabe communities, accountability and transparency were fundamentally important to the nation; decisions reached by consensus and respect for the individual citizen were interdependent. I think, as well, that it was probably easier to debate and reach consensus during this period because many people would have held a similar worldview and cultural perspective with respect to the decision-making process, planning, protocols and so on. Unfortunately, as colonization becomes more ubiquitous, division and political differences become more common.

Abuse of authority and/or political power by leadership was never an issue, since individual leaders couldn't enter into or make treaties, agree to peace or make war in isolation from the clans, their community or nation. This was unthinkable!

My father saw progress and movement forward under the *Indian Act* regime as almost impossible because of the division it created within the community of Sagkeeng. In retrospect, what my father shared with me was probably more practical than anything I had been told up to that point, because I came to understand how Ojibway, Ota'wa and Ishkodawatomi-Anishinabe communities were really about the bond between the clan (family) members, leadership and community. In many regards it had everything to do with ah-zhi-di-bah-ji-mo-wi-nan. From my father's perspective, leadership had to let the citizens of Sagkeeng retake control of the community narrative and reassert o-zhi-bi-i-gay i-nah-ko-ni-gay-win (*jurisdiction*). To him this was an important first step.

I shared my father's thoughts with an elder at one of Sagkeeng's quarterly assemblies. As he quietly smoked his cigarette and looked beyond the people sitting and moving about, he spoke of Sagkeeng's right to restore traditional leadership and governance structures. The litmus test, he felt, would be understanding and accepting what these traditional systems and structures were. For him, it was our responsibility to show how these teachings were not meant to threaten any-one, since at the end of the day Ojibway-Anishinabe leadership and governance were about forgiveness, tolerance and acceptance.

O-GI-MA-WI-WIN | TO BE ESTEEMED

But back to my earlier point regarding leadership and respon-sibility. It might sound cliché to say that Obwandiac, Tecumtha and Shingwauk embodied the spiritual and physical manifesta-tion of the cultural hero and mi-zhi-ni-way (*spirit messenger, dream helper*) who had the gift of vision and accepted respon-sibility for leadership. From my perspective, Obwandiac, Tecumtha and Shingwauk's ability to speak to the conscience of the people was what was truly remarkable about them. This is the universal meaning and reality of the prophet and leader as I see and understand it. Prophecy and leadership are such tenuous things to accept. The challenge is how you take mean-ing from stories and spirituality.

We know that prior to 1762, the Nanticoke-Anishinabeg (*Tidewater People*) were the first to resist European colonial intrusion – as early as the 1650s. For Ojibway, Ota'wa and Ishkodawatomi-Anishinabe nations, this was the beginning of the pressure placed on their societies by colonization and loss of land. In response to what was taking place, Obwandiac (1763), Tecumtha (1812) and Shingwauk (1812 and 1850) understood that only a unified political and military presence could keep the colonial violence and land loss in check.

O-GI-MA-WIN | GOVERNANCE

At a meeting at the *Ecorse River* (Michigan) in 1763, Obwandiac spoke to Neolin's dream and vision for protecting the Ojibway, Ota'wa and Ishkodawatomi-Anishinabe way of life, pointing out that political and military resistance was fundamental to maintaining Ojibway, Ota'wa and Ishkodawatomi-Anishinabe sovereignty and jurisdiction. As well, leading up to and during the War of 1812, Tecumtha knew instinctively that allied support would be critical to any military and/or political insurgency. He spoke repeatedly of this and the inherent inequity of the treaty process and negotiations taking place. In 1850, Shingwauk also sought to tackle this inequality, imbalance and inequity by addressing the question of land bi-mee-ku-mau-gay-win (*stewardship*) and ownership during the Robinson-Huron and Robinson-Superior treaty negotiations in 1850, both of which served as templates for the numbered treaty (1–11) process that began in August 3, 1871, and ended in June 27, 1921.

O-gi-ma-win, this fantastic ability to make independent decisions and enter into treaty, economic, political and military relationships, was full of purpose; it enabled the Ojibway, Ota'wa and Ishkodawatomi-Anishinabeg to assert jurisdiction and exercise political, economic, military and spiritual sovereignty over land and resources.

This is what Obwandiac, Tecumtha and Shingwauk sought to protect. Their vision of a sovereign Ojibway, Ota'wa and Ishkodawatomi-Anishinabe state based on a confederation of Ojibway, Ota'wa and Ishkodawatomi-Anishinabe nations was the outcome of at least two generations of Ojibway, Ota'wa and Ishkodawatomi-Anishinabe activism and resistance, and their success lay in their ability to reach back into the past and draw on networks of international relations that had been vibrant and sustained leading up to 1812.

DOODEM | CLAN

Fundamental to this network and organization were the seven original clans who defined the roles and responsibilities of Ojibway, Ota'wa and Ishkodawatomi-Anishinabeg. Historically speaking, the clan was woven into the political, economic, military and spiritual fabric of the community and nation. We're told this in the ah-di-so-kah-nahg, which speak to our beginning and subsequent chi-bi-mo-day-win[8] westward, and we find further meaning still in our gi-ki-do-gah-gi-bi-i-zhi-say-ma-guhk or gah-gi-gi-do-win and the creation of the N'swi-ish-ko-day-kawn Anishinabeg O'dish-ko-day-kawn. All of this oral tradition holds profound meaning in our world and describes how the clan system made it possible for Ojibway, Ota'wa and Ishkodawatomi-Anishinabe society to flourish and assert sovereignty over a broad expanse of territory.

Bawdwaywidun Banaise mentioned to me during one of our visits that we organized ourselves in this way because it enabled us to assert jurisdiction and exercise political, economic, military and spiritual sovereignty over a vast territory. The important thing to remember, he pointed out, is that the clans and seven guiding principles of kayn-daw-so-win (*ways of knowing*), zaw-gi-di-win (*love*), maw-naw-ji-win (*respect*), zoong-gi-day-win (*bravery*), gwu-yu-kaw-ji-win (*honesty*), duh-buh-say-ni-mo-win (*humility*) and de-bwe-mo-win (*speaking the truth*) provided context for Ojibway, Ota'wa and Ishkodawatomi-Anishinabe governance and sovereignty. The doodem system, he continued, came to represent the essence of the individual, community and nation.

The word "doodem" is interesting in itself, deriving from the root "de," meaning "heart" or "centre." We see its meaning throughout Ojibwaymowin and in the relationship between the words "ode" (*heart*), "oodena" (*town* or *village*), "doodem" (*clan*) and "de-we'i-gun" (*the Big Drum*). Simply stated, it's about our connectedness: physically the heart is the centre of the body and the town or village is the centre of a community. The clan is therefore accepted as the centre of identity/responsibility and the drum is the heartbeat and/or the centre of the nation.

The ethos of the o-gi-ma-wi-win and o-gi-ma-win structures had its roots in the teachings and natural laws of Anishinabe society. Ojibway, Ota'wa and Iskodawatomi-Anishinabe oral history, for example, makes it quite clear that an-o-gon-sit/ ni-gahn-no-say-wi-ni-ni-wahg and o-gi-chi-dahg responsibilities were fairly representative of the community. In times of war, their influence and authority would depend in large part on the consent of their communities and of other o-gi-chi-dahg. It's important to point out that Anishinabe o-gi-ma-wi-win had a special relationship with the people because it never set itself apart from the will of the people.

Decisions regarding whether to maintain peace or go to war, move a village or enter into trade relationships were made at national general assemblies, with the civil leadership presiding. More often than not, civil leaders were older and had probably been o-gi-chi-dahg and ni-gahn-no-say-wi-ni-ni-wahg in their younger days. However, when certain civil leaders had the respect of many community councils they would generally be regarded as a regional leader.

The colonial game plan since first contact has always been to divide and conquer. It might sound overly simplistic and cliché, but attempts to create division, dysfunction and instability have been with us for a long, long time. The colonial modus operandi has been to curry favour with individual leaders, and quite often the colonial governments would decorate these leaders with medals or gorgets in recognition of their position as "*medal chief.*"

Unfortunately, the Ojibway-Anishinabe community is still having to deal with the colonial agenda, even to this day. The *Indian Act* in this instance continues to take its pound of flesh. So all this talk about healing and reconciliation is, in my view, a political distraction intended to wreak more havoc and confusion.

At its outset, this story had two fundamental tasks. The first was to explore the meaning of leadership and the second to explore sovereignty and self-determination from the perspective of the N'swi-ish-ko-day-kawn Anishinabeg O'dish-ko-day-kawn. The specific focus on Obwandiac, Tecumtha and Shingwauk as agents of change is important because of their influence on the events that helped shape Manitou Aki.

OBWANDIAC AND THE ROYAL PROCLAMATION OF 1763

As the military and economic global conflict between Britain and France intensified in 1754, Obwandiac was this brilliant ray of sunlight that flashed brightly across the Anishinabe sky. In the period leading up to the War of 1812, Tecumtha and Shingwauk challenged the process of treaty-making and its impact on the Anishinabe collective.

The latter part of the seventeenth century was a critical period for Anishinabeg. The military and economic conflicts between Britain and France were directly impacting Anishinabe communities, their economic relationships and military alliances with each other and with other foreign nations. The surrender of Fort Ponchartrain, for example, in the autumn of 1760 forced the Anishinabe nations into a period of uneasy transition and would mark the beginning of a new era, specifically for Ojibway, Ota'wa and Ishkodawatomi-Anishinabeg.

In one of his first acts as governor general, Jeffery Amherst attempted to establish new diplomatic, military and economic guidelines by implementing a policy prohibiting gift exchanges and limiting the amount of powder, lead and guns to be traded. His actions challenged the fundamental principles of gift-giving and protocols of the nations-to-Crown relationship. This obviously reverberated throughout Manitou Aki and provided the backdrop to later events.

Both Obwandiac and Tecumtha saw the visions of Neolin and Lau-lau-we-see-kau as the symbiotic union of the Anishinabe spiritual and political world, which rejected Anishinabe dependence on a Euro-American lifestyle. By extension, they championed "*indian sovereignty*" and a return to the traditional ways. Neolin in particular was alarmed at how quickly the Lunaapewa-Anishinabeg had become dependent on European goods and white material culture after coming into contact with Swedish and Dutch traders during the early part of the seventeenth century. Amherst's "new" diplomatic policies were just the tip of the colonial iceberg, and Neolin understood that there needed to be a clearer understanding of British colonial hegemony.[9]

Visionaries and medicine people have always played an important role in understanding the true nature and intent of European expansionism and colonization and the terrorism it perpetuated. Manitou Aki has seen the coming and going of many influential Anishinabe medicine people since the 1500s and 1600s. Their visions provided not only a spiritual foundation but also the politics for resistance. During the Anglo-Powhatan-Anishinabe Wars, for example, the Powhatan-Anishinabeg were able to draw on the memory of Powhatan-Anishinabe spiritual leader Nemattenow,[10] who advised Opechancanough during the war with the British, and of Metacom (*King Philip*), who led the Wampanoag-Anishinabe resistance in 1675–78.

To reiterate, spiritual leaders and medicine people have always been central to Anishinabe society. In 1811 and 1812, Tecumtha's visit to the Creek-Anishinabeg and the following earthquakes that shook the southeastern region of Manitou Aki would come to serve as catalysts for the War of 1812. These resounding acts of nature reminded Anishinabeg of the unexplained and incredible primal power of these men and women, many of whom were skilled at travelling in the spiritual world. Historian Joel W. Martin's written description of these earthquakes and Lau-lau-we-see-kau's spiritual power is similar to the stories shared by Patricia and Norman Shawnoo and Jim Dumont.

Moses Dawson, influential owner of *The Advertiser*, a *Cincinnati* newspaper, wrote another story in which William Henry Harrison, then an army officer, demanded that Lau-lau-we-see-kau make the sun stand still and the moon alter its course to prove that he was a prophet. Soon after Harrison's challenge, on June 16, 1806, an eclipse of the sun took place. Some historians were quick to dismiss this story as nonsense, implying that astronomers travelling in the region had told Lau-lau-we-see-kau of the impending eclipse. Naturalist William Bartram, who travelled extensively throughout Creek-Anishinabe territory, wrote that there were medicine people who "were known to stop and turn back an army, bring rain and even assume the power of directing thunder and lightning."

Other spiritual leaders and medicine people were quite influential for brief periods. They include Shawnee-Anishinabe spiritual leader Peng-ah-she-ga, Scat-ta-mek (Lunaapewa-Anishinabe), who was very active from 1752 to 1775, and Munsee-Anishinabe Wang-o-mend, who influenced Lau-lau-we-see-kau for a time.

Women were also held in high regard. Lunaapewa-Anishinabe spiritual leader Beata was very prominent in the early part of the 1700s, despite the fact that many of her teachings had Christian undertones. Paiute-Anishinabe spiritual leader Wovoka led the Ghost Dance movement in the late 1800s. Seneca-Anishinabe leader and prophet Handsome Lake sought to awaken Haudenosaunee-Anishinabe spiritual consciousness. Goyathla (Geronimo) was another. These men and women came to represent the spiritual face of colonial resistance.

Lau-lau-we-see-kau's embracing of spiritualty[11] and Tecumtha's vision of a political and military confederacy were effective and powerful. Ceremony and spirituality were all manifestations of this Ojibway-Anishinabe world and spiritual power. In many of our communities, medicine people who had the ability to nah-nahn-dah-wi-i'we (*cure by sucking*), hold the jeeskahn (*shaking tent*) and Wabanowiwin (*initiate dreams and*

manipulate fire [in an] attempt [to reverse] an existing situation)
were expressions of this.

On September 3, 1783, the Treaty of Paris officially ended
the American Revolution. The British eventually relinquished
all claims to any territory south of Kitchi Gumi (*Great Lakes*).
They were, however, successful in keeping control of the northern territory. In the deliberations that followed, the Anishinabeg
sought to establish diplomatic relations with the newly created
United States. Anishinabe nations made every effort to maintain
the integrity of the middle ground and argued that the United
States had no ownership of or right to territory west of the original proclamation line and the *Allegheny Mountains*. As a result,
a third of the treaties negotiated and entered into during this
period were peace treaties. All the others were land surrenders.[12]

In the treaty negotiations that followed, Anishinabe nations
continued to argue that the British had no legal right to transfer
any territory because the lands in question didn't belong to
them. They also maintained that the N'swi-ish-ko-day-kawn
Anishinabeg O'dish-ko-day-kawn and its allied nations had
never been defeated in battle, nor had they ever surrendered.
All of this political and diplomatic wrangling becomes a precursor to the dysfunction we see today, and it really has its
roots in the 1493 papal bull Inter Caetera[13] and its implied
Doctrine of Discovery, which speaks to this struggle between
two very different worldviews and ways of life.

ZHAAGOOJI'IWE ZHIGO AGO' I-DI-WIN |
THE IDEA OF CONQUEST AND TREATY

The history of Manitou Aki is an interesting study of egregious
politics. It's also a remarkable story of integrity, honour, respect
and commitment to agreements and centuries-old conciliatory
diplomacy. Ojibway, Ota'wa, and Iskodawatomi-Anishinabe
nations and their communities have always been resolute in
their attempts to remind the Euro-Americans of biin-di-go-dah-
di-win and the bezhig onaagan gaye bezhig emikwan diplomatic

protocols that had existed prior to first contact. The Two-Row Wampum Treaty (1613) specific to the Haudenosaunee-Anishinabe Confederacy and the Dutch was one example of these protocols.

In response to the societal destruction and genocide waged, the onus has always been on Anishinabeg to "define what it meant to be human." Often, political and military resistance was the only language the foreigners understood. The Powhatan Wars (1610–14, 1622–32 and 1644–46), Pequot War (1636–38), Kieft's War with the Lunaapewa-Anishinabeg (1643–45) and King Philip's War (1675) were just the beginning of the resistance that was to follow. As well, the Treaty of Glasco that ended the war between the Wampanoag confederacy and the British in 1678, followed by the 1701 Great Peace of Montréal treaty between the French and thirty-nine nations, became the face of European-styled treaties. During the course of these treaty negotiations, the American Revolution began (1775) and ended (1776) with the United States' declaration of independence.

The Treaty of Fort Stanwix (at *Rome,* New York), the first of the *"conquest treaties,"* negotiated and signed by the Mohawk-Anishinabeg on October 22, 1784, effectively surrendered territory in what is now *Kentucky, West Virginia, Pennsylvania* and northern *Ohio.* The Iroquois ceded land they claimed between the *Appalachian Divide* and the *Ohio River.* This arrangement was dressed up as a peace treaty in an attempt to legalize the land titles of thirty thousand settlers already west of the new Appalachian Divide and Allegheny Mountains proclamation line.

From my perspective, the Treaty of Fort Stanwix was troublesome for a number of reasons, the first of which concerns the roles of *indian superintendent* William Johnson (brother-in-law to Joseph Brant), Joseph Brant (self-appointed Mohawk-Anishinabe leader) and *indian agent* George Croghan (father-in-law to Joseph Brant) in the negotiations. Johnson was just one of many land speculators who were negotiating these new treaties in an attempt to take control of large tracts of surrendered Anishinabe territory. This conflict of interest and the fact that the Mohawk-Anishinabeg Confederacy had no authority to negotiate or surrender lands that didn't belong to it in the first place were obviously troublesome to the Shawnee-Anishinabeg. The Treaty of Fort McIntosh (at *Beaver,* Pennsylvania) was negotiated and signed by George Rogers Clark,[14] Arthur Lee,[15] Richard Butler[16] and a small number of younger "hand-picked" Wendat,[17] Lunaapewa, Ota'wa and Ojibway-Anishinabe leaders on January 21, 1785. The treaty recognized American sovereignty for the first time and established a new boundary line east of the *Cuyahoga* and *Muskingum Rivers* in what is now north and southeastern Ohio.

Not surprisingly, the Shawnee-Anishinabeg refused to participate in the negotiations or recognize any part of the treaty, because the lands in question were part of their traditional territories. Realizing that they underestimated Shawnee-Anishinabe opposition to the treaty, the United States immediately sought to mitigate the damage by returning some of the surrendered lands north of the Ohio River and east of the Muskingum River.

Within a year of the Fort McIntosh treaty, on January 31, 1786, Richard Butler, Samuel Holden Parsons[18] and a small number of unknown Shawnee-Anishinabe leaders agreed to the Treaty of Fort Finney.[19] However, many of the more notable leaders in attendance took the opportunity to give the Americans a belt of black wampum as a declaration of war.

Of course, land was and remains an important consideration for the United States and the Anishinabe nations. As fragile as it was, the United States would pass the Northwest Ordinance on July 13, 1787, in an attempt to create the first organized territory of the United States. The ordinance would also establish a boundary and separation line between the Anishinabe nations and the United States and give the continental government the right to negotiate for more Anishinabe land.

Despite the opportunity for increased economic development and financial trade, the N'swi-ish-ko-day-kawn Anishinabeg O'dish-ko-day-kawn and the Shawnee-Anishinabe nation firmly opposed the ordinance because of their concerns regarding the loss of sovereignty. In their view, the lack of commitment to a more substantive treaty process jeopardized well-established economic, political and diplomatic relationships. They argued that United States policies and legislation were often duplicitous in nature, as reflected in the young republic's negotiation of a number of questionable treaties.

From the perspective of the N'swi-ish-ko-day-kawn Anishinabeg O'dish-ko-day-kawn, the political will of the United States to respect its political and legal obligations was simply not there. Despite the Royal Proclamation of 1763, which recognized Anishinabe title to land/resources and acknowledged the sovereignty of Anishinabe nations, there was serious doubt about the transition taking place.

AMERICANISM AND THE NOTION OF EXCEPTIONALISM

The nations-to-nation relationship also became more strained because the United States saw itself as qualitatively different from other nations, as manifested in the politics of *Americanism*[20] or *American exceptionalism*. French writer Alexis de Tocqueville[21] explored and referred to this ideology in his seminal work, *Democracy in America*, in the early part of the 1800s. The spirit and intent of treaties as negotiated became collateral damage to the larger political agenda of the United States.

In view of the negative politics and lack of diplomacy regarding American exceptionalism, Anishinabe nations continued to argue that treaties were analogous to *contracts* between two independent and sovereign entities. For us, land was a living embodiment of the political, economic and social relationship established by the treaty framework and was also fundamental to how we saw the universe. From our perspective, land was inalienable and held in common by all human beings to be passed from one generation to the next.

As Anishinabe opposition to Americanism deepened, Mi-chi-ki-ni-kwa (*Little Turtle*), a well-respected Myaamia-Anishinabe[22] o-gi-chi-dah and o-gi-ma-wi-win, led allied Anishinabe forces in opposition to the United States and was soon joined by We-ya-pier-sen-wah (*Blue Jacket*), a Shawnee-Anishinabe o-gi-chi-dah. During this period, generals Arthur St. Clair and Josiah Harmar, who had negotiated and signed the Treaty of Fort McIntosh in 1785, pushed to ratify the Treaty of Fort Harmar (negotiated on January 9, 1789, at *Marietta*, Ohio).[23] There was little Anishinabe support for the treaty because it ignored the most basic issue regarding non-indian settlements west of the new boundary line. By and large, many Anishinabe leaders saw it as a simple reiteration of the Fort Stanwix and Fort McIntosh treaties.

As a result of the generals' overzealousness, Harmar was defeated badly at the Battle of the Maumee on October 20, 1790, and St. Clair was easily defeated by Mi-chi-ki-ni-kwa and We-ya-pier-sen-wah on November 3, 1791. For the most part, Little Turtle's War came to represent a struggle between two very different ways of life and worldviews.

After these defeats, the United States entrusted "Mad" General Anthony Wayne with the responsibility of organizing a regular army, and at the Battle of Fallen Timbers, in August 1794, the United States defeated We-ya-pier-sen-wa. Despite the numerous accolades Wayne received, it should be noted that Mi-chi-ki-ni-kwa and We-ya-pier-sen-wah handed the United States more casualties than in the wars of Geronimo, Crazy Horse, Sitting Bull, Cochise and Red Cloud combined.

JAY TREATY (1794) AND TREATY OF GREENVILLE (1795)

The impact of the Jay Treaty (negotiated and signed on November 19, 1794, and proclaimed on February 29, 1796) was lasting, and many of our people are still reeling from it all. The treaty provided for the complete withdrawal of the British from forts and territory in the United States, but it allowed for British trade and commerce within the territory. It also saw the creation of two separate international jurisdictions – Canada and the United States.

The following year, on August 3, 1795, the Treaty of Greenville (at present-day *Greenville*, Ohio) surrendered large tracts of Anishinabe territory in what is now Ohio and also recognized the United States as a sovereign power for the first time. In return, the United States agreed to recognize Anishinabe *"ownership"* of the remaining lands and provide an *"annuity"* system of payment or services in-kind. All of this signalled a fundamental change to the nations-to-nation relationship and the politics of the middle ground.

TECUMTHA AND THE WAR OF 1812

Tecumtha was particularly bothered by Mi-chi-ki-ni-kwa's agreement to the provisions of the Treaty of Greenville. However, many believed that Mi-chi-ki-ni-kwa thought that the treaty might facilitate a process where the Myaamia-Anishinabe nation would share jurisdiction over the territory. Other leaders, including Te-ta-boh-ske (Lunaapewa-Anishinabe; *Grand Glaize King*) and Ca-te-wee-ke-sa/Ca-ta-ca-has-ca (Shawnee-Anishinabe; *Black Hoof*), saw the treaty as the new middle ground. Tecumtha was particularly troubled by this, as the treaty stood in stark contrast to Anishinabe sovereignty and jurisdiction ideals.

With the signing of the Treaty of Greenville in 1795, the United States made it clear that it was intent on developing and establishing a different type of political, economic and diplomatic relationship, one that acknowledged its control and power.

"Hand-picked" Anishinabe leaders also began to negotiate decidedly one-sided treaty agreements. Often these leaders were more than willing to accept the authority and primacy of the United States. Of course, this same approach has been used throughout the history of the colonial world, since indirect control was often more cost-effective and politically, economically and diplomatically self-serving. These same "hand-picked" leaders argued in their defence that the Northwest Ordinance (1787) and the Treaty of Greenville were attempts to accept the existence of aboriginal and treaty rights – however minimal they might have been.

In the period leading up to 1812, Tecumtha encouraged Anishinabe nations to challenge the colonial violence and land surrenders taking place. He pointed out that the majority of treaties surrendering huge tracts of land were unacceptable from a legal and political perspective, because no individual leader and/or community had the authority to surrender the sovereignty of lands that belonged to all Anishinabeg collectively.

From 1805 to 1820, editor, clergyman and lawyer Jeremiah Evarts (William Penn) made the legal and political argument that the *Indian Removal Act* would break every treaty the United States negotiated and would effectively destroy whatever humanity and national honour the country hoped to establish. Evarts saw treaties as compacts between independent communities, with each party acting through its government. In his view, the Northwest Ordinance and the Treaty of Greenville were antithetical to the legal and political understanding and application of treaties.

In fact, Tecumtha was increasingly frustrated with the complicity of Anishinabe leadership in some of the treaties and land surrenders being negotiated. As a result, he remained focused on the threat they posed toward Anishinabe lands and society. At the time, this was seen as a bold rebuke of leadership and the treaty negotiations/land surrenders that were taking place.

Many saw Tecumtha and Lau-lau-we-see-kau's politics of resistance focusing on decolonization as a catalyst for maintaining Anishinabe sovereignty and spiritual renewal. Raising the Anishinabe consciousness and pushing the idea of a multi-national alliance and confederacy was a message that reverberated throughout indian country.

During his visit with the Creek-Anishinabeg, for example, Tecumtha raised the question of land and national security and the possible extermination of their nations and societies. He also urged the Creek-Anishinabe nation to join with the N'swi-ish-ko-day-kawn Anishinabeg O'dish-ko-day-kawn and other allied nations in the resistance movement.

At the same meeting, Tecumtha received an unexpected boost from Benjamin Hawkins, an indian agent who was there to bully the Creek-Anishinabeg into accepting a federal road across their territory. Hawkins, in truth, signalled the emergence of the indian agent and indian superintendent who took advantage of economic opportunities in indian country by exploiting speculative and commercial opportunities. This was further exacerbated by the indian agent and indian superintendent's disregard for Anishinabe sovereignty and interests. In his opposition to Hawkins and others like him, Tecumtha reflected a revolutionary and bold persona that emboldened many Anishinabeg and their communities when speaking to the importance of maintaining the integrity of Anishinabe lands.[24]

How do we explain Tecumtha's visit to the southeastern United States (present-day *Georgia*, *Alabama*, *South Carolina* and *North Carolina*) and the series of goos-ko-say aki (*earthquakes*) in the region? We can rationalize it by saying it was purely coincidental, or we can try to understand it from an Anishinabe worldview that looks at the power of spirit and the universe differently and acknowledges the possibility of these types of events. The *New Madrid* earthquakes, as they came to be known, are estimated to have measured 8.2 on the Richter scale and were felt over approximately 50,000 square miles and moderately across 1 million square miles.[25] To provide some context, the 1906 San Francisco earthquake, for instance, was felt over

6,200 square miles. Many came to see these earthquakes as a reflection of Lau-lau-we-see-kau's spiritual power.

This idea of a political, social, economic and military multi-national confederacy was innovative and challenging for the period. Logistically it seemed almost impossible to organize, given the vast territory, differences in language and dialects, national focus and protocols. Despite these obstacles, Tecumtha was able to successfully articulate the commonalities in the Anishinabe struggle.

SHINGWAUK'S INFLUENCE ON PRE-CONFEDERATION AND NUMBERED TREATIES

As the fight for land increased following the War of 1812, Shingwauk questioned the land cessions taking place. For example, the surrender of 2.7 million acres of land in southern Ontario and the 1836 Bond Head Treaty on Manitou Minising (*Manitoulin Island*) were particularly troublesome, as they posed serious threats to the political, social, economic and land integrity of the Anishinabe communities.

The discovery of rich mineral and metal deposits in the *Lake Huron* and *Lake Superior* regions brought everything to a head, making it clear that a different and more equitable approach to treaty negotiations was needed. In the end, William B. Robinson was forced to negotiate the Robinson-Huron and Robinson-Superior treaties in 1850. They represented a new type of treaty and served as a template for the numbered treaties.

In retrospect, Obwandiac, Tecumtha and Shingwauk were the quintessential embodiment of leadership in terms of their brilliance as political and military strategists.

Mii i'i-way ojibway-anishinabe i-zhi-chi-gay-win.
Zhigo mii'iw eta-go o-way neen-gi-kayn-dahn zhigo
ni-gi-noon-dah-wah. Ahaaw sa. Weweni.

2

Obwandiac

THE MAN WHO TRAVELLED
AND STOPPED AT MANY PLACES

Ni-biin-daa-koo-ji-ge gaye ni' o-nah-ko-nah
ah-di-so-kah-nahg zhigo di-bah-ji-mo-wi-nan g'dah
mi-kwe-ni-mah-nahn obwandiacbun, tecumthabun,
miinwaa shingwaukbun ... Meegwetch.

IT WAS A BEAUTIFUL July day and I was looking forward to travelling to Mount Pleasant, Michigan, and visiting with members of Obwandiac's family. After all, Obwandiac was the stuff of legends. It was surreal to think that I would be talking to members of his family, people who had first-hand knowledge and personal stories of the man who had literally changed the face of this continent in 1763.

Willie Dunn's "Pontiac" played in my mind as I drove to Michigan. Incredible thing, this technology! I tried to picture Obwandiac along the ridges of mooseback mountain and the lakes of a thousand dreams, over the weeping badlands. Obwandiac raising his wampum belts of war and his efforts to drive the strangers from our shores. All of which is told to us in our stories and Willie Dunn's haunting "wiseman's tale."[1]

My first meeting with Ben Hinman, a grandson of Obwandiac, took place at the Saginaw Chippewa Indian Tribe reservation in Michigan, following an introduction by Willie Johnson, chief curator at the Ziibiwing Center. Ben and I had coffee at the Center. It was an interesting first meeting for a number of reasons. This was my first real attempt at academic research, and I was a bit apprehensive, since I've always had some issues with research generally. In fact, I tended to see the academy and any type of research as a culture-eating monster that will stop at nothing until everything is eaten or has fallen under its spell. In these instances, Anishinabe ways of knowing, language, traditions and culture are either destroyed or neatly appropriated by people playing indian.

Ben was extremely polite, and we got through the introductions. As we talked, I told him of my interest in his grandfather and how I came to undertake this journey, one that began during my first term as *Indian Act* chief. He in turn talked of Obwandiac's o-dah-bi-ji-gan and of his grandfather's concern about the violence and terrorism being perpetuated by colonization and the threat it posed to Anishinabe ancestral lands. For Obwandiac, respect for the political, social and economic sovereignty of each Anishinabe nation was central to the principles of the middle ground.

Surprisingly, no picture of Obwandiac actually exists, and there are no dramas or poems written about him apart from Dunn's song and Robert Rogers's 1766 play, *Ponteach*. As well, he would never have an audience with any future president. He was first mentioned, for example, in the documents and papers of William Johnson, who referred to a speech made by *"Pontiague, Outava chief"* at Fort Duquesne (Pennsylvania) in 1757.

During my meeting with Ben, he told me that Obwandiac was born in 1720 on the *Maumee River*, at the mouth of the Auglaize (near present-day *Fort Wayne, Indiana*), to Kuinousakis (Ota'wa-Anishinabe) and an Ojibway-Anishinabe mother whose name is unknown. Obwandiac and his wife, Kan-tuck-ee-gun (*Woman Canoe Paddler*), would have three children: a daughter, Marie Mannon le Sauvagesse de Sauteuse, and two sons, Pashshegeesh-gwashkum and Nebankkum.

In Ben's mind, Obwandiac's concept of Anishinabewiwin[2] was rooted in the consciousness and miskew ah-zha-way-chi-win of his family and the Anishinabeg. This is what guided his grandfather's efforts to overthrow the colonial and geopolitical politics taking root in the mid-1700s, cleverly pitting the British and French colonials against each other.

Later that winter, I got to meet Steve Pego, another grandson of Obwandiac's and a cousin of Ben's, at Midewiwin (*Grand Medicine Society*) mid-winter ceremonies in Mount Pleasant, and we talked about his grandfather. Steve believes that Obwandiac's knowledge of colonial power and its inherent inequality moved him to act in the period leading up to 1763.

I should point out that Steve and Ben are well known and held in high regard throughout indian country. Steve has been an elected chief of the Saginaw Chippewa Indian Tribe and Ben is a sculptor and artist of some note. Both still carry on the work that their grandfather began so many years ago and are activists to their core. There is a certain strength and quiet dignity in the way they carry themselves. I admire this.

NEOLIN

Steve and Ben told me that their grandfather heard Neolin (*The Enlightened One,* or *The Prophet*), a Lunaapewa-Anishinabe medicine person, speak for the first time during the summer of 1762 about a vision he was gifted with. Their grandfather noticed something commanding in how this man spoke to the dangers colonialism posed to the Anishinabe culture and way of life. Upon reflection, they suggested that Obwandiac might have realized that with each passing year the white man was becoming greedier and more exacting, oppressive and overbearing.

After listening and talking to Neolin, Obwandiac became convinced that supporting Neolin and his spiritual message was the right thing to do and that it would resonate throughout Ojibway, Ota'wa and Ishkodawatomi-Anishinabe territory. Returning to the *indian ways* (*ceremony, spirituality and thought*) and quitting all commerce with the white man appealed to many, because the Euro-American occupation of Anishinabe lands was wreaking havoc with Anishinabe society generally and Anishinabe communities were reeling. Even then, colonization was like a giant tapeworm reaching deep into the heart of indian country.

More importantly, Neolin added a spiritual dimension to Obwandiac's political and military message, which created a breathtaking synergy for what would take place between May 7 and mid-November 1763.

In truth, Neolin's vision addressed the political and economic issues of the day (European intrusion into *indian lands*

and decreasing economic/fur trade), which were moving
Obwandiac and Ojibway, Ota'wa and Ishkodawatomi-
Anishinabe nations toward war. From Neolin's perspective,
Ojibway, Ota'wa and Ishkodawatomi-Anishinabe survival
and stability would depend in large part on maintaining our
ah-zhi-di-bah-ji-mo-wi-nan and i-nah-di-zi-win (*way of being and
traditions*), which would be difficult given the changing demo-
graphics. Neolin's vision must have been revealing and reliably
vivid on one hand and on the other obfuscatory for Obwandiac.
That said, Obwandiac would have been able to see and experience the impact of the colonial mentality first-hand and understand the complexity of organizing an alliance of different
nations and maintaining the political and military integrity of
each within the movement, the logistics of which must have
seemed impossible.

Despite these challenges, Obwandiac was able to find his way
and was guided and encouraged by the Neolin's vision, which
called for the Anishinabeg and their leadership to reject their
deepening dependence on all things European and return to
traditional ways. Even then, colonization and the daily intrusion
into Anishinabe territory were a very serious threat to the social,
political, economic and military structures of the Anishinabe
nations. Neolin and Obwandiac sought to prevent and remedy
this. Strangely, Neolin is not mentioned in any of the war rec-
ords from the start of the war or anywhere else after that.

THE RESPONSIBILITY OF STORIES
The fact that there is little record or acknowledgement of
Neolin or of the reluctance to accept Obwandiac's role in
planning one of the most successful Anishinabe moments in
the history of Manitou Aki reeks of racial bias. Their resolve
to protect and strengthen Anishinabe society is a legacy that
remains with us still; the Royal Proclamation issued in 1763, its
treaty process and the existence of Canada itself are indicative
of this.

Our history and stories have always been shared by white historians and others through a different cultural perspective, one that is rife with racial bias. In truth, many of the white historians who attempted to tell our story and record history did so through a cultural filter. They saw people and events differently and quite often provided different interpretations of Anishinabe history, because for the most part we were savages. In *Our Hearts Are as One Fire* I want to share a different story, using an Ojibway-Anishinabe perspective and understanding of the world as we know and see it.

Ojibway, Ota'wa and Ishkodawatomi-Anishinabe oral tradition is about ah-way-chi-gay-win (*teaching by telling a story*). Viewed in this way, our belief base and everything that we are as Ojibway, Ota'wa and Ishkodawatomi-Anishinabeg is found in our sacred narrative, moral and personal stories and ceremony. They ensure good conversation, since academic discourse within western academia is prone to long-winded monologue that is often biased and racist when talking about Anishinabeg and other people of colour.

The colonial rhetoric is suffocating, making it difficult to listen to, as is the idea that only white people have the knowledge and ability to talk about epistemology, the scientific method or inductive proof that became the face of the "Enlightenment," which attempted to master the world.

Meegwetch to the Ojibway, Ota'wa and Ishkodawatomi-Anishinabe oral historians, the pictograph writers, the sacred, personal and moral story-keepers, and the family and community memorialists who have helped preserve our stories by acknowledging and recording the truth about our past with care. These men and women are responsible for preserving the most important events and public speeches.

The very idea that Ojibway, Ota'wa and Ishkodawatomi-Anishinabe ah-do-win (*self-determination*), o-gi-ma-win, di-bayn-di-zi-win and o-nah-ko-ni-gay-win (*natural law*) were central to beedahbuhn (*the new dawn*) is often surprising to non-indians, since Anishinabeg were considered less than human and without the ability to think and rationalize.

As well, di-bah-ji-mo-wi-nan that are sometimes private but almost always official were protected and nurtured by family. Personal stories and oral history often tell us what our people did, what they wanted to do and what they believed. Ironically, these stories are less prone to misrepresentation. For this reason, a clear distinction has to be made between the stories written by Euro-American historians and Anishinabe knowledge keepers and rememberers.

Accordingly, stories and interpretation of protocols by people such as Ota'wa-Anishinabe leader and historian Andrew Blackbird (Mack-e-te-be-nessy), a fluent Anishinabemowin speaker, are more on point and accurate. For example, Blackbird writes that the name was pronounced *bwon* or *bon,* which meant *his stopping* or *stopping it.* Similarly, Isabel Ozawamik and Angus Pontiac from Wikwemikong, Ontario, told Willie Johnson that the name meant *"A Man Who Travelled and Stopped at Many Places."*

To reiterate, oral history and tradition are better understood and more faithfully passed on than the written word, since text written by those with limited knowledge of language can be open to several interpretations, misinterpretations and exaggerations. In our minds, we can't move forward without looking to the past. To this end, reclaiming our stories is one of the prerequisites for our freedom and emancipation.

O-GII-WAY-EH-ZHI-MI-GOON ZHIGO GII-WAA-NI-MO GAH-GI-BI-I-ZHI-SAY-MAH-GUHK | TO CHEAT, DECEIVE AND WILLFULLY MISREPRESENT HISTORY[3]

Given what has taken place on Manitou Aki and elsewhere, it seems that colonialism still wreaks havoc. We face daily intrusions into our world, and many of us obviously take issue with this. In stories about Obwandiac there are deliberate misrepresentations of fact.

I find it incredible that even Obwandiac's nationality and name came into question! American historian Francis Parkman suggested that Obwandiac had been adopted by the Ota'wa-Anishinabeg, and J.N. Nicollet, a French mathematician and geographer, claimed that Obwandiac was Nippising-Anishinabe. These same historians even went as far as to question the meaning of the name *Pontiac* or *Obwandiyag*. It seems foolish in retrospect that Euro-American historians would question Obwandiac's heritage and the meaning of his name, given their lack of understanding of our history, language and protocols.

It's also interesting that, despite his military success, Obwandiac is sometimes compared to Patroclus of the Trojan War, because his influence was never fully appreciated in the planning of events leading up to 1763, and in other instances to Alexander the Great, because of these very successes.[4] For the most part, though, Euro-American reflections tended to understate Obwandiac's accomplishments and all that he was.

There are even questions about his role in the events leading up to and during 1763. For example, Euro-American historians, politicians and others have suggested that Obwandiac's role was greatly exaggerated and that he was merely a minor character, one of many local warriors. Other historians during this period, such as Randolph G. Adams, wrote that Obwandiac was nothing more than a menace.[5] Still others, including Howard Peckham and Michael McConnell, minimize his role in the planning and organization of the events leading up to the war in 1763, suggesting that his role was greatly exaggerated and that he was a local leader of no great significance.

Historian Richard Middleton hints that the idea of Anishinabe liberation didn't begin with Obwandiac and that Seneca-Anishinabeg Genese Tahaiadoris and Mingo Kiashuta were the men who actually conceived of and planned these efforts to oppose colonial aggression and were responsible for sending war belts to the east and west.[6] I find this incredulous because oral history suggests that Tahaiadoris and Kiashuta had neither the charisma nor the ability to organize and accomplish something of this magnitude! Their political and military reach was simply not wide enough, and it was also a well-known fact that both men were extremely disliked by Anishinabe leadership. We could probably argue as well that Neolin's spiritual vision might have languished in obscurity had Obwandiac not arrived at the time he did.

Despite the cynicism regarding Obwandiac's role in shaping the colonial politics of the day, there is absolutely no denying his role and participation in the planning of some of the war's most important battles, including the Battle of the Monongahela (Pennsylvania), where newly appointed commander-in-chief for the thirteen colonies, General Edward Braddock, was defeated.

To their credit, General Thomas Gage and Colonel John Campbell considered Obwandiac influential, a force to be reckoned with, a leader whose disposition and authority was absolute and respected by his people. In spite of his bias, Parkman did acknowledge that Obwandiac was a leader of some influence. The fact that Obwandiac's father and mother were Ota'wa-Anishinabe and Ojibway-Anishinabe was also seen as an advantage, given that these were two of the most powerful nations on Manitou Aki. Still, there were some who saw him as haughty and high-handed. Obwandiac, it seemed, couldn't win for trying.

Regardless of how Euro-American scholars and historians see Obwandiac and what was said at the time about him or his role in planning of one of the most successful decolonization movements the world has seen, he successfully laid siege to every British post west of the Allegheny Mountains, with the exception of Fort Pitt (Pennsylvania) and Fort Detroit (Michigan). Anishinabeg will always remember Obwandiac for his skill as a military strategist and as one the most charismatic political leaders the Anishinabe world has seen.

DI-BAA-KO-NI-GE-WIN NAA-WAY-I' II AKI |
THE POLITICS OF THE MIDDLE GROUND

As word of Obwandiac and his exploits in the period leading up to the French and Indian War (1754–63) spread, his influence grew considerably throughout indian country. It's important to point out that Obwandiac's influence as leader and strategist was never questioned or disparaged within indian country. In fact, he was able to straddle both worlds and articulate an Anishinabe-focused economic, political and military agenda that addressed the impact of colonial power, domination and varying degrees of complex hegemony.

Despite Middleton's skepticism regarding Obwandiac's role in the planning of the war in 1763, he did acknowledge that Obwandiac was charismatic, respectful, and brilliant in his political judgment, organizational and leadership abilities.[7] Through the sheer force of his personal appeal, he began to transform the colonial narrative and dynamic.

Steve and Ben explained that, from the outset, their grandfather had a fairly good appreciation of what was happening elsewhere in the world. He had heard of the wars that had taken place in faraway lands such as Prussia and Austria-Hungary and recognized that these conflicts would eventually find their way to Manitou Aki. This worried him, as he saw the negative influences of colonization and the terrorism it manifested. Above all, he paid close attention to Neolin's spiritual message because of its relevance to what was taking place in indian country.

For these reasons, Obwandiac saw the middle ground as an important reality because of the buffer it created between the Euro-American and indian nations. In his mind, the middle ground represented a philosophical and practical place where political, military and trading relationships and alliances were established based on the Anishinabe protocols of harmonious co-operation and mutual respect.

One interesting characteristic of the middle ground was the practice of French and British families opening their homes to Anishinabe o-gi-chi-dahg, hunters and trappers going to or coming from military or hunting expeditions. This practice had its roots in the Ojibway-Anishinabe practice of biin-di-go-dah-di-win, which allowed for diplomatic reciprocity between the Ojibway, Ota'wa and Ishkodawatomi-Anishinabeg and other nations during times of war.

In time, however, Obwandiac and Neolin saw the emergence of British colonial power as a serious threat to Anishinabe society. From Neolin's perspective, there had to be a renunciation and rejection of everything that represented British colonial power (material wealth, the comforts of western goods and trade). This was fundamental to Ojibway, Ota'wa and Ishkodawatomi-Anishinabe political sovereignty, justice and equality.

Middle ground protocols[8] and relationships were clearly defined within Anishinabe societies. There was absolutely no mistaking this! As far as the inner workings of the Ojibway, Ota'wa and Ishkodawatomi-Anishinabe nations were concerned, a specific clan would control specific trade routes, geographical areas and diplomatic protocols. Marriages were also arranged to increase the number of trading partners for the clan and extend diplomatic and economic relationships.

The middle ground was a highly functional diplomatic concept and reality through which many Euro-Americans were routinely assimilated in the Anishinabe community. George Croghan points out that the French had almost become one with Anishinabeg. We also see, for example, that within this well-defined structure, the Mohegan-Anishinabe nation had responsibility for taking news from the east to Anishinabeg in the west, and quite often this news would focus on the movement of the Euro-Americans. This was something they had done for over two hundred years!

The middle ground was about political, military and diplomatic reciprocity. From the perspective of the Anishinabeg, every citizen had a responsibility for maintaining balance and harmony. This was nationhood in its most organic self.

Although the middle ground physically separated brother and sister nations, it represented both the centre and husk of the relationship itself. The survival of Anishinabe protocols and relationships was threatened by colonial intolerance. All of this gave context to what would take place.

We also can't overlook the depth of Obwandiac's influence on international trade and contribution to the economy at this time. For example, he issued bills of credit and treasury notes in order to support the Ojibway, Ota'wa and Ishkodawatomi-Anishinabe economies and finance his war. His bills were drawn on birchbark and bore the figure of nignig (*otter*) the sign of his clan, which also included a representation of the article for which the bill was valid – a gun, bag of corn or a deer – all of which were always redeemed. This he did with the regularity of an exchequer.

At a meeting on May 5, 1763, holding at his side a red and purple wampum belt[9] given him by the French king, Obwandiac took the opportunity to remind those in attendance that Anishinabeg were gifted with self-sufficiency, sovereignty and the right to be onki-akeeng.[10] Ben and Steve told me there was a political, social and moral righteousness about their grandfather that added to his charismatic appeal that day. He must have been electrifying and provocative, they told me, smiling.

GI-MESH-KO-DIN-NAY-NAH-NIK GI-DI-BAH-JIM KAY-GO | COLONIAL FICTION

Regardless of what Francis Parkman, Howard Peckham, Francis Jennings and other historians felt or saw the need to ignore or misrepresent, Anishinabe oral tradition and history is rigorous and accurate in describing Obwandiac and Neolin's ability to harness the anger and general malaise felt throughout indian

country. Together, they challenged colonization and its
political system at its racist root. For me, the historians' bias is
nothing more than an attempt to perpetuate the idea of conquest and legitimize colonization and genocide.

Given the colonial dynamics, Obwandiac understood that
Ojibway, Ota'wa and Ishkodawatomi-Anishinabe political and
military success would depend in large part on a unified confederacy of all Anishinabe nations. He was clearly successful in
his organization, because many nations answered his call to
rise in defence of their rights.

Upon his arrival in February 1755, General Edward Braddock
was surprised by the political and military planning taking
place throughout indian country. In April of that same year,
he dispatched First Sergeant Jacob de Marsac, with seventeen
wampum belts, to meet with a number of influential Ojibway-
Anishinabe leaders from Mi-shi-ne-mack-i-naw-go (*Michilimackinac*),[11] Waw-gaw-naw-ke-zee (*Crooked Top of the Tree;
L'Arbre Croche; Cross Village*), Saganam and Ba-wi-ti-gong (*Where
the Fish Were Good and Lived Well*; present-day *Sault Ste. Marie*).[12]
Unfortunately for Braddock, his messaging failed miserably, his
impatience, arrogance and temper having got the better of him,
as he was soundly defeated at the Battle of the Monongahela
on July 9, 1755, and would die four days later. Of the 1,300
men he led into battle, 450 were killed and 422 were wounded.
For many military observers, it made clear the enormity of the
task of maintaining a British presence on Manitou Aki.

A certain tranquility blanketed the country following
Braddock's defeat, which compelled anthropologist Anthony
F.C. Wallace to compare Neolin's vision to that of Moses and
the Ten Commandments.[13] But the calm would end abruptly
with the appointment of Jeffrey Amherst to the position of governor general in September 1760. In an attempt to teach the
indians a lesson, Amherst immediately increased the trade rates
and price of consumer goods, while simultaneously reducing
the goods, gifts and money given in trade transactions. In

truth, the gift exchanges were seen as a form of rent for the outposts and forts on Anishinabe lands and as an expression of respect and friendship.

BIIN-DI-GO-DAH-DI-WIN | TO ENTER EACH OTHER'S LODGES

Generally speaking, Anishinabe–Euro-American political and trade protocols were often complex but were generally understood and respected. For example, a toll payment of wampum, furs, grain or other trade goods were paid for using certain trade routes and, in extreme situations, trespassers were killed for disregarding protocols or refusing to pay the toll charge. For this reason, control of these trade routes provided a virtual monopoly over what took place economically.

Amherst's haphazard handling of issues stood in stark contrast to Obwandiac's steady hand. Despite logistical difficulties, Obwandiac was able to organize a sizeable military and multination alliance with relative ease.

Many Anishinabe leaders considered Amherst's administrative policies an insult to the long-established middle ground economic, political, social and military protocols. Amherst took the dim-witted view that indians were conquered and therefore their political, economic and social concerns didn't matter. This position obviously undermined and complicated the notion of the middle ground. In his eyes, Anishinabeg needed to know their place.

Ota'wa-Anishinabe leader and historian Andrew Blackbird wrote that exclusive control over trapping areas and trade routes strengthened the economies of the N'swi-ish-ko-day-kawn Anishinabeg O'dish-ko-day-kawn and in turn provided opportunities for the Ojibway, Ota'wa and Ishkodawatomi-Anishinabeg to expand their communities and organizations. He pointed to Waw-gaw-naw-ke-zee, the principal community of the Ota'wa-Anishinabeg, fifteen to sixteen miles long, where there was an abundance of fruit (strawberries, raspberries and blackberries) and fish were plentiful.

Needless to say, Amherst was troubled by all the political posturing and military activity taking place in indian country and was also alarmed by Obwandiac's influence on the economy and politics of the day. He resented Obwandiac's political and military savvy and willingness to fight to protect middle ground protocols. For Amherst, the principles of the middle ground were contrary to every colonial practice that he had come to understand. Obwandiac was putting down the system and he needed to be stopped.

WE-MI-TI-GO-ZHI ZHIGO ANISHINABE MII-GAA-DI-WIN | THE FRENCH AND INDIAN WAR

The "French and Indian War" is a somewhat misleading representation of history, since the war was actually fought between *British America* and *New France*. Obwandiac and the N'swi-ish-ko-day-kawn Anishinabeg O'dish-ko-day-kawn fought independent of France, which made their successes all the more impressive.

From the perspective of the British, the war with the French began in earnest in 1754, with the attack on Fort Duquesne, at the fork of the *Monongahela* and *Allegheny Rivers* in present-day Pennsylvania. For some reason, historians can't decide whether George Washington was involved in this attack; I'm not even sure why it matters at this point. A year later, Braddock also failed to take the fort.

With defeat at hand, the French destroyed the fort in 1758 and, shortly after that, the British began construction of Fort Pitt, which became a focal point in 1763 for more nefarious reasons.

In June 1758, Amherst successfully launched attacks on Fort Louisburg and Fort Niagara, forcing the French to abandon all their posts/forts east of *Detroit*, making the defence of Fort Ponchartrain all the more important, as it represented France's last foothold in the region. Nevertheless, the fort fell to the British on November 29, 1760. Oddly enough, Fort Pontchartrain's future was decided by Amherst's capture of Montreal on September 8 and the subsequent *Articles of Stipulation*[14] making the defence of Detroit inconsequential. With the defeat of the French, Anishinabe nations intensified the political rhetoric and continued their threats of military action, which heightened an already critical situation for the British.

OBWANDIAC MII-GAA-ZO MANITOU AKI ONJI | OBWANDIAC AND THE FIGHT TO PROTECT MANITOU AKI

At a meeting on April 27, 1763, with Ota'wa, Ishkodawatomi, Lunaapewa[15] and Huron-Anishinabe delegations on the banks of the Ecorse River (*Lincoln Park,* Michigan), Obwandiac spoke to the red and black war belts[16] given him by the king of France and the Lunaapewa-Anishinabeg. It's important to note that these beads can't give false stories, since it's impossible for the man who takes the belt to alter or add to it.

Those in attendance described Obwandiac as lithe like a panther, showing intelligence, skill and charisma as an orator. He emboldened and excited many of the o-gi-ma-wi-win and o-gi-chi-dahg as he spoke to the war belts given to him and of the importance of Anishinabe sovereignty and land. This meeting proved important, as the N'swi-ish-ko-day-kawn Anishinabeg O'dish-ko-day-kawn's war council and other Ojibway, Ota'wa, Ishkodawatomi and Wendat-Anishinabe o-gi-ma-wi-win acknowledged for the first time their willingness to go to war.

Immediately following this meeting, Obwandiac visited the Midewigun to discuss the confederacy's plans. However, the lodge couldn't sanction any act of war or aggression because of its philosophical or spiritual principles. Mindful of this, Obwandiac was particularly careful about how he broached Neolin's spiritual message, which lay at the heart of his own.

He then followed this meeting with visits to the Ouiatenon, Kickapoo and Myaamia/Twightwee-Anishinabe nations east of and along the *Wabash River* and provided them with details of the fast-approaching military campaign. He also continued his lobbying efforts by sending red and black wampum war belts to the Ojibway and Ota'wa-Anishinabeg at *Saginaw Bay*, *Thames River* and Michilimackinac (Michigan). Interestingly, his lack of trust in the Mohawk and Oneida-Anishinabe nations proved a bit problematic for him; he knew they had the ability to disrupt lines of communication between Schenectady and Oswego (New York), making them useful allies.

In terms of strategy, Obwandiac understood the importance of destabilizing the British forces by taking the more established forts in Ohio, Indiana, Pennsylvania and Michigan. This became central to his military plan.

Amidst the political and military preparations taking place, Obwandiac attended another war council meeting at present-day Mount Pleasant on May 5, 1763, to discuss three main issues: the Conestoga-Anishinabe village massacre; how to respond to the lives lost at the village; and whether the British (*"those dogs clothed in red"*) should be completely removed from Manitou Aki.

Within a few days of his first meeting with Ota'wa, Ishko-dawatomi, Lunaapewa and Huron-Anishinabe delegations on the banks of the Ecorse River, on April 27, Obwandiac would begin his war for Manitou Aki, laying siege to Fort Detroit (Michigan) on May 7. This siege would last until the middle of November.

Obwandiac, for some reason, didn't take the fort, despite the fact that Thames River leader Sekahos and his force of 120 Ojibway-Anishinabe ni-gahn-no-say-wi-ni-ni-wahg and o-gi-chi-dahg arrived there on May 21, followed by Wasson's Ojibway-Anishinabe force of 200 o-gi-chi-dahg from Saginaw Bay on May 31. By June 9, Obwandiac had a force of 850 o-gi-chi-dahg under his command.[17] The sheer size of his military force made it quite clear that the fall of Fort Detroit was inevitable.

The question as to why Obwandiac didn't take Fort Detroit is certainly up for debate. However, we have to keep in mind that Obwandiac's every move was predicated on listening to the advice of his war council. More interestingly, they advised against the total annihilation of British forces.

With military precision, a number of forts were taken by Anishinabe forces in relatively short order. Fort Sandusky (Ohio), on the south shore of *Lake Erie,* surrendered relatively quickly on May 16; Fort St. Joseph (Ontario), the British forces' most westerly post, was taken by Ninivois and Ishkodawatomi-Anishinabe forces on May 25; and Fort Miami (Michigan), overlooking *Lake Michigan*, surrendered to Myaamia/Twightwee-Anishinabe forces on May 27.

Similarly, Kickapoo, Piankashaw and Wea-Anishinabe forces quickly captured Fort Ouatanon (Indiana) on June 1, and within three days, Ojibway and Sac-Anishinabe forces led by Men-neh-weh-na (*The One with Silver Tongue*)[18] had captured Fort Michilimackinac (Michigan). In a journal entry, Alexander Henry wrote that Men-neh-weh-na had spared his life following the defeat of Fort Michilimackinac, an act of compassion that surprised him.

Ojibway-Anishinabe leader Wasson would lead a force of approximately three hundred Ota'wa, Ojibway, Ishkodawatomi, Mingo, Kiashuta, Seneca and Wendat-Anishinabe o-gi-chi-dahg that quickly captured Forts Presque Isle, Le Boeuf and Venango in (Pennsylvania) between June 15 and 20. The next day, Ota'wa-Anishinabe forces attacked settlements at L'Arbre Croche and Sault Ste. Marie (Michigan and Ontario, respectively). On June 22, the N'swi-ish-ko-day-kawn Anishinabeg O'dish-ko-day-kawn lay siege to Fort Pitt at the confluence of the Allegheny and Monogahela rivers in Pennsylvania but did not overrun the garrison for specific reasons, which we'll discuss later in the story.

It's remarkable that Obwandiac – without the use of modern technology – was able to quickly lay waste to British garrisons in Fort Sandusky (Ohio), Fort St. Joseph (Ontario), Fort Miami and Fort Michilimackinac (Michigan), Fort Ouatanon (Indiana), and Fort Presque Isle and Fort Venango (Pennsylvania).

Following the failure of their surprise attack on Obwandiac's encampment on June 24, 1763, the British were faced with the possibility of losing the war. On the same day as the attack on Obwandiac's camp, they gave two smallpox-contaminated blankets and a handkerchief to Anishinabe delegates attending a meeting to discuss peace provisions at Fort Pitt.

BAH-NAH-JI-TOO-WIN ZHIGO ZHIINGENDAAGOOZHI ANISHINABEG | GENOCIDE AND THE IDEA OF INDIAN HATING

The use of germ/biological warfare was really nothing new in military campaigns in other parts of the world. The Assyrians, for example, used germ/biological warfare as a weapon and tactic in 501–600 BC by poisoning the wells of their enemies; Hannibal of Carthage was said to have used poisonous snakes against the Pergamene navy; and the Mongols and Turks often used infected carcasses to infect the water supplies of their enemies.

In this case, the use of smallpox was indicative of two things: Amherst's deep racial hatred for Anishinabeg and the difficult and serious situation the British found themselves in. The plan was detailed in a series of letters between Colonel Henri Bouquet and Amherst, in which they discussed the use of smallpox-contaminated blankets to infect Anishinabe forces laying siege to Fort Pitt. For posterity, I've taken the liberty of sharing parts of these letters here.

In one of the first in a series of letters, Bouquet wrote, "That vermine have forfeited all claims to the rights of humanity."[19] Amherst responded to William Johnson on July 9, 1763, and again on August 27, 1763, suggesting that "Measures to be taken as would bring about the Total Extirpation of those Indian Nations" and "Put a most Effectual Stop to their very being."[20]

Amherst continued, "Could it not be contrived to send the small pox among those disaffected tribes of Indians? We must on this occasion use every stratagem in our power to reduce them." Bouquet in response: "I will try to inoculate the Indians by means of blankets that may fall in their hands, taking care however not to get the disease myself" (Amherst journal entry, June 29, 1763).

On July 16, 1763, Amherst resolved to "extirpate this execrable race"[21] by using smallpox-contaminated blankets to be used as gifts to Anishinabe delegates attending a meeting to discuss peace provisions.

OMI-KWAY-NI-MAAN OBWANDIAC | OBWANDIAC REMEMBERED

In one of the campaign's last battles, the N'swi-ish-ko-day Anishinabeg O'dish-ko-day-kawn and its Seneca-Anishinabe allies soundly defeated the British at Devil's Hole (Fort Niagara, New York) on September 14, 1763. Shortly after, "Monsieur Dequindre, a French officer from Fort Chartres, arrives with the news that the peace between France and Britain was official."[22]

The influence and leadership abilities of Obwandiac were unparalleled for the time; his military success between May and November 1763 was indicative of this. We see, for example, that in less than six weeks, Forts Sandusky (Ohio), St. Joseph and Michilimackinac (Michigan), Ouatanon and Miami (Indiana) and Presque Isle, and Venango and Le Boeuf (Pennsylvania) surrendered to N'swi-ish-ko-day-kawn Anishinabeg O'dish-ko-day-kawn forces. During this period, only Fort Pitt and Fort Detroit remained in British hands.

Even before the start of the French and Indian War, Obwandiac had a clear idea that Anishinabe nations would have little or no choice but to participate in the global military and economic conflict manifesting itself on Manitou Aki. It's also important to take into consideration the fact that Obwandiac forced the British to accept that a clearer nations-to-Crown rapprochement was needed with the N'swi-ish-ko-day-kawn Anishinabeg O'dish-ko-day-kawn and its allies. For him this was essential to maintaining the notion of the middle ground.

Immediately following the Treaty of Paris (February 10, 1763) and the Royal Proclamation (October 7, 1763), an uneasy truce enveloped indian country. In effect, the proclamation was seen by many as an attempt to provide the means through which peaceful coexistence could be maintained and Anishinabe inherent/primordial title to land recognized.

With Amherst's removal in November 1763, the Anishinabe nations saw a radical shift in British policy and attitude. Amherst's replacement, General Thomas Gage, was seen as having a better grasp of diplomatic relations and of the middle ground's diplomatic and economic protocols. More importantly, he knew that Obwandiac still had approximately six hundred o-gi-chi-dahg at his disposal. Gage informed William Johnson of this in a letter dated July 2, 1764.

From the outset of the French and Indian War, in May 1763, Obwandiac knew that Anishinabe military success would depend in large part on the military efficiency of the confederacy. He also knew that political and military alliances with other Anishinabe nations would be critical.

OBWANDIAC ZHIGO DE-BWE-TAM I-NAH-KO-NI-GAY-WIN[23] | OBWANDIAC AND THE ROYAL PROCLAMATION OF 1763

Andrew Blackbird acknowledged that Obwandiac's use of economic, political and military resources was effective and absolute. He added that this convinced the British that only negotiation and accommodation would bring an end to the hostilities.

On October 7, 1763, King George III delivered the Royal Proclamation, acknowledging the primordial rights of Anishinabe nations to lands and a commitment to a treaty process that would facilitate the sharing of lands and resources on Manitou Aki. In effect, Anishinabe Bill of Rights.

Two days after learning of the Treaty of Paris, on October 29, 1763, Obwandiac ended his siege of Fort Detroit (Michigan). He was heard to say to those around him, "They can have their Fort ... we have our lands."

The Royal Proclamation for the most part defined the nations-to-Crown protocols and code of conduct between the Euro-American and Anishinabe nations. It also established legislation specific to the use of and sharing of indian land. Given its focus on treaty rights and the sharing of land/resources, the Royal Proclamation as an Anishinabe Bill of Rights became one of the mitigating factors for the American fight for independence in 1783. In retrospect, it came to mean many different things to many different people.

For Anishinabe nations, the Royal Proclamation remains important for two reasons: it was the first time the territorial integrity and ancestral title to Manitou Aki was acknowledged, and it recognized the concept and practical application of Anishinabe nationhood and sovereignty. With the proclamation, Britain legally entrenched and institutionalized a treaty-making process and made Anishinabe consent a prerequisite to the sharing of any territory and/or resources.

JEESKAHN ZHIGO MI-KI-NAAK | THE SHAKING TENT AND THE TURTLE

Obwandiac's participation in and use of ceremony to find out whether he should participate in the 1764 Niagara meetings to ratify the Royal Proclamation is interesting. The indian ways, such as the jeeskahn, madoodiswan (*sweat lodge*), gii'i'go-shi-mo (*fast for a vision; vision quest*), manitou na-ga-mo-nan (*sacred songs*), gi-ki-nah-mah-gay-wi-nan (*teachings*) and zagaswe'i'di-win opwaagan (*pipe way*), characterize a very different way of communicating with all living things, the world around us and the universe.

The use of ceremonies and stories to teach ah-way-chi-gay-win (*life lessons*) is as old as the world itself. In the past, the indian ways were our way of finding answers to questions about issues or concerns we might have had. In this instance, Obwandiac had concerns about the ratification of the Royal Proclamation and therefore sought counsel in ceremony. In the contemporary world, we look to legal and political advisors, researchers and so on.

In the period leading up to the Niagara meetings, Obwandiac continued to question Johnson's strategy of establishing multilateral relations with each of the major Anishinabe confederacies. He understood full well that his participation in any of these initiatives would be seen as a capitulation to William Johnson, who, as indian superintendent, was a polarizing figure. Obwandiac was therefore quite content keeping his distance from any of Johnson's attempts to broker any treaty or diplomatic process. Any or all of Johnson's influence and legitimacy up to this point rested solely on the shoulders of Joseph Brant.

Obwandiac's use of the jeeskahn was of particular interest to me, given my participation in several jeeskahn ceremonies and belief in the indian ways and both my own o-dah-bah-ji-gahn and that of this story. His use of the ceremony spoke volumes to me, and I was appreciative of the teaching he was able to share with me.

The elder Alexander Henry wrote that during this ceremony there were things he saw and heard that challenged his reality and could never be explained. He asked, for example, how one responds to the *Great Turtle* and other mi-zhi-ni-way-wahg (*spirit messengers, dream helpers*) who speak to one in many different ways and at different levels because one feels them, breathes them, sees them as alive and as having their own spirit life. They speak to a natural and vibrant world, complete with answers as to how we reframe, reclaim and rename. These spirit messengers, as Henry understood, "possessed unique powers of translation, which enabled Anishinabe to speak with kitchi manitou."[24] This notion of Anishinabe kayn-dah-so-win (*ways of knowing*) becomes even more interesting because the concept has been distorted beyond understanding. For some people, ceremony is seen as "old gossip" or something "sinister."

Henry described in great detail the preparation that took place, noting the placement of five different species of poles ten feet in height, which were placed in holes approximately two feet deep in a circle about four feet in diameter and bound together by a circular hoop. This would come to serve as the structure/skeleton of the jeeskahn.[25]

The ceremony began at nightfall, once the structure of the jeeskahn was covered with animal skins and the jeeskahn i-ni-ni (*shaking tent man*) was tied by the arms. At this time, the oshka-bewis (*ceremonial helper*) helped in calling the jiibayag (*spirits*), using the opwaagan and manitou na-ga-mo-nan. The tent began to shake, the shaking increasing in intensity because of what Henry assumed were the spirits entering it. The voices he heard were those of the jeeskahn i-ni-ni, Great Turtle and the spirits, who were telling Obwandiac to avoid the gathering because of the boats full of soldiers the Great Turtle had seen. Henry described how there was "a cacophony of animal sounds emanating from it, followed by a period of silence. The great turtle was heard and the Jiisakiiwinini declared the spirit's readiness to answer questions."[26] He added that Obwandiac then offered tobacco to the jeeskahn and asked "whether or not the English were preparing to make war upon the Indians and whether or not there were at Fort Niagara a large number of English troops."[27] Henry was astonished when the Great Turtle returned to tell Obwandiac that "he had visited Fort Niagara and on proceeding further towards Montreal and the river was covered with boats full of soldiers on their way to make war."[28]

Despite the British promise of peace, Obwandiac didn't attend the gathering because of what the Great Turtle told him. Instead, he asked Men-neh-weh-na to lead the N'swi-ish-ko-day-kawn Anishinabeg O'dish-ko-day-kawn delegation to the gathering. Obviously, some people will ask, "How can something like this happen or take place? It must have been Obwandiac's imagination!" In response to questions like this, I point to the indian ways and miskew ah-zha-way-chi-win that we share with the past, which enables us to experience and share in their experiences. They speak to the emotional and spiritual aspects of being Anishinabe.

The mi-zhi-ni-way-wahg speak to us using the indian ways: our ah-di-so-kah-nahg, di-bah-ji-mo-wi-nan and ah-way-chi-gay-wi-nan, our bah-wah-ji-gay-wi-nan (*dreams*) and ni-gahn-nah-ji-mo-wi-nan (*prophecies*). All are sacred items in my o-dah-bah-ji-gahn that show me and my family our peoples' memory of sacred places. They also help explain my interconnectedness with the world around me. These indian ways and o-dah-bah-ji-gahn also guide me and show me how we as Ojibway-Anishinabeg came to think this way about our reality, how and why we were placed on this land. It's a pretty expansive place, but it's also pretty finite. More often than not, these experiences will speak to our indianness/Anishinabeness and our place in this world and provide us with an opportunity to understand the Ojibway-Anishinabe ethos.

Regardless, our ways of knowing and ceremonial knowledge provide us with necessary survival skills. They may vary from nation to nation, but they are more than just a neat story to amuse kids around a campfire. They explain a complex set of relationships between man and his creator, the animals and plants, the universe and its creation. The "west" as an ideal has vigorously attempted to discredit this incredible reality and history.

We know from our stories and miskew ah-zha-way-chi-win that the west has always been about the control of people and their cultures. It's about arrogance, both intellectual and spiritual. For this reason, the stories about Obwandiac, Tecumtha, Shingwauk and the N'swi-ish-ko-day-kawn Anishinabeg O'dish-ko-day-kawn are about reframing, reclaiming and renaming.

There are varying interpretations of what took place during Obwandiac's visit to the jeeskahn. However, Henry did acknowledge that Obwandiac became very much opposed to the idea of reconciliation, and in his opinion Obwandiac understood that the future of Anishinabeg depended in large part on his decision and this troubled him.

In a letter to William Johnson, George Croghan made it quite clear that Obwandiac's importance was not misplaced: "Pontiac commands more respect amongst those nations, than any Indian I ever saw could do amongst his own tribe."[29] From 1763 until his death on April 20, 1769, at Cahokia (present-day *St. Louis, Missouri*), Obwandiac continued to push for a restored political, economic and military middle ground. His genius lay in his ability to effectively articulate Neolin's spiritual vision in a way that motivated Anishinabe nations to challenge British attempts to remove the shadow of Anishinabe title. In doing this, he was able to stand outside the colonial rhetoric and harness Neolin's spiritual message to achieve specific political and military objectives. The N'swi-ish-ko-day-kawn Anishinabeg O'dish-ko-day-kawn under Obwandiac's leadership would take nine of twelve British forts and change the face of colonial oppression on Manitou Aki.

The Royal Proclamation and its treaty framework was formally ratified at Niagara on August 1, 1764, by twenty-four[30] Anishinabe nations. Shortly after this, a number of questionable treaties were negotiated in fairly rapid succession. These treaties created a number of problems specifically for the Shawnee-Anishinabeg, because the lands being treated and surrendered represented their principal hunting territory and also because the sovereignty of the United States was acknowledged.

CONQUEST TREATIES

Four treaties were particularly troublesome for Obwandiac, Tecumtha, Shingwauk and other Anishinabe leadership from 1768 to 1795, for a variety of reasons.

The Treaty of Fort Stanwix,[31] for example, negotiated on November 5, 1768, saw the Mohawk-Anishinabeg surrender parts of Shawnee-Anishinabe ancestral territory to the newly established United States. The Shawnee-Anishinabe argue that the lands in question weren't the Haudenosaunee-Anishinabe confederacy's to treat or surrender, and that William Johnson, George Croghan and Joseph Brant had a conflict of interest, because one was a land speculator, another was an indian agent and the last had no authority to surrender any of the lands in question.

Next was the Treaty of Fort McIntosh, in 1785, which again was negotiated by the Mohawk-Anishinabeg and a group of young Wendat and Lunaapewa-Anishinabe leaders who acknowledged the sovereignty of the United States for the first time.

Following the signing of the Treaty of Fort Finney on January 31, 1786, the Shawnee-Anishinabeg gave a belt of black wampum to the United States as a declaration of war. And on January 9, 1789, the signing of the Fort Harmar Treaty effectively transferred all of Ohio to the United States.

Perhaps most troubling to Tecumtha and the N'swi-ish-ko-day-kawn Anishinabeg O'dish ko-day-kawn was the 1795 Treaty of Greenville, because it was negotiated by Mi-chi-ki-ni-kwa, We-ya-pier-sen-wah, Ca-ta-ca-has-sa and Sha-te-yah-ron-ya (Wendat-Anishinabe; *Leatherlips*). It was particularly problematic because it was seen as a capitulation to the United States.

This sovereignty acknowledgment and land surrender gravy-train continued until 1871, when the House of Representatives stopped recognizing indian tribes as independent nations, ending nearly one hundred years of treaty-making.

In time, many Anishinabe nations and leaders would come to challenge the validity of these "*conquest treaties*" because of the complicity of a number of Anishinabe leaders who were appointed by the United States and the involvement of land speculators and indian agents who had ulterior motives for the one-sided negotiations. All of this would come to serve as a rallying point for Tecumtha in 1812.

The tone of the relationship between the United States, Great Britain and the Anishinabe nations also began to change during this period. First Sergeant Jacob de Marsac, for example, used the term "father" for the first time while delivering seventeen belts of wampum to the Ojibway, Ota'wa and Ishkodawatomi-Anishinabe leadership at Michilimackinac on April 27, 1755. This was also the first time that Great Britain told the Ojibway, Ota'wa and Ishkodawatomi-Anishinabeg that it wished to adopt them as children "instead of brothers as they have hitherto been."

The political, social and economic relationship between Britain and the indian nations became more tenuous during this period as well. Obwandiac saw this as an exaggeration of Britain's perceived authority and place in indian country.

In Ben Hinman's mind, his grandfather was a man who was able to move between both societies with relative ease. A man who successfully opposed European powers, forcing them to abandon grandiose notions and pretensions of conquest. At the end of the day, Ben spoke of his grandfather's eagle staff and medicine bundle and of his commitment to Anishinabe sovereignty. Who cares that few dramas and poems were ever written about him!

**Mii i'i-way ojibway-anishinabe i-zhi-chi-gay-win.
Zhigo mii'iw eta-go o-way neen-gi-kayn-dahn zhigo
ni-gi-noon-dah-wah... Ahaaw sa. Weweni.**

3

Tecumtha

HE WALKED ACROSS

Ni-biin-daa-koo-ji-ge gaye ni' o-nah-ko-nah
ah-di-so-kah-nahg zhigo di-bah-ji-mo-wi-nan g'dah
mi-kwe-ni-mah-nahn obwandiacbun, tecumthabun,
miinwaa shingwaukbun ... Meegwetch.

PATRICIA AND NORMAN Shawnoo (grandchildren of Tecumtha)
and I were sitting in a small restaurant at Kettle and Stony
Point in southwestern Ontario on a somewhat muggy June day,
talking about some of the issues that impact our people daily.
Poverty and missing and murdered women took up most of the
discussion. Patricia is quite active on a number of other fronts,
particularly as they impact Anishinabeg politically, socially and
environmentally. She is also a staunch advocate for women's
rights and is widely respected for this in her community and
throughout the rest of Canada and the United States. Interestingly, it was Patricia who corrected me on the proper pronun-
ciation of the name "Tecumtha." She smiled as she corrected me
at a gathering years ago, and I've been mindful of it ever since.

This was my first time meeting Norman, who as a leader in
his community commanded a great deal of respect. He carried
himself with quiet dignity. As former elected community leaders
we had many things in common, and we shared a few laughs
about some of the more difficult aspects of being an elected
leader.

I-NO-DE-WI-SI-WIN | THE FAMILY

Patricia and Norman tell me that Tecumtha's father, Pu-ke-shin-
wa n'wau (*Something That Falls*), a Kispoko-speaking Shawnee-
Anishinabe, was a "great war chief, a man who was highly
regarded as a statesmen and o-gi-chi-dah," who died fighting
alongside Ho-ko-les-kwa (Shawnee-Anishinabe; *Cornstalk*) at
Kenawa during the Battle of Point Pleasant (also known as
Lord Dunmore's war) in 1774. His mother, Me-thoa-taas-kee

(*A Turtle Laying Eggs in the Sand*), a Pekowi-speaking Shawnee-
Anishinabe woman, was also held in high regard throughout
the Shawnee-Anishinabe nation and would remain an influence
on Tecumtha throughout his life.

They also tell me that his eldest brother, Chee-see-kau (also
known as Pep-quan-na-ke – *The Gun*) took over as head of the
family following the death of their father, and they're quite
certain that it was Chee-see-kau who "put out" Tecumtha for
his ma-kah-day-kay-win (*vision quest*) at the age of twelve. It's
also important to note that it was Chee-see-kau who taught
Tecumtha "to look with contempt upon everything that was
mean and instilled in him [the] 'correct, manly and honourable
principles'." For this, Chee-see-kau came to be very much
respected and admired by his younger brother.

Patricia and Norman describe Tecumtha's sister Me-ne-wau-
laa-koo-see (Te-cu-ma-pe-ase; *Flying over Water* or *Wading Bird*),[1]
who was born in 1767 and died in 1825, as an "intelligent woman
who was respected by all the women." She was also very influential in all aspects of clan, community and nation matters.
Patricia and Norman emphasize that she held considerable
sway within the N'swi-ish-ko-day-kawn Anishinabeg O'dish-
ko-day-kawn during and after the War of 1812.

Tecumtha (*He Walked Across*) was born on March 9, 1768,
during the family's return to Piqua on the banks of the *Miami
River* in Chilicothe-Anishinabe territory (Ohio).

Tecumtha also had three brothers who were triplets. Ku-mus-
kau-kau (*Star Shooting in a Straight Line over Great Waters*) died
in his first year, and Sau-wa-see-kau (*Jumping Panther*) was
killed at the Battle of Fallen Timbers on August 20, 1794.
The last, Lau-lau-we-see-kau (*The Rattle*) – or Tens-ka-wa-ta-wa
(*The Open Door*) – is forever linked with Tecumtha and the War
of 1812.

We know with some certainty that Lau-lau-we-see-kau had
two wives, four sons and three daughters, and that one of his

sons, John Prophet, married Pe-ne-e-pe-es-ce, a daughter of
Sau-coth-caw (*Spybuck*), an important Shawnee-Anishinabe
leader.[2] Tecumtha also had another sister and brother, Ne-haa-
ee-mo and We-ya-pier-sen-wah (*Blue Jacket*), who were adopted
in 1771.

Me-thoa-taas-kee and Me-ne-wau-laa-koo-see were driving
forces throughout Tecumtha's life. They taught him, for example,
that men should show compassion to all Anishinabeg and that
showing respect for women was an honourable thing to do.[3] As
a result of her neglect of their infant son, Mah-yaw-we-kaw-pa-we,
Tecumtha's first wife, Moh-ne-toh-se, was sent back to her
family. His second wife, Ma-ma-te, died shortly after giving
birth to their son Nay-tha-way-nah (*A Panther Seizing Its Prey*;
also known as Pau-kee-saa, *Crouched Cat Stalking*), in 1796.

AWENEN TECUMTHA? | WHO WAS TECUMTHA?

Despite the litany of stories, epic poems, verse romances, historical novels and biographies of Tecumtha, there are few stories
about Tecumtha the man and his emergence as leader. (There
are few personal stories of any Anishinabe leader, for that matter.) Patricia and Norman mention that he was initially known
as Sha-wa-nung (*Southern Star Falling*) to acknowledge a star
that fell across the southern sky at his birth, and this was the
name he used during the Treaty of Greenville negotiations.
Tecumtha himself can never be understood in isolation from
Obwandiac, as their successes and failures are intimately connected, both emotionally and spiritually.

Tecumtha was described as being approximately five feet
ten in height, a strongly built man of superior intelligence.
The British never really knew what to make of this Shawnee-
Anishinabe man who was known to speak, read and write in
English but spoke only Shawnee when meeting with them. A
brilliant act of arrogance. They also came to realize that he was
far superior to any British military leader in their ranks.

Midwestern literary pioneer Judge James Hall, one of the earliest writers to document the historical relationship between the United States and Anishinabe nations, described him as a man of great genius and courage, who was bold and unwavering, an orator and leader the likes of which had never been seen before.

Some compared him to Napoleon himself, and others described him as the Shawanese king, a noble and heroic man, and one of the greatest Anishinabe leaders ever to have walked Manitou Aki. William Stanley Hatch, a colonel in the American army, for example, had a bizarre fascination with Tecumtha, describing him as a noble hero with a "mouth beautifully formed, like that of Napoleon I, his eyes clear, transparent, hazel."[4] I'm not sure what to make of Hatch's reason for describing Tecumtha this way, but I think on the whole it made it easier for Euro-Americans to see and accept him as an equal.

In *Wacousta; Or, The Prophesy: A Tale of the Canadas* (1832), John Richardson, the grandson of John Askin and an Ota'wa-Anishinabe woman, used fiction and historical fact to describe events leading up to the political resistance and War of 1812. Richardson afforded Tecumtha great respect and also had detailed knowledge of Lau-lau-we-see-kau's conversations with artist George Caitlin regarding the "*indian confederation.*"

Tecumtha understood the intricacies and many complicated layers of resistance politically, militarily and diplomatically, and because of this and the leadership qualities he embodied, Euro-Americans saw and referred to him differently. William Henry Harrison, a future president of the United States, on meeting Tecumtha for the first time told everyone that "eyewitnesses were well aware of the phenomenon of the heroic Indian chief."

There are historians who promoted the racist idea that Tecumtha and Obwandiac were of mixed blood because it was simply inconceivable from their perspective that an indian could ever have the ability to formulate complex ideas or thoughts. To them, an indian was simply "merciless" and "savage."

Ironically, Tecumtha would break every stereotype known to them. It must have been particularly frustrating and unnerving for the colonial administrators and military leaders of the day to see this. In fact, Tecumtha transcended the idea of who and what an indian was and had become, which was in direct contrast to how they saw Lau-lau-we-see-kau, an indian who represented everything that the Europeans feared and hated. He was celebrated "as one of the great patriot chiefs. These accounts treat him as a unique orator and brave warrior, an exemplary Indian."[5] He was also described as one of the most gifted and transformative leaders the world has seen, one who challenged the very nature of colonial expression and exceptionalism itself. Twentieth-century leaders Mahatma Gandhi and Nelson Mandela are often compared to him because of their similar ability to move people and articulate the meaning of revolution and political movement.

ZA-NA-GI' IWE KI-TA-KA-MI-GA | COLONIAL LANDSCAPE

A number of events that took place in 1812 were clearly indicative of Tecumtha's knowledge and understanding of the changing colonial landscape. For example, he understood that a common political and military front was necessary for challenging the questionable treaty negotiations and land surrenders taking place. To this end, the authority of individual Anishinabe leaders and communities to enter into and make treaties often came into question because "Ojibway, Ota'wa and Ishkodawatomi-Anishinabe nations openly operated by consensual and limited delegation of authority and many of the chiefs and headmen who were negotiating treaties on behalf of their people did not have total authority."[6]

In the period leading up to the war, Tecumtha made it quite clear that only a federation and alliance of indian nations with shared commonalities and heritage could enter into negotiations and agree to treaties. From his perspective, individual leaders, communities and nations negotiating treaties didn't have the authority to surrender lands and territory that collectively belonged to all Anishinabe nations.

In retrospect, both Obwandiac and Tecumtha understood the subtle nuances of the colonial *realpolitik*. We see this in all their deliberations with the Euro-Americans. In this way they mirrored each other. Further, their ability to express Neolin's and Lau-lau-we-see-kau's spiritual visions politically and militarily was a thing of practicality. As well, their success in establishing military alliances with France, Britain and other indian nations was indicative of their military and diplomatic savvy. Tecumtha's orchestration of the strategic alliance between Britain and the N'swi-ish-ko-day-kawn Anishinabeg O'dish-ko-day-kawn, for example, was the first time an Anishinabe leader would lead the forces of one colonial power against another. In 1763, Obwandiac fought independent of France, making his successes even more impressive.

The alliances that Tecumtha forged leading up to the War of 1812 were important from a diplomatic and intellectual perspective, given the myriad complexities in relation to political/diplomatic ideas, identity, territorial integrity and spirituality. This was an effective response to the impact of colonization.

As the alliance between the Anishinabe nations became more entrenched, Tecumtha and Lau-lau-we-see-kau reminded Anishinabe communities and nations of past resistance movements. They spoke of Obwandiac in 1763, of Ho-ko-les-kwa's Shawnee-Anishinabe war with Lord Dunmore[7] in 1774, and of Mi-chi-ki-ni-kwa and We-ya-pier-sen-wah's defeat of General Arthur St. Clair on November 4, 1761, at the Wabash River, one of the greatest Anishinabe victories over the United States.[8] They retold stories of Wampanoag-Anishinabe sachem/leader Metacom's warning about the land surrenders taking place in 1675–76.

MISKEW AH-ZHA-WAY-CHI-WIN | THE ACT OF FLOWING, OR BLOOD MEMORY, THE THREAD THAT TIES US TO OUR FAMILIES, THE EARTH AND OUR SPIRIT

Tecumtha and Lau-lau-we-see-kau were able to harness the memory of past diplomatic relationships and centuries-old trade networks that existed long before the arrival of the Europeans. They saw the value of articulating our shared heritage and commonality, which was reflected in our indianness/Anishinabeness and our rootedness in the land.

Tecumtha understood that a well-resourced and organized alliance was essential to any successful political and military campaign. He also knew that the N'swi-ish-ko-day-kawn Anishinabeg O'dish-ko-day-kawn would have to play a fundamental role in protecting Anishinabe sovereignty and jurisdiction over indian lands going forward.

Tecumtha saw that a respectful and equitable treaty process was deliberately non-existent. Further, the treaty negotiations and irresponsible land surrenders lacked legitimate representation from the Anishinabe collective as a whole. In his mind, this was a point of fact. He believed that Anishinabe nations had to retake and reclaim control of the treaty process, exercising sovereignty and jurisdiction over lands and resources. Call it what you want – Revolution! Resistance! Insurgence! – Tecumtha knew that for all the talk, each wasn't without consequence. For that reason, the focus on reconciliation was an important issue during one of the first Ojibway, Ota'wa, Ishkodawatomi, Wendat, Myaamia, Lunaapewa, Kickapoo and Winnebago-Anishinabe assemblies to take place.

Insurgency was "often a motivated and conscious undertaking on the part of the masses"[9] and a reflection of a peoples' conscious effort to break free from oppression and colonial slavery. Tecumtha realized that insurgency was the only viable response to the idea of American exceptionalism at the time.

Even before 1812, the United States was already fearful of the threat posed by Tecumtha. Secretary of War James McHenry, one of the signatories of the US Constitution, made this quite clear in a series of letters to General Arthur St. Clair, Governor of the Northwest Territory,[10] telling him that the Shawnee-Anishinabeg were committed to protecting the boundary line, and mentioning the impending meeting with the N'swi-ish-ko-day-kawn Anishinabeg O'dish-ko-day-kawn to discuss the 1795 Treaty of Greenville (Ohio). Patricia and Norman also point out that Tecumtha had started to plan and build support for his political and military movement ten years prior to 1812.

AMERICAN DIPLOMACY

In the hope of averting a major conflict, the United States proposed a number of initiatives. The first focused on inviting Lau-lau-we-see-kau to Washington to explore opportunities for compromise. The second concerned a series of meetings (held August 1–22, 1810) with the future president of the United States, William Henry Harrison, at Fort Vincennes (Indiana). At these meetings, Tecumtha and the seventy-five Shawnee, Winnebago, Kickapoo, Ishkodawatomi and Ota'wa-Anishinabe o-gi-chi-dahg who accompanied him were adamant that no more indian lands would be surrendered. Harrison was equally stubborn about the objectives of the United States.

On the second-last day, Tecumtha called Harrison a liar and questioned the integrity of the Anishinabe leadership, who were seemingly more loyal to the United States. Tecumtha maintained that returning to a more traditional lifestyle would better serve Anishinabe sovereignty and jurisdiction ideals within the context of the middle ground. He argued that the land surrenders taking place and negotiated treaties such as the Treaty of Greenville (1795) and Treaty of Fort Wayne (1809)[11] were particularly troublesome for a number of reasons. Tecumtha asserted that the consent of all Anishinabe nations was needed before these or any other treaty or land surrenders were ratified.[12] He was also adamant that the integrity of the middle ground be respected politically, socially and economically.

Tecumtha made every effort to maintain peace because organization and readiness was central to the confederacy and alliance's military strategy. At Anishinabe war council meetings, he spoke bluntly of his frustration with the Ishkodawatomi-Anishinabeg, describing them as impetuous in their efforts to wage war. In an effort to pre-empt them, Tecumtha sent runners carrying black wampum tied with red ribbons to the Ota'wa, Shawnee, Winnebago, Kickapoo and Sac-Anishinabeg, inviting them to join him in the upcoming military campaign.

Harrison also became alarmed by the respect and interest shown Tecumtha, as many of the Anishinabe nations were excited and emboldened by his military and political genius and Lau-lau-we-see-kau's spiritual message. Even more surprising to him was the fact that Tecumtha's message and reach extended as far as Manitou Abi in the northwest, and the influence of the N'swi-ish-ko-day-kawn Anishinabeg O'dish-ko-day-kawn on the Kickapoo, Sac, Fox, Winnebago and Menominee-Anishinabe nations. All of this, coupled with Tecumtha's military strategy and political network, forced Harrison to make a pre-emptive strike at Tippecanoe[13] in 1811.

ANISHINABE PRINCIPLES OF DIPLOMACY

Many people believe that a leader like Tecumtha comes along only once in a lifetime to bring about change and revolution.[14] He was a different kind of leader, with interesting characteristics and influences. One influence that stands out was that of Me-thoa-taas-kee and Me-ne-wau-laa-koo-see. Tecumtha's mother and sister continually reminded him that respect, compassion, kindness, sharing and taking care of those in need were important principles and teachings to protect.[15] In their eyes, the middle ground and its fundamental principles of Anishinabe diplomacy – bezhig onaagan gaye bezhig emikwan and biin-di-go-dah-di-win – were about Anishinabeg having respect for life and territorial jurisdiction.

For Anishinabeg, the emphasis on sharing was so strong that almost no interaction was carried on without it, because it ensured the well-being of all the people rather than just a few. Given this discussion's focus on land, I think John Locke's discourse on life, freedom and ownership of property, which helped shape the idea of capitalism and enlightenment in the United States, has some relevance, as it was contrary to everything that was Anishinabe society. This was certainly not lost on Jean-Jacques Rousseau, who believed that the Anishinabe notion of sharing and land protection was a precursor to the communist ideologies of Russia and China. In this regard, the War of 1812 could be seen as a struggle between the political ideologies of the future.

The United States' lack of respect for established boundaries represented a pejorative condemnation of the Royal Proclamation of 1763. In fact, Edmund Burke in his essay on political emancipation stated that King George III had overstepped his authority in defending the rights of the Anishinabeg. Maybe Burke saw the proclamation as an acceptance of British defeat and surrender as well; I'm not sure, but it would be worth a future discussion.

Shortly after its declaration of independence in 1776, the United States passed the Northwest Ordinance (1787), establishing the first organized territory in the United States. This proved problematic for Tecumtha, since he saw it as a political and military act of aggression. But I'm getting ahead of myself; I'll discuss this later in greater detail.

To reiterate, all the diplomacy, political, and military jockeying taking place in indian country showed Tecumtha that survival of Anishinabe society would depend in large part on some kind of political and spiritual renaissance and/or rejection of the Euro-American way of life. To some degree, Lau-lau-we-see-kau's "spiritual voice against assimilation and for 'traditional

practices'" became an important point of convergence for him.
Lau-lau-we-see-kau's vision provided Tecumtha with a certain
strength and resolve to right the colonial wrongs taking place.
Just as Obwandiac had before him, Tecumtha visited the
Midewigun to inform it of the inevitable military conflict.
Patricia makes it quite clear that the Grand Medicine Lodge
could in no way sanction any act of war or use of violence.

It became apparent that Tecumtha's planning and advocacy
was having a major impact throughout indian country. All
of this worried William Henry Harrison, Thomas Jefferson
(president of the United States from 1801 to 1908) and James
Madison in the period leading up to 1812.

Generally speaking, the United States' colonial politic was
unnerved by all of this. As political and diplomatic talks became
more intense, the colonial bureaucracy was threatened by
Tecumtha's very vocal opposition to the Greenville and Fort
Wayne treaties.

Patricia and Norman add that Anishinabe leaders during
Treaty of Greenville negotiations repeatedly suggested that the
"treaties (as) negotiated by the 'Long Knives' were not worth
the paper they were written on"[16] because "all the fires of the
Anishinabeg did not sanction it."[17] Tecumtha refused to "touch
the pen or feather to show his consent."[18] Both Patricia and
Norman describe how General Anthony Wayne drew a line in
the earth with his sword and told everyone that the treaty
would stand with the land on one side belonging to him and
that "anyone who crossed the line would get the sword run
through him." With a smile on their faces, they tell me how
Tecumtha walked across the line and said, "This treaty is no
good and the land is still ours!"[19]

Concerned about the duplicity surrounding the treaty
negotiations, Henry Rowe Schoolcraft[20] suggested that treaty
provisions and wording were often changed to reflect the
Euro-American perspective and tended to ignore those of the
Anishinabeg. Pine Shomin points out that "the wording was

altered so that the land, which was to be reserved for the Anishinaaybeg forever, was only to be reserved for five years."[21]

Tecumtha certainly had his share of detractors, with Mi-chi-ki-ni-kwa being the most vocal, assuring United States representatives during Treaty of Greenville negotiations that the Anishinabe nations would never come together in one council. In response, Tecumtha argued that no single village or nation leader could sign away the sovereignty over lands that belonged collectively to all Anishinabeg. The Treaty of Greenville was just one tip of many icebergs.

Tecumtha's strategy on expanding the political, economic, social and military base of the N'swi-ish-ko-day-kawn Anishinabeg O'dish-ko-day-kawn was also important in the diplomatic discussions taking place at this time. In his mind, the movement had to go beyond the colonial construct. His message of an Anishinabe political, spiritual, military and nation uprising resonated throughout indian country because there was a legitimate fear that land and all its resources would "pass into the hands of the white man."[22]

MAAWANJI'IDIWAG | COMING TOGETHER

Tecumtha's political vision of a confederation of nations provided a realistic alternative to the oppressive idea of United States expansionism and colonial terrorism. This idea of a newly recharged and invigorated confederacy was incredibly bold for the period, given the complexity of Anishinabe nation protocols politically and culturally. His success in organizing an independent movement of this magnitude, despite differences in culture, politics, nation protocols and so on, was all the more incredible.

Political theorists and historians have insisted that all independence movements encounter similar difficulties when confronted with the same barriers. They have also suggested that all revitalization movements, independent of local differences, share these same common structures and processes.

Nevertheless, the complex Anishinabe nation protocols and traditional structures always had at their centre a common thread, rooted in the land itself.

Tecumtha continued to push for a military response to the treaties being negotiated and repeatedly referred to the importance of the middle ground during his travels. For him, the middle ground was a manifestation of Anishinabe social, political, military, economic and diplomatic sovereignty. With brilliance, he was able to exploit the anti-colonial sentiment to the fullest because his strategy focused on sovereignty and self-determination issues. Even then these issues troubled many of the Anishinabe nations. In fact, Tecumtha's understanding of colonial politics came from the Anishinabe resistance to Euro-American colonization since first contact.

During his travels, Tecumtha repeatedly made reference to newly negotiated treaties that were surrendering large tracts of indian land. Initially, there was little appetite for war or the confederacy of nations that Obwandiac had first broached in 1763. However, the Treaty of Greenville created a serious political schism in indian country as a result of the collusion that took place, in the form of illegal sales of land by individuals or tribes without authority, during its negotiation and eventual signing.

Regardless of the United States' proposed commitment to a revised demarcation and boundary line, Tecumtha continued to oppose the treaty and its provisions, seeing the need to object to William Henry Harrison's attempt to be the "apex of the colonial triangle" because, even then, information and communication were power. He argued and remained adamant that the United States could not initiate any treaty negotiation without consultation and meetings with the Anishinabe collective. And he then told the US representatives that he had no interest in visiting President Thomas Jefferson to discuss anything.[23] His arrogance was brilliant!

AMERICAN EXCEPTIONALISM

Tecumtha saw American exceptionalism[24] as foolish and bold in the same breath, as it was a departure from past diplomatic and political practices. In the days leading up to the United States' declaration of war, Harrison pointed to the diminishing influence of the wampum belt that spoke to the unity of the indian nations, adding that the Wendat-Anishinabeg, who were entrusted with the responsibility of safeguarding the "Great Belt [as a] Symbol of Union between the Tribes in their late war with the United States," had taken a position of neutrality with respect to the treaties being negotiated. This, of course, caused him some worry.

President James Madison's declaration of war on June 18, 1812, proved a bit more challenging for Tecumtha, because he knew that the allied Anishinabe nations were not militarily ready or organized, and they were central to his objective of going to war. Patricia and Norman point out that both Tecumtha and Lau-lau-we-see-kau were unyielding in their opposition to American expansionism because of the threat it posed to Anishinabe sovereignty and jurisdiction. They relish the excitement their grandfather created: "We know the meetings were full of excitement and the atmosphere electric ... Boy! If only! Our lives would have been so different!"

They add that their grandfather saw an interesting parallel between the Anishinabe and slave experience. Tecumtha believed the slave trade and the treatment of blacks were no different from what the Anishinabe nations were facing. He saw that the colonial practices of the day had a spatial/spiritual exile from the land and a cultural/psychological focus at their core. He knew that slavery played a significant role in the commerce of the colonial economy, and in this equation indians were simply in the way and had to be removed.

Tecumtha considered colonial politics a threat to the very idea of Anishinabe self-determination, sovereignty and the middle ground itself. Not surprisingly, his idea for self-determination and national unity drew on the strategies of resistance in use since contact, and he never once vacillated in his opposition to the large wholesale land surrenders taking place. The Greenville and Fort Wayne (Indiana)[25] treaties, in his view, added to the inequality between the United States and indian nations and seriously undermined the idea of the middle ground.

The threat to the principle of the middle ground was also exacerbated by the changing Anishinabe–Euro-American political, economic, social and military relations in the period leading up to 1812. In the autumn of 1810, for example, Tecumtha travelled to the Cherokee, Choctaw, Chickasaw, Muskogee and Seminole-Anishinabe nations in the south (present-day Kentucky, *Tennessee*, *Mississippi*, Alabama, South Carolina, Georgia, *Louisiana* and *Florida*) and Wendat, Kickapoo, Ota'wa and Ishkodawatomi-Anishinabe communities along the *Illinois* and *Fox Rivers* and northern shores of Lake Huron (Wisconsin and Illinois) to tell them of the impending war with the United States. In response, General William Hull and William Henry Harrison met with Anishinabeg near present-day Detroit and Fort Wayne in an effort to dissuade them from joining Tecumtha's resistance movement.

ONAAKONAN | THE PLAN AND STRATEGY

Tecumtha's opposition to the colonial grand design and relationship between the Anishinabe nations and colonials was deep-rooted. Patricia and Norman describe the relationship between Harrison and Tecumtha as explosive. Harrison, it seemed, felt threatened by Tecumtha and everything that he represented.

Tecumtha was also unyielding in his presentation to Harrison at Vincennes (Indiana) on August 12, 1810. "Tell him he lies! The whites will not cross the old boundary," he shouted at

Harrison, who was taken aback by this demanding indian. In response, Harrison shouted, "The United States [will] enforce the 1809 Treaty of Fort Wayne by sword if need be." Undeterred, Tecumtha told Harrison that all Anishinabeg had equal rights to the unoccupied land, that the right of occupancy was as good in one place as it was in another, and that the land belonged to the first who sat down on it with his blanket/skins. And he added that "no other man or nation has a right to the land until the first leaves it."

During the exchange, Tecumtha made it quite clear that there would be no further land surrenders without the consent of all Anishinabe nations – a stunning condemnation and indictment of American international policy! In fact this meeting convinced Tecumtha that there was absolutely no possibility of compromise or rapprochement with the United States.

There were also interesting financial and land transactions taking place during this time. For example, historian William Bergmann writes, "Land sales would not on any condition exceed two cents per acre, notwithstanding that the federal government attempted to sell the same land for as much as eight dollars per acre."[26] Throughout all of the shenanigans that were taking place, Tecumtha continued to argue that all Anishinabe lands were held in common by all Anishinabeg and therefore could not be bartered or sold without the agreement and consent of all. The problem with the land surrenders, he pointed out, was that Ojibway, Ota'wa and Ishkodawatomi-Anishinabe leadership were in no position to agree or acquiesce to provisions of any treaty without the approval of the citizenship as a whole.

Tecumtha's idea of a sovereign Anishinabe state was an expression and manifestation of the Anishinabe reality. For him, this was a fundamental piece of the anti-colonial sentiment and resistance that spanned centuries. His vision of a sovereign Anishinabe state was in fact based on a confederation of Anishinabe nations that was itself predicated on the persistence of at least two generations' worth of Anishinabe activism and resistance, which drew from a healthy and vibrant network of alliances and protocols.

Historian Rachel Buff acknowledges that Tecumtha was decidedly strategic in his opposition to United States colonial expansion and was particularly effective at articulating his political and intellectual ideas in relation to Lau-lau-we-see-kau's spiritual vision. In her view, Tecumtha helped Anishinabeg reclaim the idea of a separate Anishinabe sovereign state/jurisdiction. She adds that he was able to give some clarity to Lau-lau-we-see-kau's vision from quite a secular place[27] – a genius or gift that not many had.

The spiritual and political visions Tecumtha and Lau-lau-we-see-kau shared throughout this period were wrapped in the Anishinabe ah-di-so-kah-nahg, a vibrant piece of Anishinabe nah-nah-gah-dah-wayn-ji-gay-win. This in itself was empowering and exciting. The brothers saw the practical side of being politically and culturally separate from the vagaries that colonization and assimilation brought with them, and this message resounded loudly throughout indian country. Buff points out that "accepting the categories of 'red' and 'white' allowed the Indians to 'awaken' and unite; and draw upon traditional practices as well as the cultural and epistemological adaptations made as a response to colonialism."[28]

All of this would prove fertile ground for Tecumtha and Lau-lau-we-see-kau as they continued to challenge Harrison's pursuit of "United States hegemony and semiotic order" and the notion that he alone stood at the "apex of the colonial triangle." Coupled with the frustration that ran rampant throughout indian country and Lau-lau-we-see-kau's continued condemnation of questionable land surrenders and the focus on private property, abuse of liquor and other Euro-American practices, Tecumtha and Lau-lau-we-see-kau's messages took root.

TECUMTHA GANWIIKE | TECUMTHA REMEMBERS

Many young people were energized by Tecumtha and
Lau-lau-we-see-kau because they reaffirmed the Anishinabe
notion of independence and sovereignty. There was also something pure in reaffirming what we've always known, in terms
of where we came from, who we were and how we fit into this
world. The ah-di-so-kah-nahg, ah-way-chi-gay-wi-nan and our
own di-bah-ji-mo-wi-nan speak to this and also define our
notions of Anishinabe justice and liberation. The fact that
the brothers were willing to sacrifice their lives to change the
colonial narrative and the Anishinabe world was certainly
not lost on the young people.

Tecumtha and Lau-lau-we-see-kau continued to resist the
United States and its colonial terrorism at every turn. Lau-lau-
we-see-kau's warning of a great darkness was a defining moment
for many of the young ni-gahn-no-say-wi-ni-ni-wahg who eagerly
went to see him at *Prophetstown* during the spring of 1807.

For Tecumtha, Lau-lau-we-see-kau and other like-minded
ni-gahn-no-say-wi-ni-ni-wahg, and o-gi-chi-dahg, the N'swi-ish-
ko-day-kawn Anishinabeg O'dish-ko-day-kawn was the perfect
political and military vehicle through which to challenge the
United States. The brothers were able to harness incredible
energy and power for this specific end. No doubt the successes
achieved by Obwandiac (1763), Tecumtha (1812) and Shingwauk
(1812) were in large part due to the N'swi-ish-ko-day-kawn
Anishinabeg O'dish-ko-day-kawn and the alliances it established
with other nations.

A number of historians also make the argument that Joseph
Brant and the Haudenosaunee-Anishinabe Confederacy were
key figures in opposing the United States in the period leading
up to 1812. Just as they minimized Obwandiac's role in 1763,
they have attempted to minimize the roles of Tecumtha and the
N'swi-ish-ko-day-kawn Anishinabeg O'dish-ko-day-kawn in
1812. Incredibly, they give much of the credit to Joseph Brant

and the Haudenosaunee-Anishinabe Confederacy for the planning and creation of this large-scale Anishinabe resistance movement at a meeting that supposedly took place at *Lower Sandusky* (Ohio) in 1783.

However, our own written and oral accounts dismiss this altogether, telling us, for example, that Anishinabe nations would have rejected Brant's proposal for any kind of Anishinabe resistance movement without question because of his role in the Treaty of Fort Stanwix in 1768.

Everything that the colonial United States and Canada were and continue to be is because of the N'swi-ish-ko-day-kawn Anishinabeg O'dish-ko-day-kawn! Despite this, relatively little is known or understood about this political, economic, social, military and spiritual confederacy.

N'SWI-ISH-KO-DAY-KAWN ANISHINABEG O'DISH-KO-DAY-KAWN

The Ojibway, Ota'wa and Ishkodawatomi-Anishinabe nations established and organized themselves into a confederacy with a clearly defined governance structure, style of leadership and clan system that reflected an effective and sustainable form of Anishinabe government during the time of the *great migration*. Further, the ever-growing economy provided the N'swi-ish-ko-day-kawn Anishinabeg O'dish-ko-day-kawn with many economic opportunities.

A number of Anishinabe ah-di-so-kahn-i-ni-ni-wahg/kwe-wahg provide written and oral accounts concerning the influence of the N'swi-ish-ko-day-kawn Anishinabeg O'dish-ko-day-kawn. Ojibway-Anishinabe historians Mack-e-te-be-nessy (Andrew Blackbird), William Warren, Kah-ke-wa-quo-na-by (Peter Jones) and Kahgegagahbowh (George Copway) were probably the most prolific and accurate because of their fluency in Ojibwaymowin, and their understanding of the Ojibway, Ota'wa and Ishkodawatomi-Anishinabe kayn-dah-so-win, manitou kay-wi-nan (*ceremonies*), ah-di-so-kah-nahg, ah-way-chi-gay-wi-nan and

di-bah-ji-mo-wi-nan. For example, they tell us that following
the failure of the United States to live up to certain Treaty
of Paris[29] provisions, a number of Anishinabe nations took
responsibility for protecting the Canadian colonies and their
economies and maintaining the fur trade. The N'swi-ish-ko-day-
kawn Anishinabeg O'dish-ko-day-kawn certainly had a pivotal
role in the defence of present-day Canada. The United States
army and the British regulars in North America combined had
fewer men than the N'swi-ish-ko-day-kawn Anishinabeg O'dish-
ko-day-kawn, which had a force of over ten thousand men
ready for military mobilization. There certainly wasn't any
doubt about what the confederacy could do in the event of
military hostilities during this period.

Furthermore, there was some confusion regarding the
Haudenosaunee-Anishinabe Confederacy's role in either supporting or opposing Obwandiac, Tecumtha, Shingwauk and
the N'swi-ish-ko-day-kawn Anishinabeg O'dish-ko-day-kawn's
efforts in 1763 and 1812, respectively. However, Seneca-
Anishinabe forces were involved in the Forts Presque Isle
(June 15, 1763), Le Boeuf (June 18, 1763) and Venango (June
20, 1763) and Devil's Hole (September 14, 1763) military campaigns. As well, we believe that Sganyadai:yo (*Handsome Lake*;
Seneca-Anishinabe) might have been involved in the taking
of Fort Venango in Pennsylvania, because his uncle Guyasuta
fought alongside Anishinabe forces, and we know for certain
that he was at the Battle of Devil's Hole.

In the larger scheme of things, by the summer of 1813 the
two reservations under Sganyadai:yo's greatest personal influence – Allegheny and Tonawana – had still turned out a total
of only seven warriors. Also, a number of Mohawk-Anishinabeg
from *Grand River* enlisted to support the British,[30] and approximately 150–200 Iroquois-Anishinabeg from New York were
recruited by the United States. Of course, this would have
made for some interesting Haudenosaunee-Anishinabe internal
politics.

Trent University professor Paula Sherman questions the accuracy of some historians' attempts to paint the political, military, economic and spiritual relationship between the two confederacies as strained and constantly at political, economic and military odds with each other. In addition, Bawdwaywidun Banaise tells me that each confederacy had a healthy respect for the other's territory and jurisdiction, pointing to a "Council of Peace meeting (that) was called by the Ojibways, according to tradition, below Sault St. Marie ... This council received the deputies of the Iroquois, who concluded a treaty" during the latter part of the 1600s as a case in point. The agreement and truce remained in effect until a small Ojibway-Anishinabe hunting party was attacked by Iroquois-Anishinabeg three winters later. These hostilities continued until the Great Peace of Montréal was negotiated and signed by thirty-nine nations looking to "bury the hatchet deep in the earth" in 1701. The Great Peace of Montréal was the first recorded (on a wampum belt) Anishinabe treaty, which recognized that land was held in common by the Anishinabe collective and that the "chase be everywhere free; that landmarks and boundaries of all those great countries be raised; and that each one should find himself everywhere in his country." Both confederacies saw this as an opportunity to renew diplomatic and political relationships. Tecumtha made several references to the treaty in the period leading up to and during the War of 1812.

Tecumtha's focus on diplomacy and economic relationships was important, as it expressed a number of things, including his desire to salvage well-established nations-to-Crown protocols and Anishinabe i-nah-ko-ni-gay-win. Bawdwaywidun Banaise makes the point that a long time ago, the Haudenosaunee-Anishinabe longhouse in the east stood side by side with the Midewigun to the west, respecting each other's ceremonies and jurisdiction; this was rooted in bin-di-go-dah-di-win, a long-held nation-to-nation and nations-to-Crown protocol.

DEGANAWIDAH, AIENHWATHA AND THE
GAYANASHAGOWA | THE GREAT BINDING
LAW OR GREAT LAW OF PEACE

There's been some debate regarding the Haudenosaunee-Anishinabe Confederacy's reluctance to participate in the War of 1812. I believe that the confederacy's political and military position has to be understood in the context of Deganawidah (*The Peacemaker*), Aienhwatha (*He Who Seeks the Wampum Belt*) and the condoling (or condolence) ceremony. The ceremony itself was seen as an act of divine intervention in human affairs, which provides some explanation as to why the confederacy would have been reluctant to participate in any type of war.

For this reason, I'm careful about how I share my understanding of it, and I share it as I would in ceremony.

> **Ni-biin-daa-koo-ji-ge gaye ni' o-nah-ko-nah
> ah-di-so-kah-nahg zhigo di-bah-ji-mo-wi-nan
> g'dah mi-kwe-ni-mah-nahn deganawidah, aienhwatha,
> obwandiacbun, tecumthabun, miinwaa
> shingwaukbun ... Meegwetch.**

. . . . **❝❝** . . . .

When the Great League was created, Deganawidah visited Aienhwatha and brought with him four sacred ceremonies (Great Feather Dance, Drum Dance, Thanksgiving Song and the Peach Stone Game) and the Karihwi: io.[31]

Deganawidah spoke of one longhouse with five council fires that would come to represent one family. Deganawidah also revealed that the wampum belt would be the symbol used to convey messages of war and of peace.[32] A Tree of Peace was then planted in the centre of the chiefs with an

eagle perched on top and Deganawidah then told the
Haudenosaunee-Anishinabeg that the eagle would be vigilant
of threats and dangers to the confederacy.

Deganawidah also told the Haudenosaunee-Anishinabeg
that the white roots of the Tree of Peace would then span
its reach across the land. It would be here that the
Haudenosaunee-Anishinabe Confederacy would bury their
weapons of war. They would then bind five arrows together
and a council fire kindled, which would come to symbolize
the power and unity that comes from peace.

Following the Gayanashagowa proclamation, the condolence ceremony would replace blood revenge. Any crimes and
injustices committed from this point forward would be rem-
edied by a payment of wampum, whose reparations and
payments would be similar to the payment of fines and/or
jail terms.

That ten strings of wampum would be offered to make
amends for the loss of a man's life and twenty for the loss of a
woman. Punishment was doubled for a woman because she
could bear life. For the Haudenosaunee-Anishinabeg, the
great law is about being inclusive and respectful of the differences between "human beings."

And that the neutrality spoken of by Deganawidah in the
Gayanashagowa, condoling ceremony and the Gai wiio[33] and
Karihwi: io was expressed by the Haudenosaunee-Anishinabe
Confederacy in its commitment to peace and neutrality.
This was the message of Deganawidah as I was told and
have heard.

. . . . **"** . . . .

**Mii i'i-way ojibway-anishinabe i-zhi-chi-gay-win.
Zhigo mii'iw eta-go o-way neen-gi-kayn-dahn zhigo
ni-gi-noon-dah-wah . . . Ahaaw sa. Weweni.**

CONFLICT OF INTEREST AND DUPLICITY

The conflict of interest and duplicity in the negotiation of the Fort Stanwix (November 5, 1768), Fort McIntosh (January 21, 1785), Fort Finney (January 31, 1786) and Fort Harmar (January 9, 1789) treaties were somewhat obvious, to my mind. We see, for instance, that Joseph Brant was married to Catherine Croghan, a daughter of George Croghan (indian agent); and his sister Molly Brant was one of Indian Superintendent William Johnson's wives. Others, such as surveyor George Rogers Clark, physician Arthur Lee, Richard Butler, and lawyer and general Samuel Holden Parsons, were land speculators and military men who made acceptance of American sovereignty decidedly one-sided.

Of course, this had a definite bearing on how treaty and diplomatic relations unfolded during this period, because indian agents and indian superintendents had considerable power and latitude in dealing with Anishinabe nations. As previously mentioned, Johnson, Brant and Croghan's DNA are all over the Treaty of Fort Stanwix, which accepted American sovereignty for the first time. The treaty established a new line of property that extended the earlier proclamation line from the Alleghenies (the divide between the Ohio River and coastal watersheds) farther west, effectively transferring ownership and control of what now is Kentucky, West Virginia and Pennsylvania to the United States.

The Fort Stanwix (New York), Fort McIntosh (Pennsylvania) and Fort Finney (Ohio) treaties saw the Mohawk-Anishinabeg surrender millions of acres of Ojibway, Ota'wa, Ishkodawatomi and Shawnee-Anishinabe territory. As well, the involvement and complicity of Clark, Lee, Butler and Parsons, all of whom were government agents, in these negotiations was particularly troubling for the Ojibway, Ota'wa, Ishkodawatomi and Shawnee-Anishinabeg. The great wealth and sense of entitlement amassed by carpetbaggers and land speculators such as John D. Rockefeller, J.P. Morgan and Andrew Carnegie, men who believed they had the "special right of God" to extinguish Anishinabe title and advance the policies of manifest destiny,[34] was also a direct consequence of these types of negotiations.

In view of the land surrenders and concessions being made, it became obvious to Tecumtha that the N'swi-ish-ko-day-kawn Anishinabeg O'dish-ko-day-kawn and its allies, the Creek and Choctaw-Anishinabeg, had to be more forceful and forthright in opposing the colonial United States. For him, the N'swi-ish-ko-day-kawn Anishinabeg O'dish-ko-day-kawn and its alliances with other Anishinabe nations were an expression of sovereignty under international law; to his mind, the treaties needed to express the original *spirit and intent* of the Royal Proclamation of 1763.

As well, Lau-lau-we-see-kau gave Tecumtha strength and confidence and convinced him that Anishinabeg had to "abandon everything that the white-man introduced into the tribes; he taught them that Great Spirit was angry with them because they conformed to the habits of the white-man."[35] The brothers clearly understood that the assimilationist and expansionist policies of the United States had to be stopped. The Treaty of Fort Wayne (September 30, 1809) and its surrender of 3 million acres was a case in point. They saw protecting the land and the middle ground fundamental to Anishinabe survival, which in turn protected the social, political and economic structures of Anishinabe society.

It's important to remember that to this point Anishinabe leadership had always been guided by its sense of responsibility. Through its highly structured clan and governance system, Anishinabe society defined the responsibilities of every Anishinabe citizen.

Tecumtha and Lau-lau-we-see-kau saw the middle ground as a historical fact and reality. For them, it represented a physical and philosophical place with "a system of harmonious co-operation, based on trade and mutual respect" and "intercultural law." The policies and intent of Americanism and exceptionalism were serious threats to the geographical and diplomatic integrity of the middle ground.

At the end of the war, there was a definitive shift in attitude, policies and legislation as a result of the transition and political jockeying taking place throughout indian country and the United States. Ironically, Chief Justice John Marshall's landmark ruling in *Worcester v. Georgia* (1832) did nothing to move President Andrew Jackson toward rapprochement with the Anishinabeg; when all was said and done, Jackson simply refused to enforce federal law and allowed the state of Georgia to disregard the sovereignty of the Cherokee-Anishinabe nation.

In retrospect, the War of 1812 was an opportunity to unite Anishinabe nations and protect Anishinabe nationhood as acknowledged within the Royal Proclamation.[36] Tecumtha would die defending Anishinabe unity and nationhood at the Battle of Moraviantown on October 5, 1813, at the age of forty-nine years. To him I say meegwetch for his vision, commitment and leadership to advance the cause of Anishinabe primordial rights to land, sovereignty and self-determination.

The day ends well, with Patricia, Norman and me reflecting on the memory of their grandfather and great-uncle. It's still beautifully warm, and it seems that Tecumtha is happy that we remember and honour him, a man whose worldview was uniquely Kispoko-Pekowi-Anishinabe.

**Mii i'i-way ojibway-anishinabe i-zhi-chi-gay-win.
Zhigo mii'iw eta-go o-way neen-gi-kayn-dahn zhigo
ni-gi-noon-dah-wah ... Ahaaw sa. Weweni.**

4

Shingwauk

THE WHITE PINE,

BOSS OF ALL THE TREES,

BECAUSE IT SHARES ITS POWER

WITH THE SUN AND MOON

Ni-biin-daa-koo-ji-ge gaye ni' o-nah-ko-nah
ah-di-so-kah-nahg zhigo di-bah-ji-mo-wi-nan g'dah
mi-kwe-ni-mah-nahn obwandiacbun, tecumthabun,
miinwaa shingwaukbun ... Meegwetch.

I PASS MY TOBACCO to *The White Pine*'s family in recognition
of Shingwauk (Ojibway-Anishinabe, ah-ji-jawk doodem;
Crane clan) and Shingwaukonse. These names were used
interchangeably, Shingwauk from noon to early evening and
Shingwaukonse from early evening to sunset, to acknowledge
the sun's waning power. Shingwauk was also given the name
Sah-kah-odjew-wahg-sah (*Sun Rising over the Mountain*) by
the Wabanowiwin (*Dawn Medicine Society, men/women who had
the ability to manipulate fire and interpret dreams for healing, and
who specialized in the natural order of the earth by studying the stars,
the moon and the sun*) to acknowledge that his power came from
the sun, its position in the sky.

On a bright sunny day in June, I was sitting with the grand-
daughters of Shingwauk, Betty Lou Grawbarger and Doreen
Pine-Lesage, as well as granddaughter Lana Grawbarger and
other members of the Shingwauk family at Ketegaunseebee.
They had graciously agreed to share stories of their grandfather. There was a lot of playful banter, gentle teasing and
so on taking place as Betty Lou, Doreen and Lana got ready
to share their stories.

From a personal perspective, this long journey had gone
full circle and was coming to an end. It seemed fitting that
the journey transition to this place where it all began, with the
planning for the first contemporary N'swi-ish-ko-day-kawn
Anishinabeg O'dish-ko-day-kawn gathering, back in the late
1980s and early 1990s.

The hot sun was shining through the kitchen window. It had
a calming and soothing effect on me. Betty Lou and I began to
talk casually about her grandfather.

JF: *I've heard many interesting stories about your grandfather, the type of leader he was and his vision for the future of our people. What are your earliest recollections of him?*

BETTY LOU: My grandfather was born on Mackinac Island in 1773. This is the story we listened to – like, you know, as children – that he was born on Mackinac Island and his mother was Ogimaa-kway (*Leading Woman*), the daughter of Mahng-ah-sid (*Loon Foot*), who was a well-known Ojibway-Anishinabe ah-ni-kay-o-gi-mah-kahn-ni-wid.

JF: *Can you tell me a little about his father, who he was, where he was from and where he met Ogimaa-kway?*

BETTY LOU: There were British ships anchored at Mackinac Island; this is where Shingwauk's father, Jean-Baptiste Bart, met his mother. We were told that when Shingwauk was three or four years old, his father took Ogimaa-kway as a mistress. So anyways, let me see ... I have to tell the truth, that's why I have to tell the truth. Jean-Baptiste took Ogimaa-kway, the only daughter of Mahng-ah-sid, as his mistress, lover and housekeeper. We were also told that when Shingwauk was three or four years old, his father wanted to take him back to England. They dressed him – took his buckskins off of him – they dressed him in a burgundy velvet suit.

JF: *That's pretty special ...*

BETTY LOU: Also, I might have been about four or five years old when my aunt Charlotte, my dad's sister ... she was the one who used to come and she would undo the wooden chest, Shingwauk's chest. There were a lot of things, and stories were told as items were brought out, this little burgundy velvet suit was there in that chest and we saw it. It was wrapped in tissue and she would unwrap it, [and] as she's taking things out, she's telling stories.

JF: *I've heard that your grandfather and Tecumtha had a special*
relationship with General Isaac Brock?

BETTY LOU: Yes, and the epaulets of General Brock were in
that chest. Because he took seven hundred warriors and
went to fight, join General Brock, and when General
Brock fell, he handed his epaulets to Shingwauk to lead
his men and his warriors.

JF: *Your grandfather was known to be one of the more important*
Ojibway-Anishinabe leaders during the War of 1812 and the
pre-Confederation treaty negotiations.

BETTY LOU: Apparently he had quite a history – he ended up
a champion because that General Brock took them and he
handed them to Shingwauk – he's the leader, he said, of
General Brock's men and his own warriors.[1] So that's the
story, just because they're taking his chest out all these
stories come out and if you're a good listener and your
language is the native language, then you know what's
being talked about.

Darrell Boissoneau added during the conversation that Shingwauk's home "was near present-day *Munising*, Michigan."

Shingwauk remains alive in the oral history and memory of the
Ketegaunseebee Ojibway-Anishinabe community and family
members. This man, who was considered one of the most influential Ojibway-Anishinabe leaders within the N'swi-ish-ko-day-
kawn Anishinabeg O'dish-ko-day-kawn in the early 1800s and
one of the leading figures during the Robinson-Huron and
Robinson-Superior treaty negotiations in 1850, is omnipresent
in this region of Manitou Aki.

In one of his many discussions with Thor and Julie Conway,
authors of *Spirits on Stone: The Agawa Pictographs*, Fred Pine, a
grandson of Shingwauk, described his grandfather's travels:
"He locked the doors up. He just came out sometimes.

Someday they didn't know where he was. He's gone. But his body was still there. A long journey. *California*. Nothing could stop that man."[2] Fred added that Shingwauk was known to travel to many different places by turning himself into a bird.

In relation to Fred's story and other similar stories shared by Jim Dumont, Don Daniels, Vine Deloria Jr. and Rufina Marie-Laws, I think about these physical transformations and shape-shifting possibilities. If we're to accept Ojibway-Anishinabe ah-di-so-kah-nahg and notions of history as fact, we should accept the Ojibway-Anishinabe way of seeing the world and its unfolding events as well. Only then can we come to appreciate people who see the world in this way and participate in the reality of the dream or vision. We might also come to regard their own personal lives and histories as the mysterious bridge between the "ordinary" and "non-ordinary" reality and the unique Ojibway-Anishinabeness that enables us to feel the warmth from "the mists of unremembered time a character in our traditional narratives, the trickster transformer that continues to guide our experiences"[3] and who tells us that you can't disturb a person who turns into a soul.

GII'IGOSHIMOWIN ZHIGO MIINIGOWIZID ANISHINABE | FASTING AND ANISHINABE GIFTS

Following his first ten-day fast, at the age of ten, Shingwauk fasted another ten times for ten other gifts, one of which enabled him to change into anything – any animal and anything in the world! The family add that he fasted "not to obtain a great name and respect among his people, but because he always wished to have fine dreams and wished to keep his head and thoughts clear."

From their perspective, Shingwauk's fast ceremonies and relationships with the people provided him with a clear vision of the truth and of the importance of transparency, commitment to personal values and our relationship to the Creator.[4] During these fasts he was given guidance from his spirit helpers. The family tells me that in the last twenty years of his life, Shingwauk ate just enough to keep his body strong.

It's still humbling for me when I think of his commitment to leading a good life through ceremony, fasting and abstinence, which provided him with a deep sense of spirituality and understanding of what was taking place throughout indian country. He knew, for example, that the colonial government was becoming more contemptuous of Anishinabe nations generally. In response, he pushed a treaty and independence rights agenda with respect to land, resources and governance and in due course became the face of this sustained resistance.

As efforts to entrench colonization became more focused during this period of transition, treaty negotiations became the new battlefield. In this respect, the Robinson-Huron and Robinson-Superior treaty negotiations took on greater importance.[5]

Throughout my own journey, Shingwauk was an interesting travelling companion and one of my more helpful teachers. His stories and actions provided direction and clarity during periods of uncertainty. For this, I am forever grateful to him and his family.

**Mii i'i-way ojibway-anishinabe i-zhi-chi-gay-win.
Zhigo mii'iw eta-go o-way neen-gi-kayn-dahn zhigo
ni-gi-noon-dah-wah ... Ahaaw sa. Weweni.**

THE FAMILY REMEMBERS

Lana Grawbarger reminds me that Shingwauk understood that his work was his life and that he was entrusted with certain responsibilities and obligations, so he made every effort to prove that he was worthy of the gifts he'd been given.

She goes on to share that Shingwauk was given "a dream describing all the qualities that he needed to be a good leader."

Fasting, she continues, provided him with the ability to understand the world, which was changing in remarkable ways, and
showed him that Ojibway-Anishinabeg needed to develop new
ways of dealing with colonization and the assimilation being
forced on them. Fasting gave him the clarity of mind to make
the right decisions. As I sat with his family, his presence was
very much alive within them; in fact, I felt his presence still.

When I asked the family to shed some light on Shingwauk's
presence, Lana explained that he "always had a very immediate
presence to us and I think that's part of our culture. They're
ever-present in our lives and help us." Shingwauk thought it
was important for his children to take responsibility for the
gifts left to them, and that when people came to them in times
of need it was important to help them.

Betty Lou, Doreen, Lana and Dan Pine Jr. point out that
their grandfather had a tremendous library of books, medicines,
scrolls and other mysteries. Henry Schoolcraft described one
of the scrolls Shingwauk always kept with him: The "sun is
depicted, in several places. The pictograph is uniformly drawn
as a human head, with heavy rays, surrounding it, resembling a
rude halo, which was deemed to diffuse intelligence, as well as
light, through the world."[6]

Lana mentions that Shingwauk had three wives and that,
following his baptism in the Anglican Church in 1830, the
church encouraged him to take just one wife. What was he to
do? At the end of the day, he married the most recent wife and
continued to look after and provide for his other wives despite
church objections. Lana explains: "The church didn't want him
to have anything to do with them anymore. Even McCurry's
wife said, 'How can you expect him to do that? Those are the
mothers of his children."

Politically speaking, Shingwauk was the principle negotiator
and policy-maker during the Robinson-Huron and Robinson-
Superior treaty negotiations in 1850. More importantly, many
considered him the architect of the template for the numbered

treaty process, which provided for education, shelter, health and economic opportunities. And Shingwauk's story is forever linked to those of his nephews, Obwandiac and Tecumtha.

For the most part, Ojibway, Ota'wa and Ishkodawatomi-Anishinabe leadership have considered treaties as vehicles to protect the traditional ways and quality of life. Treaty 1, negotiated in 1871, for example, was seen as a tool for planning the economic future of Treaty 1 Ojibway-Anishinabeg and as a means for ensuring the continued access to and sharing of natural and economic resources. Beyond any doubt, during treaty negotiations leadership and spokespeople had a fairly clear idea about the value of the land they were agreeing to share, given that they initially wanted two-thirds of Manitou Aki protected under treaty.

As well, Shingwauk saw education as an opportunity to adapt to the changes taking place in the Anishinabe world. For him, education and the concept of the kinoomage gamig "(*teaching lodge*) was the "new" middle ground. However, he didn't see education as a means for assimilation or the surrender of Anishinabe identity, and it certainly didn't mean the surrender of Ojibwaymowin, ceremonies, culture and worldview!

Shingwauk accepted the burden of leadership with commitment and compassion. Lana adds, "I think that Shingwauk exemplified the idea of service leadership. He looked after his people. He lobbied for permanent housing and the right to fish and hunt because he knew how important it was to sustain ourselves."

SHINGWAUK AND THE WAR OF 1812

Both Tecumtha and General Isaac Brock, a British officer charged with the task of defending Upper Canada, saw Shingwauk's support as critical to the War of 1812 because of his military acumen and the number of men under his command. In fact, Shingwauk was so highly regarded for his leadership that the British promised him an Ojibway-Anishinabe homeland if he were to join the fight.

On July 17, 1812, following its declaration of war on June 19, the United States was immediately defeated at Fort Michilimackinac (Michigan). Fort Dearborn (Illinois) was taken by Mack-e-tay-be-nessy and Ishkodawatomi-Anishinabe forces on August 15. The battle lasted approximately fifteen minutes.

Fort Detroit (Michigan) surrendered to N'swi-ish-ko-day-kawn Anishinabeg O'dish-ko-day-kawn and British forces led by Tecumtha, Shingwauk and General Isaac Brock on August 16. The battle to take Fort Detroit was noteworthy for a number of reasons. For example, historians suggest that one of the reasons Obwandiac "lost" the war in 1763 was his inability to successfully lay siege to Fort Detroit. However, in 1812 Tecumtha, Shingwauk and General Brock easily overwhelmed the fort.

When asked by Brock about his plan to take the fort, Shingwauk responded, "I will dream about it tonight, general." The next morning, Shingwauk approached Tecumtha and Brock and told them, "I dreamed that a thick fog came so that nothing could be seen on the lake around the fort and that you attacked the fortress in front, while we attacked the Americans from the rear."[7]

No side had the military advantage because of the constant military back-and-forth. The Anishinabe and British coalition, for example, successfully took Fort Shelby and Fort Prairie du Chien (Wisconsin) in July 1814. The Americans destroyed what was left of Fort St. Joseph (Ontario) on July 23, and on August 4, 1814, the N'swi ish-ko-day-kawn Anishinabeg O'dish ko-day and British forces successfully defended Fort Michilimackinac (Michigan).

It's estimated that the United States' colonial army and militia numbered approximately 35,000 men. Their total casualty list numbered 2,200 men killed in action and 15,000 either wounded or missing in action. The British, with a fighting force of approximately 48,000 men, had 1,600 killed in action and 5,000 men either wounded or missing in action.

THE TREATY OF GHENT (1814) AND ONWARDS

At the war's end, the Treaty of Ghent, signed on December 24, 1814, established a new set of nations-to-Crown protocols and made for some interesting colonial dynamics. Just like Tecumtha before him, Shingwauk saw the millions of acres of land being treated and surrendered as tantamount to war. In response, he began questioning the established treaty process and commitments, which gave little regard to the Anishinabe collective.

The Kettle and Stony Point, Walpole Island and Sarnia treaties, signed in 1827, were a case in point, representative of the political and diplomatic atmosphere of the period. The Bond Head Treaty, which established Manitou Minising in 1836 for displaced Anishinabeg after the War of 1812, also gave Shingwauk cause for concern about the Crown's commitment to honouring its treaty obligations.

Shingwauk believed that the process of providing payment and promise of goods and annuities for large areas of indian lands favoured the British, which pushed him to petition Lieutenant-Governor Archibald Acheson (Earl of Gosford) on December 15, 1838, to apply different political protocols and strategies to address British intransigence.

Darrell Boissoneau adds that the discovery of precious metals and other resources in indian country set the stage for a new kind of confrontation. Shingwauk made it clear that non-indians couldn't come into Ojibway-Anishinabe territory and exploit resources without some type of overarching agreement, pointing to the mining activity taking place at Mica Bay.

As part of their political strategy, Shingwauk, along with his son Ogista and other Ojibway-Anishinabe leaders, including Na-bah-nay-go-jing and Ka-bah-o-sa, travelled to Montreal on

May 9, 1849, to address the issue of mineral exploration and natural resource extraction. On July 7 they issued a statement in the *Montreal Gazette* claiming all of the minerals and natural resources within Ojibway-Anishinabe territory and along the north shore of Kitchi Gumi. This was an interesting strategy – the first instance of an Anishinabe leader using print media to highlight issues and demands.

THE NEW COLONIAL REALITY

In pushing his demands, Shingwauk was aware of Britain's weakened military position[8] and certainly understood the opportunities this presented, given that he had a force of approximately eighteen thousand battle-ready o-gi-chi-dahg at his disposal, prepared to defend the territory and its resources.

At this juncture, everything that Shingwauk planned and put into motion was very strategic and calculated. Even his and Tah-gay-wi-ni-ni's acceptance of medals on September 13, 1849, for their military service in the War of 1812 seemed orchestrated: within two months, on November 14, Shingwauk, along with Na-bah-nay-go-jing and Naw-qua-gah-bow, took over the Mica Mine on Lake Superior by force.

The relative ease with which Shingwauk, Na-ba-nay-go-jing and Naw-qua-gah-bow took over the mine forced the British to accept new military, political and economic realities. In fact, Shingwauk made them "recognize the existence of native territorial prerogatives"; this represented a new starting point in treaty negotiations. The three leaders surrendered on December 4, 1849, setting the stage for the Robinson-Huron and Robinson-Superior treaty negotiations, which began in September 1850.

Amidst the political rhetoric and the treaties negotiated, including the conquest treaties of Fort Stanwix (New York), Fort McIntosh (Pennsylvania) and Fort Finney (Indiana), Shingwauk understood that reaching consensus would be difficult given the political transition taking place. During this period, for example, the N'swi ish-ko-day-kawn Anishinabeg O'dish ko-day-kawn's decision-making apparatus was being usurped by one that was hell-bent on creating division in the communities.

Following Shingwauk's armed occupation of the Mica Mine, the British Crown immediately sought to limit the damage by agreeing to negotiate a separate and distinct treaty. Shingwauk responded quickly, pushing for a new type of treaty framework, one that ensured permanent Crown obligations.

THE ROBINSON-HURON AND ROBINSON-SUPERIOR TREATIES (1850)

The resulting Robinson-Huron and Robinson-Superior treaties, negotiated in September 1850, differed fundamentally from those previously negotiated and the land surrenders that took place in southern Ontario, in that they provided for permanent government obligations in the form of lump-sum payments and the promise of reserved lands and annuities to be paid in perpetuity.

Throughout the treaty negotiations, Shingwauk continually pushed the Ojibway-Anishinabe rights agenda, arguing that "we want pay for every pound of mineral that has been taken off our lands, as well as that which may hereafter be carried away."

For its part, the British Crown focused negotiations on opening territory in what is now northern Ontario to mining and other resource development initiatives. Accordingly, Shingwauk sought to obtain a number of concessions, because he understood that these treaties would come to represent a new Ojibway-Anishinabe–Euro-American and nations-to-Crown reality and would help restore the idea of the middle ground.

As one of the period's leading policy makers and political negotiators, Shingwauk was determined to protect the primordial right to land and resources at all costs. In this regard, the Robinson-Huron treaty clearly specified the right of Ojibway-

Anishinabeg to hunt, fish and trap on unceded lands and that
"an annuity of approximately two pounds per-capita and
revenue from ceded lands would be paid."[9] He argued as well
that Ojibway-Anishinabe communities should continue to have
the capacity to exercise regulatory and protective jurisdiction
over lands closest to major water routes.

Throughout indian country, Shingwauk was deeply respected
for his political and military acumen. He was also a medicine
person held in high regard within the Midewigun and Wabano
societies. Shingwauk's place within these societies is important
to consider, as it goes beyond traditional political and military
leadership responsibilities and is rooted in spirituality and the
land itself. The colonial realities, as Shingwauk understood
them, reflected an attempt to alienate Anishinabeg from the
land – a spatial and spiritual exile, so to speak.

The Midewigun and Wabano were repositories for this
exciting spiritual history, providing medicine people with the
means to establish a spiritual union with all of the mi-zhi-ni-way-
wahg from a uniquely Ojibway, Ota'wa and Ishkodawatomi-
Anishinabe place. The men of the Wabanowiwin, for example,
interpreted dreams and healed the sick through the manipulation of fire.

Shingwauk's ability to straddle both societies, despite the
intricate responsibilities of each, was uncommon. A medicine
person and jeeskahn i-ni-ni, for example, had the ability to
"*reveal hidden truths*" and was revered as a prophet. Shingwauk
accepted Wabano responsibilities and saw their spiritual complexities as connected with quality of life, clarity of mind and
the ability to have good dreams.

The gift of vision was said to come from animiikiig (*the thunderers*) and was given to the jĕs´sakkīd´ (*revealer of hidden truths
and shaking tent man*) during their youth, so there was really no
initiation to speak of. The jĕs´sakkīd´ and jeeskahn i-ni-ni had
the power to gaze into the future and become "acquainted with

the affairs and intentions of men."[10] The jeeskahn and nah-nahn-dah-wi-i'we were all manifestations of this spiritual world.

Following my election as *Indian Act* chief, one of the community's first decisions was to hold a jeeskahn ceremony to ask how the community could address the issues of division. Up until that point in my life, I had never witnessed or participated in a jeeskahn, and it came to be a defining moment in my personal and political life.

In the days leading up to the jeeskahn, Sagkeeng was full of chatter. It seemed that the majority of people were questioning either my motives or the political appropriateness of such a ceremony; others were simply asking, "What the hell is this guy doing?" And I imagine there were others who eagerly anticipated my complete political collapse. In any event, when the night arrived for the jeeskahn, a major thunderstorm developed and it rained so hard that people were soaked after spending only a short time outside. Uh-oh, I thought. Not a good sign.

Jack Starr, who was co-hosting the jeeskahn, had asked that I go with him to talk to the jeeskahn i-ni-ni. I was a little apprehensive about this. Upon entering Jack's house, I saw the jeeskahn man sitting on an old armchair. He motioned for me to take a chair and asked whether I knew the reasons for or significance of the ceremony. He began speaking of the reasons for the ceremony:

.... 66 ....

To get some answers you have to practise and believe in the indian ways. Kitchi Manitou[11] gives everything the power. Your spirit is there. If you want the spirit, Kitchi Manitou will give it to you. If you don't want it, he doesn't give you anything. That's the way in life. Ya! You believe it, you fast and you have to live a certain life for that. You can't be a fool.

.... 99 ....

He then looked at me and asked whether the ceremony should take place. *What the – ? The jeeskahn i-ni-ni was asking me whether the ceremony should take place. What was I going to say?* I looked to Jack and other elders who were present. They said nothing. My eyes returned to the jeeskahn i-ni-ni. "Maybe we should have the ceremony tomorrow night because of the storm?" I answered. "Ahaaw! Keen anish o-gi-ma-kahn," he replied, smiling. There would be no ceremony that night.

The next day, people came to Jack's home – whether for healing, out of idle curiosity or just to visit. It was beautifully bright, hot and humid. Those who came for healing brought gifts, and the oshkabewis set them aside as the jeeskahn i-ni-ni quietly spoke to each.

It was interesting to watch the preparation for the ceremony. Everything had a purpose, and everyone instinctively knew what to do. The oshkabewis placed four poles, about six feet high, in the ground, forming a circle of about three or four feet in diameter, around which were wrapped birchbark and cloth. Ironically, I would be given this same responsibility a number of times in future jeeskahn ceremonies such as when we honoured and feasted Treaty 1 ceremonial pipes and then assisted a person who was completing their initiation to conduct the ceremony itself.

As darkness fell, everything became quiet and people readied themselves for the ceremony. The number of people who came to support Sagkeeng and its young *Indian Act* chief was surprising.

The jeeskahn i-ni-ni was tied and then placed within the tent. Songs and drumming began, and the jeeskahn moved and shook, slowly at first and then more violently. Soon the voices of the mikinak (*turtle*), mae-mae-gway-suk (*little people*) and makwa (*bear*) could be heard. I was then told to ask my questions regarding the community. In turn, a number of things that the community and I needed to do were explained.

Ni-biin-daa-koo-ji-ge gaye ni' o-nah-ko-nah
ah-di-so-kah-nahg zhigo di-bah-ji-mo-wi-nan g'dah
mi-kwe-ni-mah-nahn obwandiacbun, tecumthabun,
miinwaa shingwaukbun ... Meegwetch.

*"Zagaswe'idiwin nii-wo-gii-zhik en-daa-so-zii-gwan, nee-bin,
da-gwaa-gin zhigo biboon. Wii-konge manidoo ni-bi gaye nii-
mi'i-di-win me-gwaa a-zhi-gwa," mikinak ikido.*

*Mi omaa makwa ikido gaye, "Wi-na-waa wii-ba-ga-kaa-a-
nang-oog gi-ba-baa-mi-wizh."*

*"Bi-zin-dan weweni gaye gi-ki-na-waa-bam ga-ki-na ge-goo,"
mae-mae-gway-suk di-wiin-da-ma-gay-wahg.*[12]

Mii i'i-way ojibway-anishinabe i-zhi-chi-gay-win.
Zhigo mii'iw eta-go o-way neen-gi-kayn-dahn zhigo
ni-gi-noon-dah-wah ... Ahaaw sa. Weweni.

Mikinak, makwa and the mae-mae-gway-suk spoke softly.
I felt incredible peace and comfort as I listened to them. *How
do you explain this?* Everything you believe to be reality is
challenged. You're listening to a number of voices amidst the
singing and shaking of the jeeskahn. You can feel their presence and hear their songs. The message is simple yet pretty far-
reaching: Sagkeeng, it seemed, came together for that one brief
moment, everyone setting aside years of political and personal
animosities to further the common good of the community.

As the night wore on, people asked questions regarding
their health, family and personal relationships. Just as they
had with me, mikinak, mae-mae-gway-suk and makwa provided
answers describing certain things and ceremonies each had to

complete and herb and root medicines they were to harvest during different seasons of the year and how to prepare them.

Shingwauk's story speaks of his truth, special gifts, kindness and love for the people of his community and nation. Just as with Obwandiac and Tecumtha before him, Shingwauk's gifts enabled him to see the world from a uniquely Ojibway-Anishinabe place. His family tells me, for example, that he put his people before anything else, without fear or compromise.

I struggled with how to share things that were deeply spiritual and ceremonial, such as the ah-di-so-kah-nahg, ah-way-chi-gay-wi-nan and di-bah-ji-mo-wi-nan, given the intimate relationship between the main character in the story and the storyteller. Obviously, they resonate differently for everyone, and I understand that their spirituality has to be respected, since their stories are about taking back control of their stories and power.

Most of Dan and Fred Pine's reflections about their grand-father, and the written work of German historian Johann Kohl and Henry Schoolcraft, were important in terms of the stories themselves. Dan and Fred understood that Ojibway-Anishinabe spirituality was an expression of our indianness/Anishinabeness in its purest form, and our ceremony and songs were and still are conduits for how we come to know our history and know-ledge. In all of the stories shared up to now, we see that lan-guage, place and community are intimately connected with everything about Obwandiac, Tecumtha and Shingwauk.

From my perspective, Midewigun and Wabanow stories, prayers and songs are deeply political and emotionally, psycho-logically and spiritually revealing. They allow us to maintain a connection with the memory of our people, sacred places and most intimate thoughts and ideas. In this way, the miskew ah-zha-way-chi-win we share with our family enables us to experi-ence and share in the experiences of all our ancestors who have passed. Miskew ah-zha-way-chi-win is the centre of Ojibway, Ota'wa and Ishkodawatomi-Anishinabe strength and is the thread that ties us to our families, the earth and spirit. Their history is our history. We see the past through all of this!

In one story, Shingwauk was described as being able to contextualize the spiritual relationship between the past and present in song, prayer and scrolls: "Small shells were swallowed, and re-gorged and various transformations of legerdemain attempted ... noting the original words and translations of each song, with its pictographic signs."[13] Shingwauk embraced this. This spiritual relationship enabled him to communicate with others in the spiritual and physical realm through our gi-ki-nah-mah-gay-wi-nan (*teachings*), zagaswe'i'diwin opwaagan, bah-wah-ji-gay-wi-nan/i-nah-bayn-dam (*dreams/ dreaming in a certain way*) and manitou kay-wi-nan, which are a natural means for knowing. We are shown this in many different ways: "There is a flow in the song that reminded us of poetic-prose and the recurrence of certain syllables each of which had sacred meaning."[14] Viewed in this way, Shingwauk's special gifts gave him the ability and the credibility to find answers.

Ojibway, Ota'wa and Ishkodawatomi-Anishinabe leadership and governance are simple yet complex. Men and women gifted with spiritual ways of knowing were expected to contribute to the well-being and welfare of the community.

Obwandiac, Tecumtha and Shingwauk were able to communicate with other spiritual beings and powers of the land around them. Many of their family members and those who knew them intimately share stories of na-noo-kaa-siins (*hummingbird*) and makwa, their mi-zhi-ni-way-wahg for their understanding of medicines for healing and the zagaswe'i'diwin opwaagan, which tapped into the power of the land.

For Obwandiac, Tecumtha and Shingwauk, the ah-di-so-kah-nahg, ah-way-chi-gay-wi-nan, di-bah-ji-mo-wi-nan and manitou kay-wi-nan were the indian way of making and affirming their relationship with the land and of honouring the spiritual powers and memory of those who dwelt in these lands.

Shingwauk's first contact with white people who landed on Manitou Aki is an interesting story in and of itself, because it challenges the notion of linear time and forces you to ask, What just happened here?

Ni-biin-daa-koo-ji-ge gaye ni' o-nah-ko-nah ah-di-so-kah-nahg zhigo di-bah-ji-mo-wi-nan g'dah mi-kwe-ni-mah-nahn obwandiacbun, tecumthabun, miinwaa shingwaukbun ... Meegwetch.

. . . . **66** . . . .

Myeengun, Shingwauk, and the other educated men dreamed about people that they never saw before coming to Canada. White people. Sure enough, a few years after that, Shingwauk dreamed about a boat full of strange people. Ojibwa men went down the Lake Huron until they hit the St. Lawrence River. At the mouth of the St. Lawrence River, they went to these big rocks. Shingwauk placed his men up on steep rocks. It's pretty well flat country down there, with an occasional bluff. And that's where they signalled to each other. They watched for the ship. When the Indians knew it was near, Shingwauk performed a miracle. He made the fog settle down so the boat could not land.

Shingwauk saw the boat before the fog settled down to the Lake Huron. And they could hear the people on the boat. They could hear the anchor dropping into the water. Boh-Kuhn-Djigun. Boh-Kuhn-Dji-Gay-wigis. "An Anchor." The anchor was thrown out and the Indians could hear the cogs letting down the chain.

"Okay," Shingwauk said. "Let's go."

That's when the Indians climbed on top of the boat and started banging the fellows on the head. I don't know how the Indians knew what was in those kegs. They never seen guns or gunpowder before.

Shingwauk said, "Load up all the kegs and throw the rest of it into the water."

"Then these strangers will not be able to use their guns," he explained to the Ojibwa warriors. The Indian leaders knew the Europeans had some kind of weapon that could be used to take over the land.

That time the white man did not land. More than half were killed. The Ojibwa leaders said, "Go back." Well, the people in the boat could not understand the Indian language, but they understood the warning. So, the white people's ship went back across the ocean. But the medicine man predicted they would return. "This ocean is a big Lake Huron," he said. "It'll take them two years to return. We must prepare." And that boat just left. But another boat landed on the St. Lawrence a few years later.

Shingwauk made some of the paintings at Agawa. What was Shingwauk scared of? It was the Iroquois coming up into Ojibwa country on Lake Huron Superior. The Iroquois did not have the fears that we have here. You see, we have the best climate in Canada, in Ontario, for good furs. There's too much saltwater to make perfect fur in Quebec. It's surrounded by saltwater. Where the Iroquois came from, they didn't have the country for fur animals ... Shingwauk made the markings for the other Ojibwa headmen. The big leaders of the Ojibwa. They were coming along the shore looking for a place where they would see the markings. That's the reason Shingwauk put that mark on the rock. It's just like writing a letter to somebody. When the other Ojibwa medicine men came by Agawa, they would see the paintings. That's why Shingwauk did that. The Iroquois couldn't understand it. The Iroquois have different signs too. But the Iroquois are not explorers like the Ojibwa ...

The Iroquois knew about that route and they came over to Lake Huron Superior. My people could have stopped them at the Soo, but the Iroquois went around behind to get in Lake Huron Superior. The Iroquois got here, but they didn't stay long because old Shingwauk put the jinx on them.

Shingwauk was a powerful medicine man. He knew some-body was coming to Lake Huron Superior. He had a dream (vision) and he saw the Iroquois canoes. The south star appeared to him. There's something about Shawanung, "The South Star," that means fear. There is a bad thing about the south. The South Star causes trouble. Nothing rises in the south. Not the sun, the moon or the stars.[15]

The medicine man said, "There's something bad coming from the south." Sure enough, that is where the Iroquois came from when they invaded the Ojibwa. South. They all came from the south.

This story is hard to translate. When the Iroquois came into this area, the Ojibwa asked for help across Lake Huron Superior. The Ojibwa did not have radio. How did they get the message from one side of the Lake Huron Superior to the other? Well you know what? They had that medicine man fly over there.

He flew over there, across Lake Huron Superior. It would not take very long to get over to the south shore. The medi-cine man could use any fast bird he could get a hold of. He even used that nah-noh-kah-say. It will fly across the ocean. That's the hummingbird. He was sent for messages.

Oh, they won. My people won. Well, at Agawa, that's where the old chiefs met. So Shingwauk said, "When the Iroquois come in, I'll perform a fog on them." He made a heavy fog. Shingwauk opened up the fog. He lifted the fog so he could see a long way. That's what he did. He fogged up all of Lake Huron Superior.

Shingwauk made a large fire, and his people danced around the fire and put tobacco in it. Then he performed the miracle. He had the power to affect the atmosphere and lift the fog.

When the Ojibwa tribes went out, they went and met the Iroquois out on the Lake Huron Superior. They never landed. The Iroquois never landed here on the north shore of Lake Huron Superior. Shingwauk told the warriors to watch for the Iroquois. He placed his men on top of the cliffs around the Lake Huron Superior to watch. They covered themselves with brush like hay. And put hay all over the ground so they could not be seen. It was a camouflage.

Then the Ojibwa wrapped their paddles with beaver hides to soften the sounds. Some kind of hide. They didn't make any noise with the canoes. The Ojibwa warriors went in there just as quiet as could be. And they ran the Iroquois out. In the big battle, the Ojibwa got the jump on the enemy. They grabbed them and killed the Iroquois with wooden clubs. There were no guns in those days.

After that, Shingwauk and the other powerful headmen painted those markings on the rock at Agawa. You see, those were a warning.

Shingwauk knew everything. He was the fellow that took the Lake Huron Superior Ojibwa down to the St. Lawrence when the first white man's boats landed in North America. All of the headmen gathered at Soo, Michigan. They had big birchbark canoes thirty feet long.[16]

. . . . 𝄞 . . . .

Mii i'i-way ojibway-anishinabe i-zhi-chi-gay-win. Zhigo mii'iw eta-go o-way neen-gi-kayn-dahn zhigo ni-gi-noon-dah-wah ... Ahaaw sa. Weweni.

A number of people have raised the possibility of another person named Shingwauk, given the timing of this story, since Shingwauk was born in 1773. However, within the context of ceremony and worldview, we can't ignore the possibility of shape-shifting transformations and time-travel.

If we accept the Ojibway-Anishinabe worldview, we have to accept that this way of seeing the world and its unfolding events is possible. We have to appreciate a person who sees the world in this way, who participates in the reality of the dream or vision, one who regards his or her personal life and history as the mysterious bridge between the "ordinary" and "non-ordinary" reality.

Leroy Little Bear[17] explains that Anishinabe kayn-dah-so-win allows us to entertain the possibility of shape-shifting and time travel. Mainstream physics theories do not rule out travelling backward through time. Could this be possible, based on Einstein's theory of relativity, which "describes gravity as the warping of space-time by energy and matter"? Einstein theorized that space and time were not separate things but were fused together by a four-dimensional structure called space-time. This fusion showed us that the stark difference we see between past, present and future might be an illusion.

From an Ojibway-Anishinabe perspective, time and space are always similar because time is a continuous flow or a series of moments. Ceremonies help us picture every moment throughout the entire universe and show us that Coyote, Raven and Waynaboozho[18] create havoc wherever they go. Within this frame of reference, and when you factor in motion, the common sense of time goes out the window.

Medicine people acquire a specific knowledge. They see, taste, hear and feel the world differently, and for this reason they believe that time and space exist at once. Little Bear also makes the point that our traditions, teachings and ceremonies bring order to Ojibway-Anishinabe culture.

Long, ago, the Ojibway-Anishinabeg were recognized for their unexplained spiritual and medicine power. During the War of 1812, for example, the spiritual and medicine power of Nibakom (an Ota'wa-Anishinabe leader from Manitou Minising) enabled him to change two o-gi-chi-dahg into bats so they could travel to an American camp to spy on it. In the attack that followed, the Americans were defeated and the fort was taken. To engage in and initiate seemingly impossible transformations would seem strange from the perspective of the western worldview. However, this story questions the western reality, suggesting that transformations and shape-shifting are, in fact, possible.

Ojibway-Anishinabe ah-di-so-kah-nahg and di-bah-ji-mo-wi-nan describe many instances where these transformations took place. Because of the way we view the world and because every story relates to the human experience, events quite often unfold in this manner. People with Eurocentric worldviews ask how this is even remotely possible. But Anishinabeg realize that the ability to shape-shift, travel in time, and so on is the heart of oral tradition, where the past is remembered in stories. When the story is told properly, it's a tool that empowers listeners by touching their emotions and increasing their awareness of life.

With respect to this particular story and Shingwauk's place in it, it seems that we're looking at two different periods. If the history of Canada is correct, New France would have been established during the 1500s and hostilities between the Haudenosaunee and Ojibway-Anishinabeg would have come to a head in 1653.[19] This was followed by the Great Peace of Montréal in 1701. Of course, both events took place well before Shingwauk's birth.

Betty Lou and her family had been amazing storytellers. I asked if they would like to share other memories of their grandfather. Betty Lou nodded with a warm smile and continued softly.

BETTY LOU: He [Dan Pine Sr.] was eighteen years old when my grandfather [John Askin] died. He was visiting Charley, his youngest brother, who would have been the last hereditary chief. His cousin George was the chief.

JF: *Did your grandfather provide advice and political guidance to George during this period?*

BETTY LOU: They did it all together – he was like an advisor to his brother.

JF: *He was a very helpful and caring big brother. It must have been comforting to your uncle to know that your grandfather was there to help.*

BETTY LOU: He was visiting his brother, probably talking – maybe there was a meeting coming up. They sent for my dad to take my grandfather home. He sat him in his rocking chair. I remember when I was a kid, there were two rocking chairs in front of the cook-stove in the kitchen; one was his and the other was my Grandma's. You could tell that these rocking chairs were never moved from the place. My father sat him in his rocking chair – but as soon as he sat there, he was gone.

JF: *That's a powerful memory of your grandfather.*

BETTY LOU: I guess my dad was pretty heartbroken and he had a hard time getting over that. Even when he told stories about his dad, he would still get tears in his eyes.

At the end of the day, I visited with Doreen Pine-Lesage. She'd been an activist and community representative for most of her adult life. During my brief stay at Ketegaunseebee, she'd been one of my more gracious hosts, always treating me with kindness and offering wisdom. I've always admired her commitment to family and community; she had just celebrated sixty-five years of marriage to her husband, Harold. Her tenure as band councillor at Ketegaunseebee had also provided her with a front-row seat from which to witness the fundamental changes and transitions taking place within the community, as well as at the regional and national levels. To Doreen and her family, I offer asemaa (*tobacco*) and give my meegwetch. Ahaaw sa.

During my visit with Doreen, she shared a story about her father (Dan Sr., youngest grandson of Shingwauk) and mother's invitation to dinner with Queen Elizabeth II. Her father wore four medals left to him by Shingwauk. One of the medals commemorated the coronation of Queen Victoria on June 20, 1837; the oldest was a treaty medal with a bust of King George III, given to Shingwauk for his service to King and England. Another, given to him on September 13, 1849, was a bust of Queen Victoria. In Doreen's view, the medals are testimony to Shingwauk's personal relationship to the British crown.

Shingwauk died in 1854. In one of the last stories Fred Pine shared with the Conways, he told them that "Old Shingwauk is coming back [from the dead]. He's coming back. I believe that too," and he acknowledged that it's important to "rise with the sun, to work with the sun and work like the sun works because only then will the sun walk with and take care of us"; this is the order of the earth. Fred's stories of Shingwauk were clear and concise, with no ambiguity whatsoever, and they continue to be passed from one generation to the next.

Mii i'i-way ojibway-anishinabe i-zhi-chi-gay-win.
Zhigo mii'iw eta-go o-way neen-gi-kayn-dahn zhigo
ni-gi-noon-dah-wah . . . Ahaaw sa. Weweni.

5

N'swi-ish-ko-day-kawn
Anishinabeg
O'dish-ko-day-kawn

OUR HEARTS ARE AS ONE FIRE

THERE IS ABSOLUTELY no denying Obwandiac, Tecumtha and Shingwauk's influence on the contemporary world. The Royal Proclamation of 1763, the numbered treaties (1–11) and the existence of Canada itself are indicative of it. The fact that they were able to successfully establish political and military alliances that were unparalleled for the period also speaks to their gift of vision and their ability to be strategic in their actions.

They were able to reach into the ah-di-so-kah-nahg, gi-ki-do-gah-gi-bi-i-zhi-say-ma-guhk that described who we are and how we came to be. They came to understand how the great Ojibway, Ota'wa and Ishkodawatomi-Anishinabe migration and the creation of N'swi-ish-ko-day-kawn Anishinabeg O'dish-ko-day-kawn were important foundational elements of this fantastic knowledge.

Bawdwaywidun adds, "A long time ago, may-wi-zhuh our people, the original first peoples of this part of the world, were organized in many different ways," and the N'swi-ish-ko-day-kawn Anishinabeg O'dish-ko-day-kawn was one example of how Ojibway, Ota'wa and Ishkodawatomi-Anishinabe societies organized themselves. In time, it came to represent a political, economic, military and spiritual alliance that asserted sovereignty over a broad expanse of territory.

Strangely enough, there are some non-indian scholars who argue that the N'swi-ish-ko-day-kawn Anishinabeg O'dish-ko-day-kawn played no significant part in the events that took place in 1763 and 1812. But the fact remains that nothing could have taken place without its support or involvement.

Sovereignty and the ability to make independent decisions were woven together by n' zhwa-sho o-nah-ki-ni-gay-wi-nan (*seven natural laws*): gi-kayn-daw-so-win (*ways of knowing*), zaw-gi-di-win, maw-naw-ji-win, zoong-gi-day-win, gwu-yu-kaw-ji-win, duh-buh-say-ni-mo-win and de-bwe-mo-win. These principles or laws served to guide a highly complex and effective clan system within Anishinabe society and the N'swi-ish-ko-day-kawn Anishinabeg O'dish-ko-day-kawn.

The history of the N'swi-ish-ko-day-kawn Anishinabeg O'dish-ko-day-kawn is rooted in our creation stories and history of the Anishinabeg, which go back to the time of the great migration from the *Eastern Seaboard*.

To begin this part of the story, I acknowledge the beginning of the Ojibway, Ota'wa and Ishkodawatomi-Anishinabeg and their sacred stories by passing and offering my tobacco to Manitou Aki, and say meegwetch for this.

Ni-biin-daa-koo-ji-ge gaye ni' o-nah-ko-nah ah-di-so-kah-nahg zhigo di-bah-ji-mo-wi-nan g'dah mi-kwe-ni-mah-nahn obwandiacbun, tecumthabun, miinawaa shingwaukbun ... Mii i'i-way ojibway-anishinabe i-zhi-chi-gay-win. Zhigo mii'iw eta-go o-way neen-gi-kayn-dahn zhigo ni-gi-noon-dah-wah ... Ahaaw sa. Weweni.

The Ojibway-Anishinabeg (*the eldest brother*) were the spiritual leaders, protectors of the spiritual knowledge and writers/authors of the pictographs, and our creation, migration, sacred and moral stories, ceremonies and nation experiences that were recorded and kept on birchbark scrolls. Pine Shomin's interpretation and understanding of the word "Ojibway" is very different from the one generally accepted, which is *"to trade"*; he tells us that his ga-sha (*mother*) believed "O-ji-bion" was the correct term because of the Ojibway-Anishinabeg's responsibility as pictograph writers.[1]

Shomin's interpretation and understanding of the term "Ota'wa" – "oda" (*heart*) and "wa" (*him* or *her*), or *heart* (*land*) *person* – is fundamentally different from that of some non-indians and others. Shomin's and the non-indian interpretations of the term are interesting for a couple of reasons. Firstly, Shomin points out that the Ota'wa-Anishinabeg were responsible for safeguarding the o-dah-bah-ji-gahn of the confederacy and the individual nations during the great migration. Secondly, non-indians tell us arbitrarily that Ota'wa-Anishinabeg were often intermediaries in trade and economic relationships, thus the meaning of the term. Maybe they saw economic well-being or health as one of the key indicators for physical, emotional, mental and spiritual health.

Both interpretations are fundamentally true. However, they reveal a stark contrast in worldview, with Shomin focusing on the safeguarding of the nation's spiritual health versus the non-indians' purely economic and financial understanding.

WAYESHKAD | IN THE BEGINNING

The following Ishkodawatomi-Anishinabe interpretation of how the N'swi-ish-ko-day-kawn Anishinabeg O'dish-ko-day-kawn came to be speaks to sadness, sorrow, hope and survival that is spiritual and ceremonial, and I again pass tobacco.

> **Ni-biin-daa-koo-ji-ge gaye ni' o-nah-ko-nah ah-di-so-kah-nahg zhigo di-bah-ji-mo-wi-nan g'dah mi-kwe-ni-mah-nahn obwandiacbun, tecumthabun, miinwaa shingwaukbun ... Meegwetch.**

.... **66** ....

A long, long time ago, the Ojibway, Ota'wa and Ishkotawatomi-Anishinabeg were enemies. An Ojibway-Anishinabe man had ten children, all boys. He brought them up to be warriors and all ten sons were killed in battle. There was also an Ota'wa-Anishinabe man who had ten sons who were warriors, and they too were all killed. At the same time, an Ishkotawatomi-Anishinabe man had his ten sons killed in raids as well. Each father was left without children. All three men mourned their sons and could not see the point in living any longer. They wandered away from their villages and into the woods, looking for a place to die.

The Ojibway-Anishinabe man travelled west until he was completely exhausted. As he came to a place to rest, he saw a tree which had a long root running toward the east. The root was as long as a tree is tall, and very thick. He laid down and rested awhile, and then looked towards the south. There he saw another very long root – as long as the one which went to the east – running toward the south. He went to the west and north sides of the tree and found two other roots, each as long as a tree is high. All around the tree, the grass grew long and rich. He walked around the tree until he had come to the east, and he realized that the four roots pointed exactly in the four directions.

As he looked up at the tree, he realized that there were also four huge branches, one to the east, one to the west, one to the south and one to the north. The tree had beautiful leaves, but only had these four branches, each extending out as far as the roots. As he examined the tree, he could also see that the tree had a big root that ran straight down into the earth and a huge branch that went up from the centre straight to the sky. There were no leaves on that branch until the very top, and then there were only a few. All around the tree he could see the blue sky, and there was no wind or breeze.

As the Ojibway-Anishinabe man walked around the tree, he was happy and forgot all of his sorrow at losing his sons. He had never seen so beautiful a place. As he sat there, he heard a noise like someone crying. He looked around but didn't see anyone. At last he saw a man walking toward the tree, weeping and mourning just as he had earlier. He saw that the newcomer was an old man, just like him, and that he approached the tree from the south. As the newcomer came to the spot, he saw how beautiful it was and stopped crying. He looked around and noticed all the things about the tree and then he saw the first man. He saw that the man was mourning and asked him why.

The Ojibway-Anishinabe man, who was sitting at the base of the great tree, said, "I had ten sons and I lost them all in war. I decided I had nothing left to live for and wandered until I came to this beautiful place." The other man, an Ota'wa-Anishinabe, said, "I did the same as you. I had ten sons and they were all killed, and I did not wish to live. I wandered off to die and came to this place."

They talked over the past, and while they were talking, they forgot their sorrow and felt happy. While they talked, they heard the noise of a person crying. Far off they saw a man approaching, mourning and crying. It was an old man, about the same age as the other two, and he walked along wearily. They watched him as he came from the west and approached the west root of the tree. He stopped and examined the root, and he began to notice how beautiful the tree and the place were and wiped away his tears. As he came up to the tree, the Ojibway-Anishinabe man and the Ota'wa-Anishinabe man asked him who he was and why he was mourning. He answered that he was an Ishkotawatomi-Anishinabe and that he mourned his ten sons lost in war. Like them, he had wandered off to die.

They each told their stories and saw that the same thing had brought them to this place. The Ojibway-Anishinabe man said, "It is the will of the Great Spirit that has brought us here to meet." They all agreed. They walked around and explored the place together and saw that the air was very still and calm around the tree. It was very quiet, and it seemed to them that every word they spoke could be heard by the spirits. Together they said, "The spirits have sent us here to hold council together. There has been too much fighting in our lives." The Ojibway-Anishinabe man said, "I think I had better go back to my people." The Ota'wa-Anishinabe man agreed, saying, "Yes, I think it has been wrong for us to fight all the time. We have suffered and neglected our children. It is best for us to go home." And the Ishkotawatomi-Anishinabe man said, "All this is true. It is wrong to allow all these people to die because of the fighting between us. We should all go home and stop the fighting between our tribes and live in peace."

They lit their pipes and smoked, agreeing on what they had said. They talked a long while. As they smoked and talked, the Ojibway-Anishinabe man, having been the first to get to the tree, felt he had a right to speak first. "Our people should unite as one. I will be the eldest brother. And the Ota'wa-Anishinabeg will be our second brother. And you, Ishkotawatomi-Anishinabe, will be the youngest brother." They all agreed. The Ojibway-Anishinabe man said, "My brothers, I will make a pipe and a stem for it. When I get home, I will present it to my people. I will tell them that I had ten children who were all killed in war; but I will wash that away. I will paint the stem of the pipe blue, like the sky, and we will use this pipe when we make peace with other nations." And the Ota'wa-Anishinabe man said, "I will do the same. I will remind my people of my sons, and I will have them quit fighting." The Ishkotawatomi-Anishinabe said, "I too will make a pipe of peace. I will call a council of our people and tell them of our resolution and explain the foolishness of allowing our people to be killed." The Ojibway-Anishinabe said again, "It is good. Our spirits have brought us together at this point and have brought us to agreement." They agreed that in ten days they would all meet and bring their tribes to the roots of the tree, and at these roots their tribes would live, each sheltered by one of the great branches. And then they all went their separate ways home.

When he got home, the Ojibway-Anishinabe man took tobacco and put it in his pipe. He was not a chief, only an old man. He took the pipe to the chief and told him that it was the pipe of peace. The chief smoked it with him. The old man told all his people to make peace. He told all the head chiefs of different Ojibway-Anishinabe bands to take the pipe, and to tell his story and to explain that the pipe was to be used in friendship. The smoke from the tobacco would soothe and purify their hearts and maintain peace. The older people, who had learned the lesson of peace through their losses, would teach the messages to the younger people, who would carry it on. The same thing happened with the Ota'wa and the Ishkotawatomi-Anishinabeg.

Ten days later, they brought their people to the roots of the beautiful tree. As they all got there, each set up camp on one root of the tree. The Ojibway-Anishinabe man brought a chunk of wood, and so did the Ota'wa-Anishinabe man and the Ishkotawatomi-Anishinabe man. Together, they started a common fire and brought food so they could cook together. As they began cooking, they took tobacco and lit the pipe of the Ojibway-Anishinabe man from the fire they had built together. They were going to offer the pipe to their chiefs to smoke together, but they thought that they should first offer the pipe to the Great Spirit who had brought them together. They pointed the pipe stem straight up in the air by the tree. Then they pointed the stem to the east and offered it to the spirit of the east. Then they pointed to the south and offered it to the spirit of the south and then to the spirit of the west and lastly to the spirit of the north. Then they turned the stem down toward the central root of the great tree, offering it to the spirit that keeps the earth from sinking in the water.

After this, they offered the pipe to the Ojibway-Anishinabe chief and he smoked it and passed it to the braves and war- riors. They all smoked. The man of the Ota'wa-Anishinabe tribe did the same, as did the man of the Ishkotawatomi- Anishinabe tribe. After that, they all lived as one people, and said "We will keep this fire to represent our bond with each other, and the Ishkotawatomi-Anishinabeg will be keepers of this sacred fire." The three old men made rules for the people to live together and presented them as a path that their people must follow. From the point at which they met under the tree, they must live always in peace and friendship. From that time forward, they kept their rules and the three tribes lived in peace and intermarried with each other and came to be almost as one people.[2]

. . . .**,,**. . . . .

**Mii i'i-way ojibway-anishinabe i-zhi-chi-gay-win.
Zhigo mii'iw eta-go o-way neen-gi-kayn-dahn zhigo
ni-gi-noon-dah-wah ... Ahaaw sa. Weweni.**

From this point forward, the Ojibway, Ota'wa and Ishkodawatomi-Anishinabeg and the N'swi-ish-ko-day-kawn Anishinabeg O'dish-ko-day-kawn lived as family, with each brother having his own specific responsibility.

The Ishkodawatomi-Anishinabeg, as youngest brother, would take on the responsibility for protecting and caring for the sacred fire, the symbol of the family and the N'swi-ish-ko-day-kawn Anishinabeg O'dish-ko-day-kawn's independence and sovereignty. The Ota'wa-Anishinabeg, the middle brother, would assume the task of caring for the o-dah-bah-ji-gahn and providing for the economic well-being of the confederacy. And the Ojibway-Anishinabeg, being the eldest, would look after the spiritual ways of knowing and document and record the history and the sacred and moral stories of the three nations.

The Ishkodawatomi, Ota'wa and Ojibway-Anishinabe nations of the N'swi-ish-ko-day-kawn Anishinabeg O'dish-ko-day-kawn were able to develop a clearly defined governing, leadership and sovereign structure that was politically, economically and militarily effective. The confederacy also ensured territorial control and protection. Even then, the Ishkodawatomi, Ota'wa and Ojibway-Anishinabe nations understood that equality and consensus was best realized within a governing and justice system that ensured the agreement and the consensus of everyone.

It's important to reiterate that, as the European colonies expanded and encroachment into Anishinabe territories increased, the N'swi-ish-ko-day-kawn Anishinabeg O'dish-ko-day-kawn recognized that a clearer understanding was needed regarding the use of land and how it was to be shared. The confederacy recognized that the European concept of land ownership differed considerably from its own, which was about sharing and taking responsibility for maintaining its beauty.

Sweeping territorial grabs, commercial competition and international differences between Britain and France saw the N'swi-ish-ko-day-kawn Anishinabeg O'dish-ko-day-kawn drawn into all four of the major conflicts between 1698 and 1763.

ISHKODAWATOMI-ANISHINABEG | THE YOUNGEST BROTHER

For the Ishkodawatomi-Anishinabeg, the N'swi-ish-ko-day-kawn Anishinabeg O'dish-ko-day-kawn itself was an important element of their political, economic and social fabric. As the youngest brother and protector of the sacred fire, the symbol of the confederacy's independence and sovereignty, the Ishkodawatomi-Anishinabeg had responsibility for nurturing the ideas of sovereignty and independence, which was no small task!

Their economy also provided opportunities to establish larger independent communities that enabled the nation to develop complex social institutions and advance a common front and unified voice during times of crisis or war. This was fairly evident in their economic and trade relationships, particularly with the French, and when mobilizing forces for their own defensive or offensive action.

Generally speaking, the Ishkodawatomi-Anishinabe nation was seen as a valuable ally for a number of reasons. For one thing, they were a formidable force politically and militarily, with a decision-making apparatus that was both decisive and effective. As well, their knowledge of geography, waterways and water transportation (canoes) enabled them to establish successful local and long-distance economic and trade relationships with the French, British, other European and Anishinabe nations.

As the nation increased in population and influence, the Ishkodawatomi-Anishinabeg acquired greater control over the major waterways that became the main links in the development of the N'swi-ish-ko-day-kawn Anishinabeg O'dish-ko-day-kawn, Manitou Aki and European economies. Again, their understanding of the physical geography played a defining role in shaping their political world and international relationships. From a military and economic perspective, this led to a greater influence over what took place during the 1700s and 1800s and saw the Ishkodawatomi-Anishinabeg enjoy a higher standard of living and greater influence and prestige than most of the other Anishinabe nations.

The economic, political, social and military success enjoyed by the Ishkodawatomi-Anishinabeg also provided unprecedented wealth and a sense of security that enabled them to support a relatively large and mobile population, often a prerequisite for trade and military action.

The Ishkodawatomi-Anishinabeg obviously had the wherewithal to develop social and political organizations that encouraged expansion. Further, as each community became more independent, they also had the inherent flexibility to make most decisions. However, when decisions were required to support the nation as a whole, a grand council was called. All of the Ishkodawatomi-Anishinabe communities would come together to debate issues and matters of national concern.

WKAMEK, OTOTEMAN AND INAAKONIGE |
LEADERSHIP, CLANS AND TO DECIDE THINGS
IN A CERTAIN WAY

Community wkamek (*leaders*) were expected to lead these discussions and debates in which wkamek, elders, women, men and youth would all have the opportunity to participate. Once issues had been fully debated and an agreement reached, the speaker would chant and/or speak the words of the agreement. From the eldest to the youngest, everyone stood to sing or shout out their acceptance of the decision, proclamation and declaration.

Consensus-seeking public assemblies regarding ototeman (Ishkodawatomi-Anishinabe term for *clans*), community and national issues were held regularly, and it was understood that once a decision was reached there was little room for back-biting or complaint. The focus on consensus, public discussion and decentralization of political power therefore ensured equality within the ototeman, community and nation. As well, nothing took place in isolation from the ototeman, because it was fundamental to everything that was Ishkodawatomi-Anishinabe.

It's important to understand that the five major ototeman and the thirty-three sub-clans were deeply rooted in the identity of each Ishkodawatomi-Anishinabe citizen. It was a family of citizens/individuals related to each other by a line of male ancestors going back to the beginning of time. The ototeman was and still is about loyalty and obligation to each member and to Ishkodawatomi-Anishinabe society generally speaking.

The ototeman was a partnership in the truest sense, in that each ototeman had certain responsibilities for property and territory. The Great Sea ototeman, for example, was responsible for building canoes, and only the Buffalo ototeman could organize the buffalo hunt. The ototeman system in this way provided a societal, political, military and economic framework for the communities and nation. More importantly, it provided a spiritual and moral compass for the people, all of whom were tightly woven into the fabric of the community. The truth from our perspective lies in Ojibwaymowin and the land. It isn't as simple as looking at our communities; living in our communties is important for understanding Anishinabe truth. Too many non-indians and self-professed allies believe that they can speak to our truth, worldview and understanding of the universe simply by looking at and visiting this world.

AANDAAKONIGE | THE CHANGING OF LAWS
As military hostilities between the French and British increased, a new way of doing business was also becoming entrenched. The previous social, economic and political relationships, which had focused on addressing and meeting the needs of Ishkodawatomi-Anishinabe society using Ishkodawatomi-Anishinabe political, economic and diplomatic protocols, was now evolving into a multifaceted capitalized market economy. Obviously, the Ishkodawatomi-Anishinabe experience was not dissimilar to what was being experienced by the Ota'wa and Ojibway-Anishinabe nations. As this new economic system became more established, there was also a growing dependence on foreign goods and technology, which had a considerable impact on Ishkodawatomi-Anishinabe society.

Further, as French and British hostilities became more intense and this new market-driven economy took root, a number of Ishkodawatomi-Anishinabe communities and traditional economies began to experience societal and economic upheaval. Coupled with the political changes taking place, the wkamek begin to find themselves in a difficult situation.

Unlike the French, who made every effort to apply themselves to and respect Ishkodawatomi-Anishinabe protocols, the British approach to leadership responsibility, consultation and consent was based on a more Eurocentric worldview. For example, they believed that wkamek should have had the ability to make their authoritative decisions binding on Ishkodawatomi-Anishinabe citizens, communities and nation as whole.

Wkamek had limited power, and whatever power they did have was contingent on the clan, community and nation as a whole. They did have some influence over some matters, but these were few and far between. However, responsibility for the leadership for the most part remained within the ototeman, which was a uniquely Ishkodawatomi-Anishinabe approach to leadership and government.

Given the social, political, economic and diplomatic changes taking place in Ishkodawatomi-Anishinabe society and the influence of the British way of doing business, wkamek were now expected to win concessions, which was seen as important for maintaining influence within the community. The position of leader was transitioning to a more parochial and political role.

During this period, an incredible amount of pressure was being placed on the leadership and the Ishkodawatomi-Anishinabe nation, as the British, free traders and missionaries were in full competition mode for greater access to the leadership and their communities. Ishkodawatomi-Anishinabe society was still able to achieve some territorial and economic success, but these changes marked the beginning of an economic, political and social disintegration that manifested itself in the fragmentation of Ishkodawatomi-Anishinabe communities for the first time.

ZHAAGOOJITOON WEMITIGOOZHI | DEFEAT OF THE FRENCH

With the waning influence and defeat of the French in 1700s, the Ishkodawatomi-Anishinabe communities and nation were forced to re-evaluate their political and economic relationship with the British. This had serious repercussions for most Ishkodawatomi-

Anishinabeg. For one thing, it became increasingly difficult for them to act collectively in international matters. They also understood that their position as a major economic, political and military player would change considerably with the emergence of unregulated free traders and increasing British control. It was during this time of societal upheaval and unrest that Neolin (Lunaapewa-Anishinabe) and Obwandiac gained recognition. Again, the excitement generated by both emboldened many.

At an April 27, 1763, meeting on the banks of the Ecorse River (Michigan), the Ishkodawatomi-Anishinabe war council, along with Ota'wa, Lunaapewa and Huron-Anishinabeg, listened as Neolin and Obwandiac spoke of resistance, spiritual renewal and rejection of the European way of life. This message resonated with the Ishkodawatomi-Anishinabe war council because it spoke of survival and the immediacy of the past. The Ishkodawatomi-Anishinabeg came to see their future and survival as closely linked to the old ways.

In the four months between May 16 and September 14, 1763, Ishkodawatomi-Anishinabe forces would fight alongside Obwandiac and other allied nations and successfully lay siege to and capture Forts Sandusky (Ohio), St. Joseph (Ontario), Miami (Michigan), Ouatanon (Indiana), Michilimackinac (Michigan), Presque Isle (Pennsylvania), Le Boeuf (Pennsylvania) and Venango (Pennsylvania) and defeat the British decisively at Devil's Hole (Fort Niagara, New York).

Obwandiac's military success created a bit of a conundrum for King George III. He knew, for example, that Obwandiac was fighting independent of France and had the military power to force the surrender of Fort Pitt and and Fort Detroit if he so chose, and that Britain's military and political options were limited. King George surrendered and issued the Royal Proclamation on October 7, 1763.

The Royal Proclamation ushered in a new era in diplomacy and established a buffer between Anishinabe territory and non-indian interests. It also established a treaty framework that was intended to keep peace, sustain trade and economic relationships, and control westward expansion.

THE AMERICAN REVOLUTION AND THE CONQUEST TREATIES

The American Revolution began in 1775 and ended in 1776, with the Declaration of Independence clearly outlining the attempt by the United States to create a new narrative, one that was inherently different from that of other nations. World history from this point on would have to take notice of the American notion of exceptionalism and its dystopian vision of a democracy, positioning itself as the *"first new nation."*

The Treaty of Fort Stanwix, one of the first of four conquest treaties negotiated on October 22, 1784, saw Mohawk-Anishinabeg effectively surrender territory in what is now Kentucky, West Virginia, Pennsylvania and northern Ohio in an attempt to legalize thirty thousand land titles. It also sought to allow settlement west of the new Appalachian Divide and Allegheny Mountains proclamation line.

Indian Superintendent William Johnson, self-appointed Mohawk-Anishinabe leader Joseph Brant and indian agent George Croghan were key players in these negotiations, raising serious questions of conflict of interest and collusion. Keep in mind that Johnson was just one of many land speculators who were negotiating these new treaties, which sought to take control of large tracts of surrendered Shawnee-Anishinabe territory.

The Treaty of Fort McIntosh recognized American sovereignty for the first time and established a new boundary line east of the Cuyahoga and Muskingum Rivers in Ohio. The treaty was negotiated and signed by George Rogers Clark, Arthur Lee, Richard Butler and a small number of younger hand-picked Wendat and Lunaapewa-Anishinabe leaders on January 21, 1785. The Shawnee-Anishinabeg refused to participate in

these negotiations or recognize any part of the treaty
because the lands in question were part of their ancestral/
traditional territory. Realizing the extent and depth of Shawnee-
Anishinabe opposition to the treaty, the United States sought
to mitigate the damage by returning some of the surrendered
lands north of the Ohio River and east of the Muskingum
River.

At the Treaty of Fort Finney negotiations, on January 31,
1786, the Americans were given a belt of black wampum in
opposition to the Mohawk-Anishinabeg's surrender of millions
of acres of land between the Appalachian Divide and Ohio
River. This was closely followed by the Northwest Ordinance
(1787) and the Fort Harmar Treaty (1789), which attempted to
give the United States authority and ease hostilities between
the Ishkodawatomi, Wendat, Detroit Ojibway, Ota'wa, and
Lunaapewa-Anishinabeg.

These treaties saw the emergence of Tecumtha, a leader who
was bold, brash and intelligent and who became the voice and
face of resistance. Together with his brother Lau-lau-we-see-kau,
Tecumtha would challenge the colonial and treaty politics of
the day and articulate a different vision of what the Anishinabe
world should be.

The Treaty of Greenville, negotiated in 1795 between Anthony
Wayne and Mi-chi-ki-ni-kwa, established the United States as a
new sovereign power under the guise of conquest. This was the
breaking point for Tecumtha. The treaty itself was also never
sanctioned by the N'swi-ish-ko-day-kawn Anishinabeg O'dish-
ko-day-kawn or any of its allied nations, something that would
prove problematic for the Ishkodawatomi-Anishinabeg.

It was during these negotiations that Tecumtha was first
mentioned. Patricia and Norman Shawnoo describe how
Tecumtha refused three times to accept the pipe passed to him,
telling Wayne that "you have to treaty with all Anishinabeg,
not just some of us." They add that he was adamant that

treaties be ratified by all of the Anishinabeg. Largely because of Tecumtha's advocacy and resistance, the United States eventually agreed to pay for land with cash and/or services and recognized Anishinabe title to the remaining lands.

The Treaty of Greenville and the Jay Treaty were challenging for Anishinabe nations for a couple of reasons. A number of Anishinabe nations had acknowledged the United States as a foreign power. And the Jay Treaty established an international boundary that separated the United States from Canada, creating two separate international jurisdictions.

Tecumtha was also adamant that Anishinabeg had never been conquered or subjugated,[3] which was seemingly a quid pro quo for accepting United States sovereignty. This exchange was noteworthy because it raised other questions regarding the treaty process itself and established that only the president and the Senate could legally authorize and ratify treaties and land exchanges.

As well, from 1793 to 1830, with no bureaucracy or army to speak of, the United States remained focused on establishing its own legitimacy. In fact, its Congress couldn't collect a tax to save its life, and the pseudo-empire was millions of dollars in debt. Treaties and land surrenders or exchanges often provided an opportunity for the young country to resolve its war debt.

KITCHI MOOKOMAAN AKI – OSH-KA-YA'AA | THE UNITED STATES – A NEW MANITOU AKI REALITY

During this period of transition in the diplomatic and political relationship between the United States and Ojibway, Ota'wa and Ishkodawatomi-Anishinabe, several treaties were negotiated and a number of states were established in relatively short order: Indiana (1800), Ohio (1803), Michigan (1805) and Illinois (1809). Many Anishinabe nations began to question the accuracy and validity of the treaty provisions as written, because they found them be different from what was verbally expressed and agreed to. The promise of goods, rations, one-time cash payments, annuities for a fixed number of years and services of various kinds, including provisions for teachers, blacksmiths and farmers, just didn't cut it. For the most part, the process of assimilation and forced dependence on Euro-American goods and services was a source of concern. Land surrenders and the creation of these new states were also concerning for many Anishinabe nations, because internal conflicts were becoming more common. As well, a number of Anishinabe nations had begun to incur large trade debts and financial deficits. (It's ironic that "one per cent of the population in the United States own more than 90 per cent of the property";[4] old money and "blue-blood families" such as the Whartons, Morgans, Rockefellers and Carnegies amassed their wealth on the backs of and in their dealings with Anishinabeg.)

Land surrenders proved to be disconcerting for the N'swi-ish-ko-day-kawn Anishinabeg O'dish-ko-day-kawn and the allied nations. Patricia and Norman remind me that Tecumtha noted this and was sensitive to the anxiety in many of the Anishinabe communities during his travels leading up to 1812. For him, the idea of a federation of Anishinabe nations was a re-articulation of what had been and could be again. Further, Tecumtha and Lau-lau-we-see-kau challenged and rejected the colonial hegemonic structure and changes taking place and argued that spiritual, political, economic and military resistance was in the best interest of Anishinabeg generally.

AANZINAAGO | METAMORPHOSIS
Shortly after the War of 1812, the United States began to develop new policies focused on civilizing and assimilating the Anishinabeg, the rationale being that once Anishinabeg became comfortable with the idea of being farmers, their need for land would be reduced. I'm at a loss to understand this logic; nevertheless, land was now being seen as a commodity to be bought and sold.

The second part of this policy front was the complete removal of Anishinabeg from their ancestral lands. This created a problem for the United States because it had no territory west of the 1795 Treaty of Greenville line. With this in mind, American policy makers set about negotiating new treaties and more ambiguous agreements to fulfill their objectives.

The *Indian Removal Act*, for example, in 1830 provided the emperor (President Andrew Jackson) with new clothes and, more importantly, the legislative authority to move Anishinabeg west of Michigan and the *Mississippi River*. To deal with this new piece of legislation, Ishkodawatomi-Anishinabe leadership gathered in the small village of Zhi-gahg-gong (*Chicago*) on September 26, 1833, to negotiate the Treaty of Chicago for lands west of Lake Michigan to *Lake Winnebago* in Wisconsin and Illinois. In return, the Ishkodawatomi-Anishinabeg were promised a cash settlement and replacement lands west of the Mississippi River. In the last treaties, the United States effectively transferred title to the last remaining lands and moved the Ishkodawatomi-Anishinabeg to the new indian territory.

The indian removal industry proved to be quite profitable. Salaries paid to Americans acting as removal superintendents, enrolling agents or teamsters were substantial, and the industry provided many opportunities for financial profit and gain. This situation hasn't changed much; non-indians continue to reap the benefits of wealth and opportunity at our cost – from lawyers who help negotiate the many land and residential school claims to post-secondary institutions that seek to indigenize the academy and construction companies and contractors that negotiate impact benefit agreements and partnerships. It seems that we're still a thriving industry.

OTA'WA-ANISHINABEG | THE MIDDLE BROTHER

As mentioned previously, Shomin's interpretation of "Ota'wa" – *heart (land) person* – differs fundamentally from non-indian historians and authors' understanding of the term as "*to trade*."

In spite of differences in worldview, both interpretations and responsibilities are for the most part correct and seem appropriate given that the Ota'wa-Anishinabeg were entrusted with the responsibility of safeguarding the Ojibway, Ota'wa and Iskodawatomi-Anishinabe o-dah-bah-ji-gahn during the time of the great migration. As well, from the time of first contact with the Europeans, they assumed responsibility for acting as intermediaries in trade and economic relationships. To put this discussion in proper context, it's important to understand who we are as a people and where we came from.

Mii i'i-way ojibway-anishinabe i-zhi-chi-gay-win. Zhigo mii'iw eta-go o-way neen-gi-kayn-dahn zhigo ni-gi-noon-dah-wah . . . Ahaaw sa. Weweni.

APIITENDAN GI-KI-NAH-MAH-GAY-WI-NAN | TO VALUE TEACHINGS

Ota'wa-Anishinabe society in the main was governed by three core values. The first suggested that no one individual could determine the fate of another. This was a sacred, societal and moral obligation.

Sharing was also fundamental to the people, because survival often depended on being supported by your clan and community. Sharing and the ododem (Ota'wa-Anishinabe term for *clan*) were the social security and safety net of the day. A person's wealth simply meant that he/she had more to share and therefore had the ability to give more of what he/she had. Individuals who shared more of what they had through gift-giving and trading, gained greater respect. This emphasis on sharing was so strong that almost no interaction could be carried on without it. This was simply a fact.

The Ota'wa-Anishinabeg also saw the interconnected relationship of all Anishinabeg with the natural world as fundamental to the natural order of Manitou Aki. Everything in the natural order was real and sacred! Everything that was sacred was spiritual! The natural order of the world was the sum of its whole. Nothing could exist without the other. Therefore, co-operation was seen as necessary.

Collectively, Ota'wa-Anishinabe society didn't look favourably on an ododem if its people and/or communities wanted more power and wealth. Ododem relationships were defined by humanity and a set of principles and teachings that were of the land and that linked all individuals to each other. The well-being and security of the community and nation depended on this.

ODODEM | THE CLAN, ITS PERSONHOOD AND ITS RESPONSIBILITIES

The ododem was created to respect the order of creation, including those that flew and swam and those that crawled and walked. A world without animals would have been unimaginable. There wouldn't be order as we know it and the world wouldn't have made any sense.

> **Ni-biin-daa-koo-ji-ge gaye ni' o-nah-ko-nah ah-di-so-kah-nahg, ah-way-chi-gah nan zhigo di-bah-ji-mo-wi-nan ... Meegwetch.**

··············**66**··············

At our beginning, the animals helped by nourishing newborn infants with fruits, vegetables, berries and drink, while the birds and butterflies brought joy. The bear who loved the newborn beings offered his flesh so that Anishinabeg would survive. Following the example of the bear, the deer, moose, porcupine, beaver, groundhog, grouse and goose and almost every other animal offered him/herself for the well-being of their human brothers and sisters.

··············**99**··············

Mii i'i-way ojibway-anishinabe i-zhi-chi-gay-win.
Zhigo mii'iw eta-go o-way neen-gi-kayn-dahn zhigo
ni-gi-noon-dah-wah ... Ahaaw sa. Weweni.

These living beings possessed and reflected character and
so became the clan symbols for the Ojibway, Ota'wa and
Ishkodawatomi-Anishinabeg and others. The ah-ji-jahk (*crane*)
had the eloquence of leadership, mahng (*loon*) fidelity, makwa
(*bear*) strength and courage, waa-bi-zhe-shi (*marten*) single-
mindedness and guardianship, giigoo (*fish*) a gift for teaching,
bineshi (*bird*) spiritual leaders with the gift of vision and
waa-wash-shke-shi (*deer*) grace as poets and artists.

Humanity's five basic individual and social needs – leadership,
protection, sustenance, learning and physical well-being – gave
structure to Ojibway, Ota'wa and Ishkodawatomi-Anishinabe
societies, government, defence and social units; each represented
one form or aspect of social duty. The ododem provided for
individual and social needs. Similar to their younger and older
brothers, the Ota'wa-Anishinabeg saw the ododem as important to their society.

From an Ota'wa-Anishinabe perspective, it was the responsibility of the ododem to maintain a close working relationship
with each Ota'wa-Anishinabe citizen regarding trade, political
activities and ceremonies. Language and behaving in accordance
with the natural laws ensured the survival of the nation. Member-
ship in an ododem meant an obligation to provide food, assistance, shelter and hospitality to ododem members from other
communities and nations. The ododem also determined citizenship within the nation, which enabled the Ota'wa-Anishinabeg
to establish who was and who was not Ota'wa-Anishinabe. The
ododem was an important reality for the Ota'wa-Anishinabeg,
as it was for their younger and older brothers.

As the Ota'wa-Anishinabe communities increased in size
and exponentially expanded their power, wealth and territory

between the 1500s and 1800s, the community and the ododem continued to be the centre of activity for the nation, although increased economic, political and military interaction with other nations created some uncertainty for them.

In summary, almost every aspect of life in Ota'wa-Anishinabe society, as well as in Ishkodawatomi and Ojibway-Anishinabe societies, was controlled by the ododem, which also had considerable influence over the essential tasks of everyday life.

NIIGI' ONJIGOZID | INCREASED DISPLACEMENT

As the European immigration to Manitou Aki continued during the early 1600s, the French established trade relations almost immediately with the Wendat-Anishinabe out of necessity and for survival. These trade relations unfortunately proved to be the undoing of the Wendat-Anishinabeg, because by 1650, Huronia[5] had been all but destroyed through ongoing military conflict with the Iroquois-Anishinabeg, who sought to upset this trade imbalance and take control.

In response, the Ota'wa-Anishinabe nation, which included parts of southern Ontario, Ohio, Michigan and Wisconsin, provided safe refuge for displaced Wendat-Anishinabeg and inadvertently intensified hostilities with the Iroquois-Anishinabeg. As these hostilities escalated, the Ota'wa-Anishinabeg sought the protection of their older brother to deal with the Iroquois-Anishinabe threat, which culminated in a battle near present-day Sault Ste. Marie in 1653, where the Ota'wa and Ojibway-Anishinabeg easily defeated the Iroquois-Anishinabeg.

The Ota'wa-Anishinabe control of trade and their application of a toll for the use of waterways through Ota'wa-Anishinabe territory was an interesting aspect of the colonial world. Control of these waterways gave the Ota'wa-Anishinabeg a virtual monopoly over the colonial economy and also provided them with other trade opportunities as well.

In many instances, the Ota'wa-Anishinabeg's economic success, military power and control of major trade routes enabled them to forge a direct trade, economic, political and military relationship with the French and other Europeans. Most of the essential business was done exclusively on Ota'wa-Anishinabe terms.

Despite the economic success experienced by the French, from the early to mid-1700s they sought to lessen their economic and trade dependence on the Ota'wa-Anishinabeg by attempting to curry trade, economic and political favour with other Anishinabe nations.

As a rule, though, the N'swi-ish-ko-day-kawn Anishinabeg O'dish-ko-day-kawn thought it important to control the nature of economic and political agreements, because profit and stability were always mitigating factors in and incentives for maintaining these relationships.

OBWANDIAC GII-MOOKID | THE EMERGENCE OF OBWANDIAC

In the period leading up to 1763, Obwandiac saw the economic, political and territorial success enjoyed by most Anishinabeg throughout Manitou Aki as problematic, because it was intricately tied to a growing dependence on French and British goods.

He had heard of the wars, plagues, genocides and other events that had taken place in Europe, precipitating immigration to Manitou Aki, and he had a clear understanding of the damages that colonialism brought with it. Without question, these economic and diplomatic concerns and the international conflict between the French and British had economic, political and military repercussions for the N'swi-ish-ko-day-kawn Anishinabeg O'dish-ko-day-kawn during this period and were important factors in Obwandiac's decision to challenge colonial hegemony.

Obwandiac understood the spiritual relevance of Neolin's vision as well because he saw first-hand the negative influences of colonialism, and he was encouraged by the Anishinabe response to Neolin. At one of their first meetings, Obwandiac listened as Neolin shared his bah-wah-ji-gay-win[6] of this mi-zhi-ni-way who came to him and warned him of the dangers that Europeans posed to Anishinabe survival.

THE FRENCH AND INDIAN WAR?

I've always had difficulty with the description of what took place in the mid- to late 1700s as the "French and Indian War," because it undeniably reflects a British perspective. Obwandiac, the N'swi-ish-ko-day-kawn Anishinabeg O'dish-ko-day-kawn and other Anishinabe nations saw the international conflict between the British and French in a different light. In their minds, it was about colonial greed. The British and French were fighting to preserve what Obwandiac and Neolin were speaking against.

The Treaty of Paris, signed on February 10, 1763, by Britain, France, Spain and Portugal, ending the French and Indian War and placing all of the strategically located forts and territory held by the French under British control, is a case in point.[7] The international political wrangling between the French and British led to fundamental changes in the economic, political and military protocols that the Anishinabeg were accustomed to. However, Obwandiac and the N'swi-ish-ko-day-kawn Anishinabeg O'dish-ko-day-kawn were fighting independent of France and were therefore not signatories to this treaty. Regardless, Anishinabeg believed that Manitou Aki and all of its resources still "belonged" to them. The Royal Proclamation would acknowledge this in the autumn of 1763.

OBWANDIAC GABENAAGE | OBWANDIAC'S SUCCESS

In a span of only four months (May 16–September 14, 1763), Obwandiac and the N'swi-ish-ko-day-kawn Anishinabeg O'dish-ko-day-kawn would successfully lay siege to Forts Sandusky, St. Joseph, Miami, Ouatanon, Michilimackinac,

Presque Isle, Le Boeuf and Venango and would defeat the British at Devil's Hole. Obwandiac would also end his siege of Fort Detroit (Michigan) on October 29, telling those around him, "They can have their fort; we have our land."

Obwandiac and the N'swi-ish-ko-day-kawn Anishinabeg O'dish-ko-day-kawn's success in the war of 1763 was a remarkable military feat in itself, given the period. Obwandiac's military success forced King George III to establish a treaty process and framework that acknowledged Anishinabe title to Manitou Aki on October 7, 1763.

THE AFTERMATH OF THE ROYAL PROCLAMATION OF 1763

General Jeffrey Amherst, governor general under King George III, believing that Britain was entitled to do whatever it wanted despite losing six of its eight major forts, immediately sought to manage his relationships. Giving little thought to possible repercussions, Amherst looked to downsize and economize the British administration by increasing trade rates and reducing goods, gifts, money and so forth. The colonial policies that he attempted to implement completely disregarded traditional protocols and the diplomacy of the middle ground. To his mind, the indians were conquered, and the traditional protocols and politics of the middle ground didn't matter in this instance.

Obwandiac, on the other hand, saw the middle ground and its long-established protocols as the reality of the colonial world. Contemporary historians such as Richard White also see the middle ground as a place of co-operation and mutual respect, and the foundation on which the Anishinabe-European relationship[8] was built.

The Royal Proclamation, issued in 1763, immediately created unrest within the thirteen colonies[9] as well because of the issue of land and primordial rights. The thirteen colonies simply refused to accept the principles of the proclamation and completely disregarded the proclamation line. Further, disregard for the proclamation line by land speculators, fur traders and settlers also created some concern within the indian nations. We can't ignore this fact.

After the British assumed control of the northern territory in 1763, the fur trade was still a going concern. At the same time, hostilities between the N'swi-ish-ko-day-kawn Anishinabeg O'dish-ko-day-kawn, Dakota, Fox, Sauk, Menominee and Winnebago-Anishinabe nations continued to simmer, creating a specific problem for the colonies, both British and French.[10]

THE UNITED STATES AND THE TREATY OF PARIS REDUX

The second Treaty of Paris, signed on September 3, 1783, officially ended the American Revolution. It's interesting to note that during these treaty negotiations, the British argued that the middle ground should continue to be respected and a buffer state be established. Yet they would relinquish it all, and their claims to territory south of Kitchi Gumi, in order to maintain control of the northern territory.

In their relationship with the newly created United States, Ojibway, Ota'wa and Ishkodawatomi-Anishinabe nations maintained that the young country had no title or right to territory west of the Alleghenies. They argued, for example, that the British had no legal right to surrender or transfer any territory or land at all because it didn't belong to them in the first place, and the N'swi-ish-ko-day-kawn Anishinabeg O'dish-ko-day-kawn was never defeated in battle and had not surrendered or transferred any title to the British.

As young and fragile as it was, the United States understood that it couldn't risk going to war with the N'swi-ish-ko-day-kawn Anishinabeg O'dish-ko-day-kawn and its allied nations. However, its Continental Congress was brash and cocky enough to pass the Northwest Ordinance on May 20, 1785, as an expression of its sovereignty and jurisdiction imperative. This land ordinance sought to pledge fair treatment of Anishinabeg with respect to the sharing and treatment of land. It also established a boundary line between the Anishinabe nations and the young country and gave the continental government the right to continue to trade and buy – but not seize – Anishinabe land.

Regardless of this and the other political and pseudo-diplomatic wranglings taking place, the N'swi-ish-ko-day-kawn Anishinabeg O'dish-ko-day-kawn had serious doubts about accepting the ordinance at face value. From its perspective, the American political will was simply not there, and from 1774 onward the United States did everything in its power to avoid going to war while attempting to satisfy its hunger for land and resources. The treaties negotiated often reflected this pattern.

The United States' economic, political and diplomatic relationship with the Anishinabe nations could be described as schizophrenic and duplicitous at best, since the Royal Proclamation acknowledged the sovereignty of Anishinabe nations and recognized their primordial title to land and resources. Of course, this created a serious dilemma for the United States, which manifested itself in a number of movements or political ideologies.

Americanism and the notion of exceptionalism

The new colonial ideology of Americanism and American exceptionalism became more pronounced during and after the American Revolution. Underpinning this ideology was the belief that the United States was qualitatively different from other nations. Americanism would also become uniquely tied to the policy of manifest destiny.[11]

The treaties for the most part were contracts signed with Anishinabe nations using Anishinabe protocols. This is a simple fact. Because of the relative weakness of the United States, nearly a third of the treaties signed were meant to keep peace; the rest were land surrenders, the validity of which is still being challenged today.

At the time, the United States and Canada attempted to mitigate their Anishinabe problem by establishing the reserve system. Paradoxically, these same reserves and reservations represent the centre of Anishinabe resistance today.

The concept of land as a living being was fundamental to the way in which Anishinabeg saw Manitou Aki. From the Anishinabe perspective, land was to be shared and held in common by all, to be passed from one generation to the next. Land was a birthright and inalienable. However, we begin to see the stark contrast between the Anishinabe and Euro-American philosophies in the treaties that were to be negotiated.

Conquest treaties?

The Treaty of Fort Stanwix (1768), negotiated under the pretense of conquest by William Johnston, Joseph Brant and George Croghan, was the first of the conquest treaties. As previously mentioned, Johnson and others who negotiated this treaty and others were often land speculators, the same people the Royal Proclamation and new treaty framework were intended to control. The Fort Stanwix treaty was an absurd attempt by the United States to legalize land titles of the thirty thousand non-indians already established west of the proclamation line.

By design, the treaty purposely surrendered land in what is now Kentucky, West Virginia, Pennsylvania and northern Ohio and casually extended the proclamation line west of the Appalachian Divide and Allegheny Mountains, beyond the Ohio River. It's not surprising that the Shawnee-Anishinabeg objected to the land surrender, because the land in question was part of their principal hunting territory.

In the same vein, a number of lesser-known Wendat, Luna-apewa, Ota'wa and Ojibway-Anishinabe leaders with no authority to speak of negotiated the Treaty of Fort McIntosh (1785), which also recognized American sovereignty and established a new boundary line.

Because of his financial inability to provide for his army, General Arthur St. Clair negotiated the third of the conquest treaties at Fort Harmar (1789) with Sac, Chippewa, Ota'wa, Ishkodawatomi, Wendat and Lunaapewa-Anishinabeg in an effort to further American peace efforts. The Shawnee-Anishinabeg again dismissed the treaty, pointing out that the Anishinabe nations who agreed to it had no authority to do so. In support of the Shawnee-Anishinabeg, the N'swi-ish-ko-day-kawn Anishinabeg O'dish-ko-day-kawn publicly condemned the treaty and admonished Anishinabe representatives responsible for its ratification. As payback, in an attempt to put things right, Mi-chi-ki-ni-kwa (*Little Turtle*) and We-ya-pier-sen-wah (*Blue Jacket*) defeated St. Clair decisively in one of the Anishinabeg's greatest victories.

In 1795, the treaty negotiated at Fort Greenville established the United States as a sovereign power. The United States in return agreed to recognize Anishinabe "ownership" of the remaining lands and provide payment (in cash or services) for these surrenders. Additionally, the Anishinabe nations that were signatory to the treaty were allowed to have access to and use of the land until the United States needed it. The Treaty of Greenville was the first treaty that Ota'wa-Anishinabe representatives participated in and signed. The last would be the Treaty of Detroit (1855).

The Jay Treaty, ratified in 1796, provided for British withdrawal from forts and territory in the United States, ending British authority in the northwest. Of course, the N'swi-ish-ko-day-kawn Anishinabeg O'dish-ko-day-kawn and its allied nations were affected the most because of the international boundary and the two separate jurisdictions it established.

In summary, these treaties, signed with no real authority, acknowledged the conquest of the N'swi-ish-ko-day-kawn Anishinabeg O'dish-ko-day-kawn and its allied nations and the legitimacy of United States sovereignty, and extended the proclamation line westward in order to legalize thirty thousand land titles – all in the name of peace, harmony and good relations.

ANISHINABE RESISTANCE

Anishinabe resistance took root once again in 1802, led by Tecumtha, who saw the treaties of Paris (1783), Fort Stanwix (1768), Fort McIntosh (1785), Fort Finney (1786) and Greenville (1795) as dismissive of the Royal Proclamation's principles. From Tecumtha's perspective, these treaties were negotiated by Anishinabe "leaders" who didn't have the authority to negotiate or surrender lands.

The Shawnee-Anishinabeg obviously refused to accept the terms of any of these treaties because they weren't involved in any of the negotiations and the land surrendered "belonged" to them. In response, at the signing of the Fort Finney treaty in 1786, they presented a black wampum belt to the Americans as a declaration of war.

The confusion created by and opposition to the treaties forced Tecumtha to demand an end to the land surrenders and negotiations taking place. In fact, he suggested that all treaties from 1768 on be reviewed and that the proclamation line be more controlled so as to restrict movement west of the Appalachian Mountains. He was also committed to having the integrity of the middle ground respected and its principles reaffirmed.

Tecumtha pointed to Lau-lau-we-see-kau's warnings regarding the dangers that Euro-American and colonial hegemony posed for Anishinabeg. He also declared the removal of Anishinabeg from traditional lands to be a forced spatial and spiritual exile. Displacement from the land, stories and language was something Tecumtha couldn't ignore; it manifested itself in a spiritual and physical trauma. He therefore began advocating for an alliance of all Anishinabe nations to join the Shawnee-Anishinabeg and the N'swi-ish-ko-day-kawn Anishinabeg O'dish-ko-day-kawn in opposing what was taking place.

Lau-lau-we-see-kau's visions of a spiritual identity were also firmly rooted in the political, economic, military and spiritual structure of the N'swi-ish-ko-day-kawn Anishinabeg O'dish-ko-day-kawn – in direct contrast to the racial and colonial hierarchy that Euro-Americans seemed to thrive on.

A DECLARATION OF WAR (JUNE 18, 1812)

In the period leading up to 1812, there was little development in terms of treaty negotiations and land surrenders. The Fort Wayne and and Fort Vincennes treaties, negotiated in 1809 and surrendering 3 million acres of land in southern Indiana and Illinois, were an exception.

In response to the United States' declaration of war on June 18, 1812, the N'swi-ish-ko-day-kawn Anishinabeg O'dish-ko-day-kawn and British forces led by Tecumtha and General Isaac Brock took Fort Detroit on August 15–17, 1812. The N'swi-ish-ko-day-kawn Anishinabeg O'dish-ko-day-kawn and allied nations were relatively successful in most of the ensuing battles over the following year.

For Tecumtha, the idea of an independent sovereign reality established on a centralized confederation of Anishinabe nations was a fundamental objective. He saw the impacts of westward expansion on Anishinabe communities – and the devastation. Hastily drawn-up treaties and land surrenders were particularly troubling for him, as the representatives often had no authority to negotiate these one-sided and questionable treaties. Further, these representatives and communities were surrendering lands and resources that weren't theirs to begin with. The treaties of Fort Stanwix (1768), Fort McIntosh (1785), Fort Finney (1786) and the Treaty of Greenville (1795) were blatant examples of this.

The political movement and military resistance that Tecumtha led had at its core a spiritual message that Lau-lau-we-see-kau helped narrate. To them, Anishinabe governance and sovereignty was a return home from the spatial exile that the Euro-Americans and colonies had forced on the Anishinabeg.

The Treaty of Ghent, signed on December 24, 1814, officially ended the War of 1812. And with the end of this war, another political, social, economic and military transition began for the Anishinabeg, a movement from alliance to irrelevance.

THE AFTERMATH

Immediately after the War of 1812, the Americans were eager to put a stranglehold on Anishinabe lands. In many instances, their policies were deliberately designed to choke the Anishinabeg into submission.

Under the Royal Proclamation of 1763 and the rules of international law, treaties legally recognized Anishinabe primordial title to Manitou Aki. Land transfers from Anishinabe nations to non-indians could only be conducted under the umbrella of a treaty. However, the land requirements and economic interests of the United States very quickly superseded this legal reality, creating a dilemma in relation to law and the nature of the treaty framework. The United States in time began to see Ota'wa-Anishinabeg as an obstacle to its interests and its manifest destiny policies.

During this period, the United States also began to explore various assimilationist policies and legislation, often social Darwinist in scope because of their notion of racial superiority. The United States and the proponents of these policies actually believed that once Ojibway, Ota'wa and Ishkodawatomi-Anishinabeg saw their culture and lifestyle as inferior, they would willingly adopt the non-indian way of life, one that included Christianity, farming and assimilation into non-indian society.

Given the schizophrenic and duplicitous nature of US policies and attitude, an interesting dichotomy soon developed. For example, some wanted to civilize Anishinabeg, and others wanted their complete removal or extermination. Still others believed that Anishinabeg were mentally and physically incapable of adapting to civilization. Regardless of attitude, American legislation now focused on addressing – and erasing – the *indian problem.*

INDIAN REMOVAL ACT (1830)

One of the biggest threats to Anishinabe nations at this time was President Andrew Jackson (1829–1837), who was maniacal in his legislative and physical opposition to Anishinabeg. In 1830, his administration passed the *Indian Removal Act,* which effectively removed Anishinabeg from present-day Ohio, Indiana, Illinois, Georgia, Alabama and Mississippi.

The *Indian Removal Act* made it quite clear that the United States was beginning to distance itself from the original intent of the Royal Proclamation. It also suggested that the United States never really understood or believed in the treaty rights and obligations negotiated.

The political and legal haranguing that took place was referred to in Chief Justice John Marshall's *Cherokee v. Georgia* (1831) and *Worcester v. Georgia* (1832) rulings. In fact, Marshall's decisions were in direct contrast to Andrew Jackson's racist criticisms and legislation. For example, in *Cherokee v. Georgia,* Marshall established that the Cherokee-Anishinabeg were a domestic dependent nation whose relationship with the United States was similar to a "ward to its guardian." However, he determined that the federal government had sole responsibility for dealing with Anishinabe nations[12] and that the states had no jurisdiction in the indian nations whatsoever.

A year after *Cherokee v. Georgia,* the *Worcester v. Georgia* ruling established a new foundation or framework for Anishinabe sovereignty, making the *Indian Removal Act* illegal and unconstitutional. Jackson responded, "John Marshall has made his decision, now let him enforce it." And despite the fact that Marshall's decisions acknowledged that states had no jurisdiction whatsoever in indian country and that the *Indian Removal Act* was unconstitutional, Jackson ignored the international meaning of nationhood with respect to the Cherokee-Anishinabeg; Cherokee, Creek, Chickasaw, Choctaw and Seminole-Anishinabeg were forced to relocate in 1838.

As the United States moved westward, it also passed a series of laws that sought to destabilize Anishinabe society. The 1887 *Dawes Act*, for example, became the legislative vehicle for dividing communities and nations. The legislation allowed for the division of reservations into individual parcels or allotments of 158 acres for each family head and 79 acres for each single Anishinabe citizen over the age of eighteen years – completely disregarding the Anishinabe concept and practice of bi-mee-ku-mau-gay-win. The legislation stipulated that each allotment would be held in trust for a period of twenty-five years, during which the land could not be sold, mortgaged or taxed. At the conclusion of the twenty-five-year period, each Anishinabe nation would receive a patent to the land, and the allotment could then be sold, taxed and passed from Anishinabe hands to non-indian hands.

Societal upheaval resulted in Anishinabe territory throughout Manitou Aki, because approximately two-thirds of the land held in patent was transferred to non-indians by way of foreclosure. The legislation also impacted the economic integrity of the Anishinabe nations because most of the traditional territories were lost in the process. Complex situations often developed as more treaties were negotiated. For example, consensus became more difficult to achieve because of economic, political, social and military instability – especially with the land surrenders and the economic challenges that were dividing the Ota'wa-Anishinabe communities. The Ota'wa-Anishinabe nation no longer had the wherewithal to challenge what was taking place. However, the nation's mixed economy (fishing, hunting and agriculture) also prevented a complete economic collapse and provided a good source of food when other nations were without. As well, its traditional territory included vast tracts of forest in Michigan.

During the mid-1830s, the demand for land increased exponentially. For example, the state of Michigan now wanted clear
title to all of Ota'wa-Anishinabe territory. American politics
also began to change with the election of President Zachary
Taylor in 1841 and, strangely enough, Michigan legislators peti-
tioned the federal government to give Ota'wa-Anishinabeg citizenship in order to let them remain in Michigan, arguing that
citizenship would give them stronger legal rights and make
their forced removal west of the Mississippi River unconstitutional. In 1850, the Michigan constitution granted the Ota'wa-
Anishinabeg citizenship and the right to vote on the condition
that they renounce their Ota'wa-Anishinabe citizenship. A
strange quid pro quo.

The two Treaties of Washington, negotiated on March 28,
1836, and February 22, 1855, were an issue for the Ota'wa and
Ojibway-Anishinabeg because they "surrendered" most of their
territory.[13] Only twenty-one of the one hundred recognized
o-gi-ma-wi-win endorsed the Treaty of 1836, and many of the
leadership who supported the land surrenders were later killed.

From an Ota'wa-Anishinabe perspective, both treaties
attempted to sever any remaining spiritual connection the
Ota'wa-Anishinabeg had with the lands by establishing a system
of individual parcels of land. The idea and policies of manifest
destiny continued to perpetuate the land theft, acts of Congress,
indian agents or simple appropriation.

The treaties themselves, however, were quite different from
those previously negotiated, which on the whole had recognized
Anishinabe nations as sovereign and independent.

OJIBWAY-ANISHINABEG | THE ELDEST BROTHER

Throughout history, philosophers and political observers have
analyzed political power and a nation's greatness in many
different ways. In view of the discourse regarding power and
authority, we could argue that the Ojibway-Anishinabe nation
was truly one of the world's great nations. We know, for example,

that the sun rose and fell on Ishkodawatomi, Ota'wa and
Ojibway-Anishinabe territory and that the Ojibway-Anishinabe
were powerful enough to control communication and travel
from the Eastern Seaboard, to Kitchi Gumi, to Manitou Abi
and then to the asinii-wajiw (*rocky mountain*).

In the same manner as the societies of their younger brothers,
Ojibway-Anishinabe society was firmly rooted within g' doodemonaanik ki-nah-mah-gay-wi-nan (*teachings of our clan system*).
Despite discrepancies and confusion within academia regarding
the way clans came to the Ishkodawatomi, Ota'wa and Ojibway-
Anishinabeg, we look to the sacred stories and birchbark scrolls
that describe how nigig (*otter*) broke through a sandbar at the
start of the migration, and it was then the ah-ji-jahk that led the
giigoo, mahng, waa-bi-zhe-shi, makwa and waa-wash-shke-shi
doodem westward. Even today, many Ojibway-Anishinabeg
still trace their ancestry back to these original families.

The stories and scrolls describe how the megis shell rose out
of the water seven times during the migration, beginning at an
island that was shaped like a mi-ni-si (*turtle*) or Mo-ni-yang
(*Turtle Island*), with major stopping places at Ki-chi-ka-be-kong
(*Place Where the Water and Thunder Meet*; *Niagara Falls*), Wa-wii-
a-ta-nong (*Where Two Bodies of Water Are Connected* – connects
Lake St. Clair and Lake Huron to Lake Erie; *Detroit River*),
Manitou Minising, Ba-wi-ti-gong (*Where the Fish Were Good and
Lived Well*; present-day *Sault Ste. Marie*), Wi-kwe-dong (*Spirit
Island*) and Mo-ning-wun-a-kawn-ning or Zha-ga-wa-mi-kahg
(*Turtle-Shaped Island*; *Madeline Island*).

DOODEM | THE CLAN

The importance of the doodem can never be understated,
because it represented everything that was and still is important
to Ojibway-Anishinabe society, as it was and still is for their
younger brothers. The Europeans found it necessary to work
with the doodem because of its political, economic, social and

military influence and the fact that Ojibway-Anishinabe society was governed by specific protocols and responsibilities. With its focus on security and well-being, the doodem was important to Ishkodawatomi, Ota'wa and Ojibway-Anishinabeg; nothing functioned without it. As mentioned earlier, the sharing of one's wealth and property was seen as a practicality for Ojibway, Ota'wa and Ojibway-Anishinabe society. In the context of community and society, it made sense to ensure and provide for the security and well-being of all people rather than just a few.

The doodem and o-gi-ma-wi-win were two fundamental pillars of Ojibway-Anishinabe society. But there were many different types of leaders within the community, men and women who were expected to be fair-minded and act in the best interests of the people. Often these leaders gained prestige and were renowned for their courage in battle, for their medicine powers or for being genuine in their approach to mino bi-mah-di-zhi-win (*good life*).

From a Euro-American and non-spiritual perspective, power is dependent on a hierarchical and authoritative structure. In contrast, Ojibway-Anishinabe society saw di-bish-ko (*equality*) and maada 'oo-ni-di-wahg (*sharing*) as fundamental to clan/community di-bayn-di-zi-win (*autonomy*) and gah-na-we-nin-di-zo-win (*self-sufficiency*). It also saw men and women in leadership positions as responsibile for assisting citizens in being safe, secure and self-sufficient.

As we've seen with the Ishkodawatomi and Ota'wa-Anishinabeg, decision-making was always achieved by consensus rather than by authoritative action. Of course, decisions would depend on the urgency of the situation or the matter at hand. Today, it seems that dissension and division are the result of citizens, communities and nations having limited options open to them. Under these circumstances, Anishinabe citizens often don't work together to further the collective well-being of the community.

Ojibway-Anishinabe society – like most Anishinabe societies – was and still is an oral culture. Public speaking was practised and perfected so that we might "hold up a mirror to nature" and see ourselves in the story. The ah-di-so-kah-nahg, di-bah-ji-mo-wi-nan and ah-way-chi-gay-wi-nan pass the values of society from one generation to the next, showing the range of emotions and actions inherent in the story. This was and remains important!

Of course, we know that Ojibwaymowin is beautifully descriptive, enabling speakers to vividly recall events and recreate strong events with words. We ask to remain true to their visions and stories and give thanks to the traditional ah-di-so-kahn-i-ni-ni/ kwe-wahg for sharing the ah-di-so-kah-nahg and their di-bah-ji-mo-wi-nan that help guide and teach us.

Ni-biin-daa-koo-ji-ge gaye ni' o-nah-ko-nah ah-di-so-kah-nahg zhigo di-bah-ji-mo-wi-nan g'dah mi-kwe-ni-mah-nahn Pine Shomin, obwandiacbun, tecumthabun, miinwaa shingwaukbun ... debwewin onji ... Meegwetch.

············ 66 ············

My Ga-sha told me many times that Chippewa, the English way of pronouncing Ojibwa, was not the right word to use when describing these Anishinaaybeg. The correct word is *O-jib-i-on,* pronounced O-shib-i-on. To those who belong to the Three Sacred Fires, this word means "Picturegraph Writers." This is the duty they took while on our migration. They kept these writings on sacred scrolls of birchbark and deer hides. The scrolls were stored in a hollowed-out Ma-no-na (Ironwood log), and then lowered with a rope made of Wi-ga-beesh (Basswood bark) over the side of a cliff to be hidden.

Our history relates that a prophet came to them and said that strange people would come here and try to destroy our way of life. It also says that when we are able to practice our way of life freely again, there will be a young boy who has had a vision quest and he will lead us to these sacred scrolls.

O-ji-ba-wa is another story. At the time when the Anishinaaybeg migrated from the east coast to the area of the Apostle Islands in Lake Superior (Northern Wisconsin), they went too far west at first – somewhere into what is now called lower Wisconsin. A boy dreamt that they must go back to the area where Walpole Island is today. At that time, lower Michigan was all swamps, marshes and big rivers. Some of the Anishinaaybeg left the migration, not wanting to cross these watery places. These Anishinaaybeg were called O-ji-ba-wa, meaning they left the migration.[14]

. . . . **❝** . . . .

Mii i'i-way ojibway-anishinabe i-zhi-chi-gay-win. Zhigo mii'iw eta-go o-way neen-gi-kayn-dahn zhigo ni-gi-noon-dah-wah . . . Ahaaw sa. Weweni.

Many of our stories help us make sense and meaning of how we came to be and our existence. Storytelling provides us with some context for this and the beginning of our own narrative. Our stories tell the world that we are human, not blood-thirsty savages and inhuman. They are also complex and, in many ways, different from academic historiography (the methodology of historians and the way history has been told and written) because Ojibwaymowin and our other languages are interwoven with our relationship to the world around us and to the land. In acknowledging their truth, we find some understanding of Anishinabe oral history.

The stories describe how we came to be, our place in this world and how our relationships with other Anishinabe and European nations developed. They describe Jacques Cartier and Étienne Brûlé's first meeting with Anishinabeg (c. 1500–1600) on the Eastern Seaboard of Manitou Aki and at Bawetigong (*Place of the Rapids; Where the Fish Were Good and Lived Well*). From these stories we also come to know that Samuel de Champlain was committed to establishing economic, trade, political and military relationships with the Ojibway-Anishinabeg because he knew that French survival was dependent on establishing and maintaining friendly relations with them.

We know from the stories that nothing took place without the N'swi-ish-ko-day-kawn Anishinabeg O'dish-ko-day-kawn, because the Ojibway, Ota'wa and Ishkodawatomi-Anishinabeg controlled everything economic, political and military. The Haudenosaunee-Anishinabeg Confederacy sought to upset the economic, political and military balance of power by waging war on a number of Anishinabe nations. However, as we know, Ojibway-Anishinabe forces completely overwhelmed and defeated an Iroquois-Anishinabe war party at *Iroquois Point* on Lake Superior in 1653, ending the Haudenosaunee-Anishinabe pestering.

The French were obviously concerned by the defeat of their main economic, political and military ally and immediately sought to establish peace in the hope of bringing some calm to the region, by helping to negotiate the Great Peace of Montréal on August 4, 1701. Again, in the aftermath of hostilities, the Wendat-Anishinabeg were forced into Ojibway-Anishinabe territory by the Iroquois-Anishinabeg, who had also been at war with them since 1648.

As economic and trade wars and hostilities between the French and British continued to escalate, the Ojibway-Anishinabeg were inevitably drawn into them but were quick to adapt to the market-style economy that was introduced. The French made attempts to manipulate trade prices, while the Ojibway-Anishinabeg simply began trading with the Hudson Bay Company, which had been established in 1670.

As economic and trade relations with the British became more entrenched, immigration to Manitou Aki also began to increase exponentially. All of this started a new struggle for control of the economy and the land. Predictably, Anishinabe nations were drawn into this international conflict playing out in their backyard, which also intensified animosities between the Ojibway and Iroquois-Anishinabe nations.

The following is a story shared by Kahgegagahbowh (George Copway) in 1847. Again, I share the story as I would in ceremony.

Ni-biin-daa-koo-ji-ge gaye ni' o-nah-ko-nah kahgegagahbowh ah-di-zo-kah-nan zhigo di-bah-ji-mo-wi-nan debwewin onji miinwaa g'dah mi-kwe-ni-mah-nahn obwandiacbun, tecumthabun, shingwaukbun ... Meegwetch.

The Ojibway annually sent me of their number to trade with the French at either Quebec or Montreal. A party of these was waylaid and killed by the Iroquois. Threats of reprisals were treated by the Iroquois with scorn. After a second party had been similarly attacked and slain, a council of the nation was held, resulting in some of their chiefs being sent to confer with the Iroquois. The meeting was held at Saugeen (Southampton) and resulted in the Iroquois agreeing to pay a bale of furs for each man that had been killed and in addition granted permission to the Ojibway to pass peacefully on trade trips to Montreal. This treaty held good for three years when bands of Iroquois waylaid simultaneously several parties of Ojibway returning from a trading journey. This happened in the fall of that year ...

In the meantime, runners were sent to the various allies in the coming war. In the month of May following the combined forces gathered in two parties, one at Lake St. Clair and the other at Sault Ste. Marie, seven hundred canoes being there assembled. This latter party divided into two bands. One advanced on the enemy by way of the Ottawa Valley, while the other proceeded to Penetanguishene. The Lake St. Clair division at the same time came up the east coast of Lake Huron to the mouth of the Saugeen River, where a fierce battle was fought with the Iroquois who ultimately gave way and fled before the onslaught of the Ojibway.[15]

.............**66**.............

**Mii i'i-way ojibway-anishinabe i-zhi-chi-gay-win.
Zhigo mii'iw eta-go o-way neen-gi-kayn-dahn zhigo
ni-gi-noon-dah-wah ... Ahaaw sa. Weweni.**

Territorial acquisition was traditionally seen as a sign of military power and control. The Ojibway and Iroquois-Anishinabe wars were no exception. The Great Peace of Montréal included thirty-nine nations that came to Montreal to "bury the hatchet deep in the earth." The treaty was intended to bring an end to the Iroquois wars. Peter Schmalz describes how, in return for peace and friendship, the five Haudenosaunee-Anishinabe nations extracted promises of protection and security from the British, particularly with respect to their territory around Lakes Erie, Huron and Ontario.[16]

The military strength of the Ojibway-Anishinabeg at this time was such that nothing took place without their agreement and, although the treaty was signed, the Ojibway-Anishinabeg continued to wage war with the Iroquois-Anishinabeg in order to keep their trade routes open to the United States and further entrench themselves in southern Ontario.

The concept of trade from an Ojibway-Anishinabe perspective is interesting and provides some insight into the nation's move westward. Trade was certainly not a foreign concept to the Ojibway-Anishinabeg because of their vast, continent-wide trade network prior to first contact. For the Ojibway-Anishinabe, trade could impact many things. In establishing trade relationships with other nations, the Ojibway-Anishinabe sought to establish/maintain alliances and friendly relations. For example, there was always the expectation that any gift given would be reciprocated. This form of bartering and relationship building had governed Ojibway-Anishinabe social relations since the beginning of time. The idea of sharing was so fundamental to Ojibway-Anishinabe society that nothing took place without it. The European concept of trade and economic exchange, on the other hand, was very narrow in scope. It ignored the political and social aspect of these relationships.

British customs and new protocols also muddied the water during this period. We see, for example, the appointment of trading captains to negotiate treaties and trade agreements. These British-appointed leaders wore special hats (top hats with trade-silver bands) and coats with brass buttons. (Interestingly, an elder from Sagkeeng asked that I return to the wearing of this uniform in recognition of my status as chief under the *Indian Act*.) These customs and positions inevitably bound the Ojibway-Anishinabe nation to the British in some weird deliberate way.[17]

Westward expansion and control of the lucrative economic and fur trade were factors contributing to the military conflict that eventually took place. In the autumn of 1760, the surrender of Fort Ponchartrain at Detroit effectively ended the exclusive relationship between the French and Anishinabe nations.

Again, Governor General Jeffrey Amherst's policy to stop the practice and tradition of gift-giving became an issue for many Anishinabeg, because the exchange of gifts itself had always been respected and accepted as diplomatic protocol. Unwittingly, Amherst destroyed a spirit of reciprocity that had existed since first contact and set off a chain of events that carried on well into the 1800s.

More importantly, the Anishinabe dependence on and acceptance of European goods and services was proving problematic for the Anishinabeg as well. Neolin, Obwandiac, Lau-lau-we-see-kau and Tecumtha saw the dangers that this dependence brought. For this reason, Neolin's warning resonated with and became a focal point for Obwandiac and other Anishinabe nations in the period leading up to May 1763, as did Lau-lau-we-see-kau's message and Tecumtha's efforts in the early part of the 1800s.

Not surprisingly, the thirteen colonies were upset by the Royal Proclamation, believing that King George III had overstepped his authority. In this regard, I find it interesting that there is still debate as to when the American Revolution actually began. Some historians tell us that the Americans took to arms immediately following the issuing of the Royal Proclamation in 1763, while some suggest it began with the Battle of Lexington in 1775. Still others suggest that for us it never stopped. However, one thing we do know with certainty is that the Treaty of Paris was signed on September 3, 1783.

The political and military duplicity during this period proved troublesome for many Anishinabe nations, and the Northwest Ordinance of 1787, which established the Northwest Territories (including Michigan), intensified this unrest and created new threats for the Anishinabeg, as non-indian land speculators began to move beyond the proclamation line.

The Treaty of Greenville in 1795 also started a series of treaty negotiations that were substantively and fundamentally different from those previously negotiated and ushered in a new era, with the United States still focused on westward expansion. Prime real estate along the major waterways also proved to be a hot commodity for land speculators, and the United States jumped head-first into the treaty business, full of bluster and deceit.

While it could be argued that the treaties were and are a good thing, the fact remains that the United States and Canada saw treaties as a necessary evil and a means to an end. In many instances, the smoke and mirrors were amplified by the appointment of Anishinabe leadership independent of the community and nation.

Tecumtha challenged the societal dysfunction these appointments were causing and pointed out that individual leaders and communities could not and did not have the authority to surrender lands and traditional territories that belonged to all Anishinabeg. This was his fundamental argument with respect to the Royal Proclamation and in the events leading up to 1812.

It's not surprising that a number of treaties allowed for co-operation and unity between the territorial leaders and federal officials. There were many instances where territorial governors acted as federal agents during treaty negotiations, which obviously muddied the waters.

Tecumtha saw the territorial integrity of Anishinabe lands being disrespected rather casually and without regard. For him, the notion of Anishinabe i-nah-ko-ni-gay-win was about a spiritual connection to the land and its protection for all future generations. Tecumtha sought to preserve and protect this inherent right in the War of 1812, and soon after, in response, the United States negotiated a number of treaties in relatively short order.[18] They promised prosperity and citizenship, but in reality they gave full legal effect to and ratified the transfer of lands already occupied by non-indians.

By the late 1800s, fundamental changes in the economic, political, diplomatic and military discourse were taking place. In an attempt to move with these changes, many Ojibway-Anishinabe communities had established sturgeon fisheries and trade centres in the Great Lakes region of Michilimackinac and Sault Ste. Marie. Despite this success, the continued western migration of the British placed great strain and societal pressure on the Anishinabe community and nation.

WAH-BISH-KI-WAY GI-MA-KAN-DI-WAYD O'OW AKI |
ACTS OF COMPASSION AND OTHER MISHMASH

The *Indian Removal Act* (1830) passed by the United States Congress and strongly endorsed by the Jackson administration was a means to gain greater access to Anishinabe lands and resources. The Treaty of Washington (1836) attempted to resolve the land issue once and for all in what is now Ohio and Michigan, but when all was said and done, the treaty was simply a removal treaty. The Ota'wa-Anishinabeg argued that they were never fully compensated for their lands in what was now Michigan and therefore didn't recognize the treaty.

> Ni-biin-daa-koo-ji-ge gaye ni' o-nah-ko-nah
> ah-di-so-kah-nahg zhigo di-bah-ji-mo-wi-nan g'dah
> mi-kwe-ni-mah-nahn Pine Shomin, obwandiacbun,
> tecumthabun, miinwaa shingwaukbun ... Meegwetch.

. . . . **66** . . . .

He said Apoksogon was offered a pile of money, all coin. Andrew then held his hand above the floor about two and one-half feet, signifying this pile. The negotiator at Washington told Apoksogon, "This money will all be yours

if you sell us your land in A-shig-a-ning" (Michigan today).
Apoksogon answered, "We do not need your money. We do
not wish to sell. You keep your money; we will keep our land."

The Odawa's then left the treaty negotiations. Apoksogon
and the other Headmen that had left Harbor Springs for
Washington in the fall of 1835 did not sign a treaty with the
United States Government. Apoksogon name appeared on
the document, but he did not sign it.[19]

. . . . **"** . . . .

**Mii i'i-way ojibway-anishinabe i-zhi-chi-gay-win.
Zhigo mii'iw eta-go o-way neen-gi-kayn-dahn zhigo
ni-gi-noon-dah-wah ... Ahaaw sa. Weweni.**

The Treaties of Washington and Detroit (1855) were essentially designed to terminate Anishinabe citizenship and ownership of land under the guise of setting aside lands for the
Ojibway and Ota'wa-Anishinabeg, which allowed for individual
allotments they would earn title to and hold as private property.
This was a new approach to treaty making. Of course, treaties
during this period were contemporaneously chronicling the
demise of the traditional and spiritual notions of citizenship
and land. The *Dawes Act*, passed in 1887, for example, was the
legislative tool that divided Anishinabe lands into individual
parcels and promised Anishinabeg the opportunity to enter the
United States as equal citizens. Obviously, reformers attempted
to pass this piece of legislation off as the indian Magna Carta,
despite the fact that it facilitated the loss and transfer of Anishinabe lands to non-indians because of taxation requirements.

This and assimilation became the new guiding principles.
Pure and simple! Tax payment defaults were often facilitated

by corrupt officials who withheld notification that taxes were overdue. When taxes were not paid, the non-indian would often cover off the back-taxes and gain title to the land. The loss of land was always followed by the loss of traditional economies, and the social disintegration and poverty that followed became relatively commonplace throughout Anishinabe country.

OBWANDIAC, TECUMTHA AND SHINGWAUK IN RETROSPECT

Obwandiac fought for the integrity of Anishinabe lands and the Anishinabe right to protect and live on these lands in 1763. The resulting Royal Proclamation acknowledged Anishinabe primordial title to these lands, and the treaty framework it created became the legal process for recognizing this title and agreement to share its use.

In the period leading up to 1812, Tecumtha challenged the legal abuses and lack of free, prior and informed consent of the Anishinabe collective in treaty negotiations. From his perspective, it was impossible for Euro-American or self-appointed "leaders" to surrender lands and title that belonged to the Anishinabe collective.

For his part, Shingwauk forced the British Crown to adopt a treaty process that was committed to sharing and being more respectful of each nation's needs in the 1850 Robinson-Huron and Robinson-Superior treaties, which would come to serve as the template for the numbered treaties (1871–1921). For example, Shingwauk was firm in his belief that treaties should recognize the Anishinabe primordial right to hunt, trap and fish on shared lands. He argued as well for a provision that would pay approximately two pounds per capita in shared revenue for resources.

TREATY 1 (AUGUST 3, 1871)

The numbered treaty process began in 1871 with Oo-za-we-kwun's (*Yellow Quill*) refusal to let non-indian settlers travel west of present-day *Portage la Prairie*. During Treaty 1 (Stone Fort

Treaty) negotiations, the Ojibway-Anishinabe leadership took
a very hard line with respect to the provisions of the Selkirk
Treaty signed in July 1817.

Leadership wanted specific concessions and provisions high-
lighted in the treaties. This showed that they had an idea of and
were familiar with what Obwandiac, Tecumtha and Shingwauk
sought to achieve with respect to land and treaties. Oral history
suggests that they were certainly aware of what had taken place.

More importantly, the Ojibway-Anishinabeg saw the treaty
as a form of economic planning and a means for ensuring continued access to natural and economic resources. They demanded
what they saw as a fair economic exchange for sharing the land
and its resources. It's obvious that they had a clear estimate of
the value of the land and resources. At one point, the Crown's
treaty negotiator suggested that their demands were excessive
and that he had difficulty in getting the Anishinabeg to acknowledge the views of the Crown.

Initially, during Treaty 1 negotiations, Ojibway-Anishinabe
leadership demanded two-thirds of *Rupert's Land*[20] and shared
access to its natural resources. These demands were based on
estimates of what they thought their communities and nation
would need to support themselves in the years to come. Not
surprisingly, during Treaty 1 negotiations in 1871, the federal
Crown argued that aboriginal title to northwestern Ontario,
Manitoba, the Prairie provinces, *Vancouver Island* and vast tracts
of the *Canadian North* was extinguished. Conversely, Ojibway-
Anishinabe leadership argued that Manitoba in 1870 was an
illegal entity, regardless of the Hudson's Bay Company's claim
to Rupert's Land.[21]

Anishinabeg have experienced increased intervention in our
internal affairs that began with the *Act for the Better Protection
of the Lands and Property of Indians in Lower Canada* (1850), the
*Act to Encourage the Gradual Civilization of the Indian Tribes of
Canada* (1857), the establishment of the Dominion of Canada
itself in 1867 through the *British North America Act* (1867), the

Enfranchisement Act (1869), the Department of the Interior
(1872), the *Indian Act* (1876; sought to consolidate all other
existing legislation), the *Indian Advancement Act*[22] (1884) and,
of course, the *Davin Report* in 1879, which recommended implementation of the residential school system. It's been a difficult
road to navigate because the rules are always changing. However, the one constant is Canada's continued focus on getting
rid of the indian problem.

The Anishinabeg and the N'swi-ish-ko-day-kawn Anishinabeg
O'dish-ko-day-kawn have been part of our history. Everything
that the American and Canadian republics are today is because
of the Anishinabeg. In fact, *Grenada, Quebec* and Florida also
owe their existence to Obwandiac and the N'swi-ish-ko-day-kawn
Anishinabeg O'dish-ko-day-kawn, and we should acknowledge
this. It's an amazing thing when you think about it.

Mii i'i-way ojibway-anishinabe i-zhi-chi-gay-win.
Zhigo mii'iw eta-go o-way neen-gi-kayn-dahn zhigo
ni-gi-noon-dah-wah ... Ahaaw sa. Weweni.

6

Meegwetch
bi-zhin-dah-wi-yeg

THANK YOU

FOR LISTENING TO ME

OUR HEARTS ARE *as One Fire* is an expression of Ojibway, Ota'wa and Ishkodawatomi-Anishinabe history and Anishinabeness (our culture, place and philosophy). It speaks to our collective history and opposition to the colonial terrorism that we've experienced since 1492. If anything, this story has shown that to influence laws and effect change, we have to take back control of the political, social and economic agenda that impacts our lives on a daily basis. The onus has always been ours to explain how to make our lives matter. There is absolutely no arguing this point.

The task today is not to create something entirely different and new but rather to take what has worked in the past and give it a modern-day application. We have to re-evaluate our societal, political and economic relationship with Canada and its provinces and territories. One question that immediately comes to mind is whether diplomacy and working within the Canadian body-politic and federalist paradigm are necessary for ensuring our treaty rights to land, water, fishing and hunting. It is difficult to answer this. One thing we know for sure is that the task of ending the Canadian stranglehold on policy and legislation is our responsibility. The fight for Ojibway-Anishinabe governance, sovereignty and self-determination will remain a "blood struggle."

We've seen the Canadian *realpolitik* misappropriate the Anishinabe narrative and commit cultural rape for far too long. This abusive relationship has to come to an end at some point. In many ways, we've been complicit in perpetuating the untruths and have been far too accepting of Canadian euphemisms regarding democracy and racial tolerance. Canada has to own up to its racist and oppressive policies as well, and these endless apologies have to stop!

One could ask what racism and oppression have to do with Anishinabe leadership and governance. But in many ways the systemic racism and oppression experienced by Anishinabeg on "both sides of the creek" moved Obwandiac, Tecumtha and Shingwauk and the N'swi-ish-ko-day-kawn Anishinabeg O'dish-ko-day-kawn to move.

It's incredible that there are so many people who believe that, because of all the apologies, Anishinabeg are living in a post-colonial society free from oppression and terrorism, that we've healed from the trauma and are on the road to reconciliation, and that Canada has been absolved. Despite the abject poverty, youth suicides, manipulation of laws and government oppression, we're told that we are free at last!

From its beginning, this story sought to explore Ojibway, Ota'wa and Ishkodawatomi-Anishinabe leadership and governance leadership from a uniquely Ojibway-Anishinabe perspective. The stories of Obwandiac, Tecumtha, Shingwauk and the N'swi-ish-ko-day-kawn Anishinabeg O'dish-ko-day-kawn are, after all, our stories! This unique Ojibway-Anishinabe approach spoke of the origin and history of Ojibway, Ota'wa and Ishkodawatomi-Anishinabeg as told to us in our ah-di-so-kah-nahg, ah-way-chi-gay-wi-nan and di-bah-ji-mo-wi-nan. In turn, these stories have always been nurtured within our medicine bundles and indian ways that help give context to who we are as a people and why we were placed on Manitou Aki. The medicine bundles and indian ways enable us to dream and have vision. Together with the gi-ki-nah-mah-gay-wi-nan, manitou na-ga-mo-nan, manitou kay-wi-nan and miskew ah-zha-way-chi-win, they provide an understanding and a pathway to a unique way of seeing the world. In many respects, the indian ways help us see, hear, taste and feel things differently, and throughout this journey I was always mindful of this.

It's important to reflect on our Anishinabeness and history because it humanizes each of us. This story was an attempt to explain how we interpreted the world around us from the perspective of our gah-wi-zi-mah-ji-say-muh-guhk, which are fundamental to our own bish-kayn-di-ji-gay-win (*pedagogy*) and nah-nah-gah-dah-wayn-ji-gay-win. These stories tell us explicitly where we came from, who we are, how we fit into this world and how we came to know and learn things.

> **Mii i'i-way ojibway-anishinabe i-zhi-chi-gay-win.**
> **Zhigo mii'iw eta-go o-way neen-gi-kayn-dahn zhigo**
> **ni-gi-noon-dah-wah. Ahaaw sa. Weweni.**

It's also important to point out that our truth and principles are rooted in i-nah-di-zi-win, which helps define our personal responsibilities and expectations. They also explain our interconnectedness with the universe and land.

Truth and history are powerful tools for sure. The Euro-American pedagogies that I've come to know have all been about power, systemic violence and institutionalized racism. It's about both "in your face" and nuanced violence. Admittedly, we have all been victims of this conflict at different times and for far too long. Enough!

The Canadian government's violence and injustice toward Anishinabeg have been well documented in the reams of commission and inquiry reports. In fact, we're burdened by all of it. To my mind, all this talk about reconciliation is just talk!

From termination policies and initiatives such as residential schools to the White Paper (1969), Bill C-31 (1985) and more recent legislation, the Canadian politics of distraction and intent have always been the same. But we continue to resist!

In retrospect, this journey took me to many different places and levels of understanding. It showed me a society intent on looking after and caring for its people in a very natural and organic way, a society that valued inclusivity, transparency and respect for all living things. I also came to see how the clan system ensured the social, political and economic stability of the nation and mutual trust between its leadership and citizens.

Every social, political, economic, military and spiritual element of Anishinabe life was defined by the clan system, including beliefs,[1] values[2] and worldview. The clans were about everything and anything! In this respect, the clan system was about life itself. Ojibway, Ota'wa and Ishkodawatomi-Anishinabeg were taught from the beginning of time that the clans were the Creator's gift and that creation gave each of us certain responsibilities. The clans remain centre of and brilliant spark to our world. We came to understand the leadership responsibilities of the ah-ji-jahk and mahng doodem, and the healing and protection responsibilities of the makwa; members of the giigoo doodem were seen as the philosophers and mediators, and those of the waa-bi-zhe-shi doodem were responsible for providing for and protecting the community.

We were also taught that before Ojibway, Ota'wa and Ishkodawatomi-Anishinabeg were placed on Manitou Aki, members of the waa-bi-zhe-shi doodem were sent ahead to see what Ojibway, Ota'wa and Ishkodawatomi-Anishinabeg needed to survive, and we were also told that it was the waa-wash-shke-shi and bineshi doodem who had responsibilities for beauty and reconciliation.

The clans promoted the co-operative and integrative organization of Ojibway, Ota'wa and Ishkodawatomi-Anishinabe society. Ojibway, Ota'wa and Ishkodawatomi-Anishinabe sovereignty could not by its inner dynamics function in any way other than an interdependent and supportive manner. This incredible system of social order and structure was one of the original laws of creation, which came to represent life itself.

Ojibway, Ota'wa and Ishkodawatomi-Anishinabe communities and nations also understood that sharing provided individuals with respect and prestige. A person's wealth simply meant that he or she had more to share and was therefore able to give more of what he or she had. Sharing was such a fundamental characteristic of Ojibway, Ota'wa and Ishkodawatomi-Anishinabe life that almost no interaction could be carried out without it.

It's become very clear to me that the clan system is still about de-bwe-win, bi-sa-nii-we-win (*peace*), ish-payn-du-go-si-win (*honour*), mash-ka-wi-zii (*strength*), be-jig-wen-da-mo-win (*unity*) and i-nah-ko-ni-gay-win or sa-ga-katch (*social order*).

The Roseau River Anishinabe Nation (1992) is one of the few Ojibway, Ota'wa and Ishkodawatomi-Anishinabe communities that governs outside the *Indian Act*, using specific elements of traditional clan government. For example, within Roseau River's traditional system, the giigoo doodem is responsible for maintaining balance and integration in government, the mahng doodem is entrusted with ensuring the community's security and the ah-ji-jahk doodem is the guardian of the Ojibway, Ota'wa and Ishkodawatomi-Anishinabe worldview and integrity of relationships.

In many regards, Ojibway, Ota'wa and Ishkodawatomi-Anishinabe society was pragmatic, particularly when it came to matters of national concern. The objective was always to speak with one voice and reach consensus when deliberating on community and nation issues. Many acknowledge that Ojibway, Ota'wa and Ishkodawatomi-Anishinabe i-nah-ko-ni-gay-win only became reality when consensus was reached.

Today, sovereignty and self-determination vis-à-vis Ojibway, Ota'wa and Ishkodawatomi-Anishinabe and Euro-American relations have evolved into ambiguous rhetoric because of the American and Canadian governments' unwillingness to enter into serious discussions regarding their true meaning and application. Unfortunately, this ambiguity has given way to an unhealthy and dysfunctional political, social and economic relationship.

For example, with the *Appropriations Act* (1871), the United States was more forthright in its opposition to Anishinabe sovereignty and self-determination. It dismissed the idea of sovereignty altogether, suggesting that Anishinabeg would no longer be acknowledged or recognized as independent and sovereign. In his landmark Marshall Trilogy[3] rulings, Chief Justice John Marshall acknowledged the domestic nature of Anishinabe sovereignty. Not surprisingly, each of his rulings focused on the Doctrine of Discovery, suggesting that Anishinabeg held no title to the land, only a right of occupancy. Unfortunately for Anishinabe nations, these rulings have become the foundation of American and Canadian indian law.

Anishinabeg have been waiting with bated breath for the United Nations and its nation-state club to come riding on some white horse to help us reclaim our sovereignty and self-determination. In fact, I was once told jokingly that if I held my breath waiting for this to happen, it would be hazardous to my health. So we should all be mindful of the dangers of holding our collective breath. The United Nations, for all its godly intent, has some serious detractors. Its five permanent members – France, United Kingdom, China, Russia and the United States – for example, have been guilty of different types of human rights violations throughout the last century. Yet they're entrusted with the responsibility of addressing and remedying injustices throughout the world. It's become clear to me that treaty, land and resource issues have to be resolved outside of the international arena and within our own backyards.

From my perspective, the United Nations Declaration on the Rights of Indigenous Peoples has had little impact on improving the lives of Anishinabeg in Canada – or for Anishinabeg elsewhere, for that matter. We're told, for example, that under international law another nation cannot unilaterally force another to do anything. Yet the United States, Russia, China and other countries have flagrantly ignored and dismissed issues they consider a threat to their national security.

Human rights violations are committed by a number of nations every day, and I'm not sure the United Nations Security Council would risk going to war over them. Fundamental rights, such as the right to freedom of conscience, thought and religion; protection from torture, cruelty and slavery; and the right to freedom of expression and opinion, are attacked every day. I think it's admirable that an institution that seeks to maintain international peace and security, protect human rights, deliver humanitarian aid, promote sustainable development and uphold international law exists. But we're witness to its systemic failure daily.

The recent hate-filled rhetoric and bigotry in the United States, the humanitarian crises in Yemen and Syria, the crackdown on journalists and political activists in Turkey, the detention and execution of human rights and Shi'a activists, and the Rohingya genocide and refugee crisis are cases in point. The international human rights arena is a pretty dangerous place for the most part, and the United Nations seems ill-equipped to take on the right-wing political demagoguery, deliberate human rights violations, refugee crises, and genocides taking place throughout the world. But this discussion is best left to another day.

There have been leaders of revolutionary and liberation movements who have brought the colonial beast to its knees. Mahatma Gandhi's approach to liberation, for example, was embodied in peaceful and civil protest. For Gandhi, freedom was a movement of self-purification. He understood that independence and freedom from oppression had to be secured from within; this was his prerequisite for successful revolution. Frantz Fanon, on the other hand, encouraged freedom and liberation movements to develop plans and working models that avoided duplicating the nation-states that oppressed them.

This fantastic journey provided many profound and sometimes unexplainable experiences. I came to understand how our miskew ah-zha-way-chi-win enables us to share in the experiences of our families and past generations. It reminds us that what is going on now and what has happened to us in the past was and is still mostly about power and the oppression of the Ojibway, Ota'wa and Ishkodawatomi-Anishinabe narrative. In this way, it frees us from exploitive history itself.

This story is about having the opportunity to reclaim and reaffirm our own power and history. I think this is truly an amazing place from which to talk about Ojibway, Ota'wa and Ishkodawatomi-Anishinabe leadership and governance, because Ojibway, Ota'wa and Ishkodawatomi-Anishinabe gah-gi-gi-do-win, kayn-dah-so-win and ah-zhi-di-bah-ji-mo-wi-nan have influenced one generation to the next since the beginning of time.

I thought about this history and responsibility on being elected to the position of *Indian Act* chief at Sagkeeng, because the term "chief" lent itself to a more distorted and bastardized representation of leadership. It was clear to me that any attempt to reconcile the past with the contemporary was next to impossible, given the dysfunctional political process and intrusive government policies in the community.

Political stability was and still is important to most Anishinabe communities and nations, because the *Indian Act* and government policies continue to run roughshod and impact the Anishinabe community. In fact, the *Indian Act* continues to be successful in its divide-and-conquer strategy with the elected council system that had its beginnings in 1867.

Bawdwaywidun Banaise and Vine Deloria Jr. make it quite clear that we've always used our ways of being and indianness/Anishinabeness to come together and understand our differences. As oppressed peoples, we've always used our own pedagogy to restore our humanity as individuals and human beings. By simply fighting for our humanity, we restore our own generosity and understanding of who we are. *Who better to understand oppression and impact of social degradation? Who better to understand the importance of liberation?*

This story evolved spiritually for me as well. As I participated in ceremony and visited with Anishinabe storytellers
throughout Manitou Aki, I came to see that we are all active
participants in the processes of the natural world and in the
mysteries of universe. I continue to be amazed by this as
we search for answers to our questions and clarity in our
experiences.

Anishinabeg have always been aware of these responsibilities
because we grew up learning from those who went before us.
We know that when you have ceremony and collective memory
you don't need a committee to show and tell you what to do.
Everyone talks to each other and does what's needed.

The purpose of this story was to explore and clarify some
of the responsibilities of Ojibway, Ota'wa and Ishkodawatomi-
Anishinabe leadership within a N'swi-ish-ko-day-kawn
Anishinabeg O'dish-ko-day-kawn governance framework and
construct. We've seen throughout this story that great civil
and war leaders such as Obwandiac, Tecumtha and Shingwauk
had definitive responsibilities within Ojibway, Ota'wa and
Ishkodawatomi-Anishinabe society, which moved them to
oppose and resist the social, political and economic changes
threatening the Ojibway, Ota'wa and Ishkodawatomi-
Anishinabe way of life.

We've also seen that Ojibway, Ota'wa and Ishkodawatomi-
Anishinabe communities have traditionally chosen leaders from
their respective clans. I admit that there were times when leaders were chosen simply because they were the most capable.
However, for the most part, traditional governments understood this and were respectful of people who could serve the
community best. This is how traditional governments really
worked. We understood as well that leaders such as Obwandiac,
Tecumtha and Shingwauk were renowned for their intelligence,
compassion, empathy, medicine powers and courage.

The ah-di-so-kah-nahg, ah-way-chi-gay-wi-nan and di-bah-ji-
mo-wi-nan told us long ago about the importance of having

responsible societies. A system of governance based on nationhood was and is still fundamental to the notion of Ojibway,
Ota'wa and Ishkodawatomi-Anishinabe sovereignty and
independence as a whole. From a Canadian perspective, there
is a belief that Section 35(1) of the *Constitution Act, 1982* affirms
this and that an Anishinabe order of government already exists
in Canada. However, the question remains as to who has
responsibility for defining these rights and in what context.
Viewed in this way, Section 35(1) of the *Constitution Act, 1982*
is purposely vague. When Anishinabe sovereignty and rights
recognition are discussed, the word "existing" is ambiguous,
because it places the onus on Anishinabe nations to prove
that our treaty and primordial rights actually exist. Further,
the Canadian government has tended to take an incremental,
piecemeal approach to recognition and implementation of
these rights. Therefore, support for transformative change
in terms of how things get done is often fleeting and
inconsequential.

Anishinabe social, political and economic independence can
only be achieved through sustained resistance and/or revolution
because colonial governments generally don't hand over power
and independence without some kind of struggle or pushback.
South Africa and India might be exceptions to the rule as a
result of critical mass and collective action.

To this end, Anishinabe leadership has continually reminded
Canada that we as Anishinabe nations never surrendered our
sovereignty and/or primordial rights in exchange for giving
Euro-Canadians the opportunity to settle parts of Canada without the threat of war. This is the concept of treaty at its root.
The federal Crown understood that it was more efficient and
safer to work with Anishinabeg than to fight.

Contemporary Anishinabe governments have pushed for
full legislative and policy-making capacity throughout all this.
These same governments have also argued the right to legislate
and have authority over economic development initiatives, land

and resource laws, social development renewal, changes to child and family protection, and effective education and justice systems. They've also continued to argue for the right to develop health and financial services that are respectful of Anishinabe traditions and that have the capacity to address future needs. This is the contemporary dilemma we find ourselves mired in.

In terms of the practical application and implementation of these objectives, it remains to be seen whether this can be done under Section 91(24) of the *Constitution Act, 1867* and/or Section 35(1) of the *Constitution Act, 1982* – or better yet, within an independent and sovereign Anishinabe construct.

It's possible that Anishinabe governments could demand and negotiate funding arrangements similar to European independent protectorates and principalities (Monaco, San Marino, Liechtenstein and Andorra) or have agreements similar to the Canadian constitutionally entrenched formula of transfer payments. Regardless of the path chosen, the authority to allocate these dollars would be under the purview of Anishinabe citizens and their government within a treaty and fiscal framework.

For non-treaty Anishinabe nations, a framework structured on the task of reclaiming and implementing traditional systems of governance and legislative power of government would remain for the people and be of the people. The creation of such a framework would not require any kind of constitutional haranguing; the Indian Commission of Ontario, the Indian Specific Claims Commission and the British Columbia Treaty Commission were established under such a process.

We know, for example, that an Anishinabe system of government has existed and continues to exist. Section 35(1) of the *Constitution Act, 1982* tells us and supposedly affirms this. We know as well that Anishinabe governments represent a community of people who share similar communal sentiments and languages and are united through a shared history and culture.

Obwandiac, Tecumtha and Shingwauk fought to preserve and protect this indianness/Anishinabeness, and their spirit blankets everything written and shared within this conversation.

In an ideal world, we know that one nation cannot be subjugated by other nations, as every nation is a contrasting web of people, values and historical experiences. Unfortunately, oppression and genocide have been the end result of colonization since the beginning of time. Returning to my earlier point about colonialism and the destruction it has wrought, I wonder how we recover from the abuse and violence perpetuated by colonial governments. *Our Hearts Are as One Fire* is intended to find some resolution to this question.

To my mind, social change has to be predicated on some kind of commitment to the free communication of ideas and opinions. Traditionally it was understood that no citizen could ever be prevented from stating his/her opinions, which was important to Ojibway, Ota'wa and Ishkodawatomi-Anishinabe society and government. Consensus-seeking debates were indicative of this. During Ojibway, Ota'wa and Ishkodawatomi-Anishinabe nation assemblies, for example, all of the communities would be in attendance. The leaders would debate issues long and hard until consensus was reached, one that was fully acceptable to all communities. Once that was done, the elders, men, women and youth would stand behind their leader.

We need to have an open and serious dialogue about the practical opportunities for Anishinabe nations, communities and citizens. We can then begin a new round of constitutional discussions with Canada, with the intent of entrenching some notion of Anishinabe sovereignty and self-determination.

Supreme Court judgments might give the appearance of facilitating some movement toward acknowledging sovereignty and self-determination. In *R. v. Guerin* (1984), the Supreme Court held that the Canadian government had a fiduciary-like duty with respect to "aboriginal" title, which was defined as having *sui generis* (of its own kind/genus or distinct in its characteristics) rights. Further, *R. v. Delgamuukw* (1997) determined that aboriginal title existed in Canada and was accepted as common law.

If Anishinabeg were to choose to remain on the Canadian bandwagon, Section 35(1) of the *Constitution Act, 1982*, which affirmed and recognized "existing" aboriginal and treaty rights, might be helpful. However, as I stated earlier, it's too ambiguous. Keep in mind that Section 35(1) also specified that only the federal government had the authority to deal with aboriginal land rights pursuant to Section 91(24) of the *Constitution Act, 1867*, but the provinces still have a major influence over policies and their implementation.

To avoid conflict, Canada would be better served by having this conversation sooner rather than later. If the United States, Canada, and Central and South America were to move beyond their colonial and terrorist pasts, they would have to redefine the legal character of North America. This would mean that treaties and traditional governments would have to be acknowledged and their provisions implemented within a true nations-to-Crown partnership. This approach would also dispel the misinformation and colonial propaganda regarding conquest that has been perpetuated.

For Treaty 1 people, this has been our understanding since 1871 and we still see treaties as an opportunity to establish a new middle ground with new protocols regarding land, resources and treatment of our people. In effect, the pre-Confederation, numbered, modern-day treaties and recognition of traditional governments would help re-create Canada.

All of this is about making our world a better place. To achieve this, we have to be aggressive in the defence of our treaty and primordial rights. There is no other way. Many legal scholars suggest without reservation that if there were no treaties or body of intercultural law, we would have been displaced to the point of irrelevance and would have become just another ingredient in Canada's melting pot.

The question of citizenship and political autonomy within the Canadian framework has also been intriguing to me. Meegwetch to John Diefenbaker for giving indians the right to vote in July 1960 and redefining our citizenship. Maybe we should have refused this gesture, since it's been a more difficult road ever since.

In another one of our discussions, Bawdwaywidun Banaise made it clear amidst all the confusion regarding citizenry that Ojibway, Ota'wa and Ishkodawatomi-Anishinabeg are Ojibway, Ota'wa and Ishkodawatomi-Anishinabeg first. There is nothing else.

JF: *One fundamental question that has to be asked of Anishinabe peoples is whether they see themselves as Canadian citizens or as independent and sovereign peoples? The First Peoples National Party of Canada in its policy paper states that Ojibway, Ota'wa and Ishkodawatomi-Anishinabeg have been free and independent since the beginning of time. It is a right that is inherent as described by our creation stories, ah-di-so-kah-nahg and di-bah-ji-mo-wi-nan. The First Peoples National Party (FPNP) also recognizes that Anishinabe peoples did not surrender sovereignty or their right to governance.*

BAWDWAYWIDUN BANAISE: Absolutely correct, but who knows and who cares.

JF: *In light of this, the FPNP supports a referendum that would raise the question as to whether Anishinabe peoples would continue to participate in the Canadian political process or continue to build on a "two-row" wampum process. This declaration of sovereignty would support the development of a constituent and/or constitutional assembly process. This is not an overwhelming or daunting task, as there is an organizational and operational infrastructure in the regional, national and territorial treaty organizations (i.e., Assembly of First Nations, Federation of Saskatchewan Indians, Grand Council of Treaty Three). Would you agree with this and would it be a practical response?*

BAWDWAYWIDUN BANAISE: In the 1970s a gathering took place on the Stoney reservation in Alberta. There were huge differences of opinions between the Christian natives and the traditionals. This seemed like a "two roads" reality among native peoples, which sounds like white Christians trying to convert the natives. A select meeting with all the traditionals re: Midewiwin, Sundance, waubeeno's, Aztecs and others were held. The Sami, the Arctic Circle natives, joined us. Among respected elders who came were Albert Lightning, Ernest Tootoosis, John Snow and Jack Starr from Fort Alex and others mainly from the United States, Dakotas, Lakotas and Navahos.

As being of the American Indian Movement, but identifiable as an Ojibwe Midewiwin, I was asked to chair or facilitate the long, long discussion. The first one ended after sunrise the next morning. When we passed tobacco, we announced that all pipes should be present according to a spiritual code and protocol. The response was immediate without question. Members of the Native American church, the Peyote religion and Christian indians refused to participate. But they sat and watched. I asked Philip Deere and Albert Lightening to speak after I had finished passing tobacco and initially speaking to the spirit, explaining why we were gathered.

The result was to energize and bring the traditional Anishinabe circle together, which in turn gave the elders, men, women and young people a sense of unity. This prevailed throughout the conference and brought forward that "we are Anishinabe first."

The question regarding citizenship, which seems to be the elephant in the room, has to be resolved at some point. We know full well that it has to be central to any discussion concerning Ojibway, Ota'wa and Ishkodawatomi-Anishinabe sovereignty and self-determination. From my perspective, it's absolutely necessary for Ojibway, Ota'wa and Ishkodawatomi-Anishinabeg to decide whether we see ourselves as Canadian citizens or as independent and sovereign peoples. It was a question raised by Obwandiac in 1763, Tecumtha in 1812 and Shingwauk in 1850. This fundamental question is still debated by independence movements throughout the world.

Independence leaders have rationalized that an active and informed citizenship is a prerequisite for political independence and sovereignty. They see independence as the beginning of economic and social self-sufficiency. Of course, we understand that the degree of sovereignty in many former colonies, protectorates and principalities varies. I think for the most part that sovereignty and freedom depend on the circumstance and degree of oppression.

I ask Bawdwaywidun Banaise about the use of European approaches to decolonization for Ojibway, Ota'wa and Ishkodawatomi-Anishinabe nations. In turn, he talks of Ojibway, Ota'wa and Ishkodawatomi-Anishinabe sovereignty and its endless possibilities. We continue to talk at length about the European experience. He's quick to respond that the European experience was good for the Europeans, but he is adamant that Ojibway, Ota'wa and Ishkodawatomi-Anishinabe freedom, sovereignty and self-determination be rooted in our Anishinabeness, spirituality, language and the land.

JF: *Must Ojibway, Ota'wa and Ishkodawatomi-Anishinabe nations reclaim sovereignty and assume stature similar to the principalities of Liechtenstein, Andorra and Gibraltar?*

BAWDWAYWIDUN BANAISE: No. Absolutely not! To pattern Ojibway, Ota'wa and Ishkodawatomi sovereignty upon Euro-systems is not sovereignty.

JF: *What is self-determination?*

BAWDWAYWIDUN BANAISE: The importance of self-determination from an Ojibway, Ota'wa and Ishkodawatomi reality is reflected in the principles of the N'swi-ish-ko-day-kawn Anishinabeg O'dish-ko-day-kawn. It speaks to the right of Ojibway, Ota'wa and Ishkodawatomi to determine our own economic, social and cultural development. The concept of self-determination is based upon the principles of the seven teachings and living accordingly.

JF: *Is constitutional reform possible within the Canadian framework?*

BAWDWAYWIDUN BANAISE: We could return to the constitutional table to press for fundamental change in terms of how Anishinabe nations govern themselves and the degree of sovereignty they exercise are treated. Are these practical alternatives utilizing existing political and judicial processes to and re-define the anishinabe relationship with the federal and provincial levels of government? Obviously! This process question is an issue of moral, ethical and political importance to Canada because it would enable the country to "complete the circle of confederation," as the Inuit have referred to it.

This discussion provided food for thought. A number of other alternatives are possible, given the existing Canadian constitutional framework and its limitations. If Anishinabe nations and Canada were truthfully committed to reconciliation, one of the first alternatives would be to lobby for fundamental change within the Canadian constitution and question the idea of Confederation itself.

Non-indian scholars have suggested a number of considerations, the first of which would be to revisit Section 37 of the *Constitution Act, 1982* and convene a first ministers constitutional conference to discuss reconciliation. Many people point to the failed Kelowna Accord in 2005 as an example of what might have been possible. This is a moot point, though, since at the end of the day there was no accord. They add that the non-derogation clause[4] has to be re-examined in light of the Supreme Court's understanding of the existing nations-to-Crown relationship. I think Ojibway, Ota'wa and Ishkodawatomi-Anishinabeg are tired of the same old song that "white is always right" and that only the Canadian government knows what's good for Ojibway, Ota'wa and Ishkodawatomi-Anishinabeg.

The sad reality is that Ojibway, Ota'wa and Ishkodawatomi-Anishinabe nations have been at war. Ancestral territories and jurisdiction have been under siege by federal/provincial government policies and legislation that seek to undermine Ojibway, Ota'wa and Ishkodawatomi-Anishinabe governments at every turn. Both levels of government have continually undermined Ojibway, Ota'wa and Ishkodawatomi-Anishinabe national security in critical areas such as education, child and family welfare, gaming and natural resources.

In 1969, for example, the Liberal government believed that our ethnicity and unique treaty status was the major cause for our inequality and isolation. Jean Chrétien and Pierre Elliot Trudeau believed that our salvation lay in the Canadian notion of equality and liberty. For them, a made-in-Canada solution was fundamental to Anishinabe survival, and they moved to implement the White Paper. Dressed up as an opportunity to provide individual equality leading to full and equal participation in mainstream society, the White Paper was federal policy aimed at taking its pound of flesh. But Anishinabeg understood that "the emperor wore no clothes" and argued that the proposed legislation was an attempt by Canada to rid itself of the indian problem without an actual physical war.

Economist John Kenneth Galbraith has said that "education breaks the accommodation to the culture of poverty. As poverty has a culture all its own. If it has existed for a long period of time, people come to terms with it."[5] In some instances, third and fourth generations are living on social assistance. Sadly, these families have become the face of community social disintegration and extreme poverty, ceasing to struggle against what seems fairly commonplace and is considered the norm.

The real answers to poverty and hunger are, of course, education, economic development, and employment. However, unemployment has reached catastrophic proportions, and many of these same communities attempt to deal with the poverty plunge (the less you have, the less you can do and so the less you have) with one arm tied behind their backs. As poverty rates continue to rise, more than half the people falling below the poverty line are indian children. Why is this acceptable? How do we explain to children why we let them go hungry? Sure, we can talk about it, raise our arms in anger and frustration, but the sad fact remains that it's all just talk.

The abysmal state of the child welfare system also remains a national disgrace. Half the Anishinabe population (750,000) is under the age of twenty-three years and approximately 27,000 children are currently in care and/or have been removed from their families. The system that claims to protect our children is taking them away from families and communities in much the same way as the residential school system did.

For many Anishinabe communities burdened by debt, new policy and financial regimes support painful restructuring and austerity programs. In many cases, the debt crisis leads to a growth crisis and often living standards plummet, public and community services decline, and capital investment required for economic development is simply not there.

As well, successive Liberal and Conservative-Reform federal governments since 1989 have continued to cap funding for the

Post-Secondary Student Support Program, despite the consist-
ent and significant increase in the number of eligible Anishinabe
post-secondary students and tuition. What does this actually say?

Despite Canada's reluctance to do right, there are options
that we can initiate ourselves. For example, Anishinabe nations
could issue a declaration of sovereignty. The main stumbling
block, of course, would be securing political recognition from
other nation states and specifically the United Nations Security
Council, which is responsible for approving new member states
of the United Nations, and then translating this official statement into a practical political reality.

A declaration of sovereignty might also facilitate the establishment of a constituent assembly and constitutional convention, which would be a logical and practical first step. The
United States, for example, held a constitutional convention
in 1787 and developed its own constitution.

Further, a constituent assembly might allow for the creation
of an Anishinabe parliament, should Anishinabeg express the
need for one. The Sami-Anishinabe parliaments in Norway,
Sweden and Finland offer interesting examples. Despite having
limited powers, the Sami-Anishinabe parliament does have
some relevance because of its practical application. Depending
on the circumstances, Anishinabe nations could theoretically
elect its representatives to a national decision-making forum
that would include participation in the development and draft-
ing of new Anishinabe nations-to-Crown protocols and i-nah-
ko-ni-gay-wi-nan (*laws*). All of these possibilities might render
the Assembly of First Nations, Assembly of Manitoba Chiefs
and other regional organizations irrelevant and meaningless,
which is fine with me.

There are so many possibilities! But we need to begin having
these discussions. The question of suffrage is not even an issue,
since the right to vote is a basic Anishinabe (human) right regardless of age.[6] In one of my last visits with William Commanda,

an elder from Kitigan Zibi Anishinabeg First Nation in Quebec, we talked of the middle ground and the idea of peaceful coexistence that was expressed in the Royal Proclamation of 1763 and the treaty process it had given birth to. In his eyes, the concepts of sovereignty and self-determination were clearly about equality and consensus.

Despite all the rhetoric, the future of our sovereignty and liberation is really in our hands. The decisions we make with respect to our liberation and freedom will depend in large part on whether we choose to push for change within a governance structure, such as the N'swi-ish-ko-day-kawn Anishinabeg O'dish-ko-day-kawn, which is rooted in our Anishinabeness, the land and history, or maintain the status quo and stay within the limitations of the Canadian confederation.

Obwandiac (nigig), Tecumtha (mizhibizhi) and Shingwauk (ah-ji-jahk) represented Ojibway, Ota'wa and Ishkodawatomi-Anishinabe o-gi-ma-wi-win at its most organic and purest. The empathy they expressed gave human shape to Ojibway, Ota'wa and Ishkodawatomi-Anishinabe morality. In fact, their vision transformed Manitou Aki and guides us still. Ahaaw sa. Weweni.

> **Ni' biin-daa-koo-ji-ge gaye ni' o-nah-ko-nah ah-di-so-kah-nahg zhigo di-bah-ji-mo-wi-nan g'dah mi-kwe-ni-mah-nahn obwandiacbun, tecumthabun, miinwaa shingwaukbun. Ni' meegwetch i' wayn-dam o-gi-ma-wi-win onji gaye a-no-kii-taw anishinabeg.**
> (I pass tobacco and ceremonially call upon the sacred narratives, stories of personal experience and spirit of Obwandiac, Tecumtha and Shingwauk. I give thanks for their leadership and work for the people.)

**Mii i'i-way ojibway-anishinabe i-zhi-chi-gay-win.
Zhigo mii'iw eta-go o-way neen-gi-kayn-dahn
zhigo ni-gi-noon-dah-wah.**
(This is the Ojibway-Anishinabe way, and this is
as much as I know and have heard.)

Mii i'iw.
(That is all.)

Geyaabi go g'doo bi-ma-di-zi-min.
(We're still here.)

Wayekwaase

IT IS FINISHED

THIS STORY ENDS as it began, in ceremony. I had the opportunity to travel to Winnipeg, Obishikokaang (*Land of the White Pines; Lac Seul First Nation*) in Treaty 3 territory and the Saginaw Chippewa Indian Tribe in Michigan in September 2019 at the invitation of Ojibway-Anishinabe community activist Mona Gordon; first-degree Midewiwin and Cree-Anishinabe justice advocate Chantal Barker; and Potawatomi and second-degree Midewiwin and Ojibwe-Anishinabe educator Shannon Martin.

Mona has been working alongside Ojibway-Anishinabe Midewiwin and ceremonialist Tom Chisel, from Obishikokaang, in reclaiming Midewiwin ceremonies in the community, and was one of the planners and organizers for the September 2019 Elders and Youth Clan Gathering, which focused on embracing Ojibway, Ota'wa and Ishkodawatomi-Anishinabe history and inherent laws. Ojibway, Ota'wa and Ishkodawatomi-Anishinabe clan elders and ceremonial, law and knowledge keepers from across Manitou Aki came to speak and share their knowledge on customary approaches to teaching, healing, philosophies and sacred protocols and institutions. I was struck, but not surprised, by the synergy created by the youth and elders as they provided their visions for the future.

Meegwetch as well to Chantal for her cutting-edge work on restorative justice, and to Shannon for taking back our stories through the Ziibiwing Center's Diba Jimooyung (*Telling Our Story*) project. Chantal points out that the province of Manitoba has the highest incarceration rate in the country; she maintains that the justice system and the Anishinabe communities are like jagged worlds colliding, with the obvious result. She adds that Anishinabe-focused restorative justice is about reclaiming jurisdiction, healing and restoring the balance between the victim and offender within our communities.

Shannon is a well-known and respected educator who's spent much of her life focusing on cultural and historical preservation, collections and archival management and Ojibway, Ota'wa and Ishkodawatomi-Anishinabe language revitalization in her role as executive director at the Ziibiwing Center.

Each woman looks at the world and the issues impacting our people from a uniquely Ojibway, Ishkodawatomi, and Cree-Anishinabe worldview. They're fierce in letting the world know these issues. It's this pride in our people that struck me when I first met Mona, Chantal and Shannon, years ago. I think this pride is fundamental to the task of reclaiming our ceremonies, reclaiming our justice protocols through restorative justice, and speaking about the importance of education and believing in ourselves. They truly are a breath of fresh air. Meegwetch to them again for providing me with opportunities to speak about this book and my thoughts on treaty, justice, leadership and custom governance.

Ceremony as an intellectual and spiritual concept has come to define my indianness/Anishinabeness, which are anti-colonial and anti-pan/indigenous to their core. For me, that's what this story and discussion is about. It's also about finding empowerment and a disavowal of assimilation, integration, reconciliation, indigenization and all those other catchwords that seek to distract us from our dysfunctional relationship with Canadian values, and the systemic violence it imposes on our people daily. But this matter is best left for another day.

Obishikokaang is a spiritually empowering place as well. Maybe because of *The White Pine*? I'm not sure, but you feel a certain spiritual tranquility there that embraces and warms you. The land and people have a quiet resilience that you become a part of. It tells you that everything will be all right.

I struggled with the title for this book for a long time, because so much of it is about Ojibway, Ota'wa and Ishkodawatomi-Anishinabe spiritual history, ceremony, moral and personal stories. Honouring the memories and accomplishments of Obwandiac, Tecumtha and Shingwauk in a respectful way also weighed heavily on me. It would be negligent and grossly offensive to ignore or discount the N'swi-ish-ko-day-kawn Anishinabeg O'dish-ko-day-kawn in any story of Manitou Aki. I had to do right by these men and the confederacy. I needed to do the right thing! This was my responsibility and commitment.

With this in mind, I approached my good friend Ozawa Ginew (James Roach; ah-ji-jawk doodem from Ketegaun-seebee) and passed tobacco to him. I asked him to take this question into ceremony. Some people might find it odd that I would put this much faith and trust into something intangible and metaphysical. My response is quite simple: it's important to understand that this book is very much about the past, present and future and the different layers of consciousness and ways of knowing. I certainly have no difficulty with this.

Following the ceremony, Ozawa Ginew mentioned that the spirit messengers were excited and seemed full of anticipation, telling him that "a-yaa-ba-naa-bid ani-akii-wahng/waa-bahng i-naa-ba-ji-toon Ojibway-Anishinabe osh-kiin-zhi-goon zhigo n'swi-ish-ko-day-kawn anishinabeg o'dish-ko-day-kawn."[1] I mentioned to him that I was travelling to Lac Seul to participate in a gathering of youth and elders and would probably take this to a jeeskahn. He agreed with my doing this.

My presentation on sovereignty and treaties at the Elders and Youth Clan Gathering goes reasonably well, and I am happy to be given the opportunity to speak to matters that I'm passionate about. That evening, Pasha Onee Binace (Ralph Johnson), kinozhe doodem (*Pike clan*) from *Seine River*, Ontario, holds a jeeskahn ceremony at the ceremonial grounds at Frenchman's Head, one of three Obishikokaang communities. It's bitterly cold and wet. The darkness and drizzle is broken by the sacred fire in the distance. Despite the cold breeze off the lake, hearing the laughter and people talking in Ojibwaymowin is warm and reassuring.

Pasha Onee Binace is standing and talking to the people as I sit myself down. He is explaining what will take place during the ceremony and is reminding people that they should make ready with their tobacco and food offerings. He also asks those who are visiting the jeeskahn to talk to him in case they need help with translation or if they have questions about what will take place. Songs and teachings are also shared during this time. It is pretty exciting to be part of the ceremony once again.

We talk briefly. I mention to him the reason for my coming to the jeeskahn, telling him that Ozawa Ginew was told in ceremony that "a-yaa-ba-naa-bid ani-akii-wahng/waa-bahng i-naa-ba-ji-toon Ojibway-Anishinabe osh-kiin-zhi-goon zhigo n'swi-ish-ko-day-kawn anishinabeg o'dish-ko-day-kawn" was a good, strong title for the book.

Mona's friend, Sheila Cameron from Wabaseemoong (*White-dog*), makes sure I have my tobacco and food offering. The kindness and caring shown me by Mona and Sheila is reflective of Ojibway-Anishinabe i-zhi-tah-win (*ways and customs*) and debweyendamowin (*belief*), which Ojibway-Anishinabeg and other Anishinabe nations are trying to reclaim piece by piece, teaching by teaching. Meegwetch again to these two Ojibway-Anishinabe ikwewag (*women*) for walking the talk.

After the sharing of tobacco and food, the ceremony begins. One by one, people visit the jeeskahn. Each of the spirit messengers talk and examine their conscience, find out who they are connected to and working with. They tell everyone that they want to do the right thing and that sometimes this is not easy. However, this spiritual technology is such a fantastic thing; the jeeskahn is like a time capsule, taking you to different places.

As I lie down and settle myself on the ground, the bell begins to sound and the jeeskahn begins to shake back and forth, and then it stops. Makwa is with us and begins talking with the jeeskahn i-ni-ni. Makwa is talking in a deep, guttural voice. I'm not even sure how you can describe it. In my mind it is part of Obishikokaang, the people, and all of our history and memories. It is soothing and grandfatherly but also spiritually electric.

This spiritual energy gives me calm as I lie on the ground with my hand holding one of the lodge poles. I listen as Makwa and the jeeskahn i-ni-ni talk. I make out "di-baa-jim ongowe gichitwaawibii'igan, kitchi-apiitendaagwad ge-go zhaag-we-nim weweni mi-kwe-ni-mah-nah-nik ongowe o-gi-ma-wi-nik, ba-zi-gwiin anishinabeg mash-ka-wi-ga-bo-wid."[2] These are the words and the message: "*Our hearts are as one fire, this is our vision for the future.*"

Mii i'i-way ojibway-anishinabe i-zhi-chi-gay-win.
Zhigo mii'iw eta-go o-way neen-gi-kayn-dahn zhigo
ni-gi-noon-dah-wah ... Ahaaw sa. Weweni.

APPENDIX

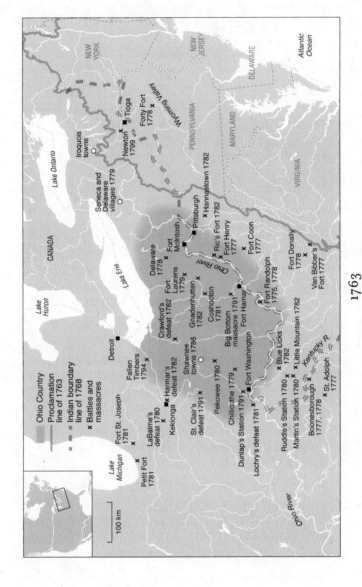

1763

Source: Adapted from "Ohio Country's Croghan," online at
http://Ohiocountry.us/index.php?p=1_10_Ohio-Country-s-Croghan.

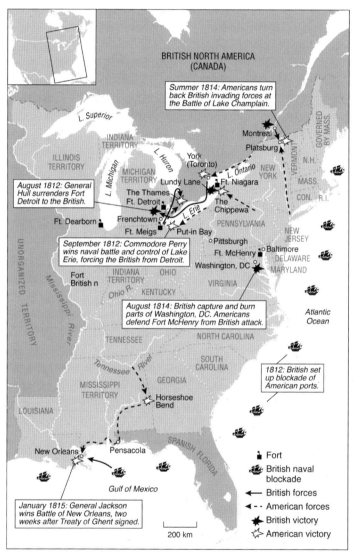

BRITISH NORTH AMERICA (CANADA)

Summer 1814: Americans turn back British invading forces at the Battle of Lake Champlain.

August 1812: General Hull surrenders Fort Detroit to the British.

September 1812: Commodore Perry wins naval battle and control of Lake Erie, forcing the British from Detroit.

August 1814: British capture and burn parts of Washington, DC. Americans defend Fort McHenry from British attack.

1812: British set up blockade of American ports.

January 1815: General Jackson wins Battle of New Orleans, two weeks after Treaty of Ghent signed.

L. Superior

INDIANA TERRITORY
ILLINOIS TERRITORY
L. Michigan
L. Huron
MICHIGAN TERRITORY
Montreal
Platsburg
York (Toronto)
L. Ontario
VERMONT
N.H.
NEW YORK
MASS.
CON.   R.I.
GOVERNED BY MASS.
Lundy Lane
Ft. Niagara
The Thames
Ft. Detroit
The Chippewa
L. Erie
Ft. Dearborn
Frenchtown
Ft. Meigs
Put-in Bay
PENNSYLVANIA
NEW JERSEY
UNORGANIZED TERRITORY
Pittsburgh
Baltimore
Ft. McHenry
DELAWARE
Washington, DC
MARYLAND
Fort British n
INDIANA TERRITORY
OHIO
Ohio R.
KENTUCKY
VIRGINIA
Atlantic Ocean
Mississippi River
TENNESSEE
NORTH CAROLINA
Tennessee River
SOUTH CAROLINA
MISSISSIPPI TERRITORY
GEORGIA
Horseshoe Bend
LOUISIANA
SPANISH FLORIDA
New Orleans
Pensacola
Gulf of Mexico

Legend:
- Fort
- British naval blockade
- British forces
- American forces
- British victory
- American victory

200 km

The War of 1812

Source: Adapted from http://jb-hdnp.org/Sarver/Maps/War%20of%201812.jpg.

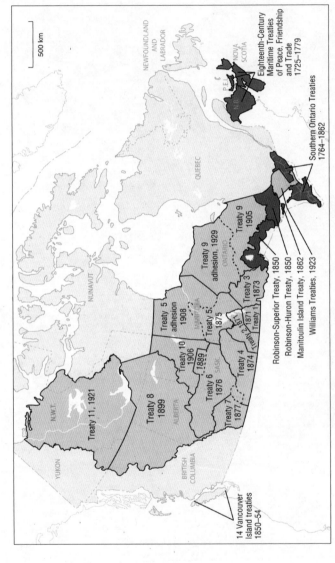

Historical Indian Treaties, 1850–1923

Source: Adapted from "A Commemorative History of Aboriginal people in the Canadian Military," online at https://www.Canada.ca/en/department-national-defence/services/military-history/history-heritage/popular-books/aboriginal-people-Canadian-military.html.

TIMELINE

1653   Ojibway-Anishinabe defeat an Iroquois-Anishinabe war party at the site of present-day Iroquois Point on Lake Superior.

OBWANDIAC

1747   Obwandiac's political and military profile as ni-gahn-no-say-wi-ni-ni and o-gi-chi-dah is one of increasing presence.

1754   November 7: First Sergeant Jacob de Marsac departs for Ba-wi-ti-gong by order of General Edward Braddock.

1755   APRIL 27: Jacob de Marsac arrives at Mi-shi-ne-mack-i-naw-go (Michilimakinac) with seventeen wampum belts.

JULY 9: General Braddock is defeated at the Battle of the Monongahela (Pennsylvania), one of the most disastrous defeats for the British.

1757   Obwandiac is first mentioned by name and in print by William Johnston at Fort Duquesne (Pennsylvania).

1758   Jeffrey Amherst is appointed governor general.

1760   November 29: Fort Ponchartrain (Detroit) surrenders to the British.

1762   APRIL 27: Ojibway, Ota'wa, Ishkodawatomi and Wendat-Anishinabe o-gi-ma-wi-win, o-gi-chi-dahg, ah-ni-kay-o-gi-mah-kah-nah-wahd and ni-gahn-no-say-wi-ni-ni-wahg meet to discuss their discontent and frustration with Amherst's actions.

British North America is merely a seaboard strip about a thousand miles long and one or two hundred miles deep.

1763 FEBRUARY: Treaty of Paris signed.

APRIL 19: The death of Teedyuscung, the king of the Delaware-Anishinabeg, moves the war council, which includes Ni-ni-vay (Ishkodawatomi-Anishinabe), Ta-ke (Wendat-Anishinabe), Mack-a-te-pe-le-ci-te (Ota'wa-Anishinabe) and Obwandiac, to move quickly, rather than later as originally planned.

APRIL 21: N'swi-ish-ko-day-kawn Anishinabeg O'dish-ko-day-kawn receive a war belt from the Delaware-Anishinabeg, who are asking for assistance to avenge their defeat at Kittaning (Pennsylvania) in 1756.

APRIL 27: Four hundred Ishkodawatomi, Ota'wa and Huron-Anishinabeg meet with Obwandiac on the Ecorse River. He tells them of the war belts given to him by the French king.

MAY 5: Second council meeting takes place to discuss three points: the Conestaga-Anishinabe village massacre, avenging the loss of Anishinabe life and the wish to "drive off those dogs clothed in red." The war council decides that they will take to war on May 7.

MAY 7: Siege of Fort Detroit (Michigan) begins.

MAY 16: Fort Sandusky (Ohio) falls.

MAY 25: Fort St. Joseph (Ontario) is taken.

MAY 27: Fort Miami (Michigan) surrenders.

JUNE 1: Fort Ouatanon (Indiana) is captured.

JUNE 4: Fort Michilimackinac (Michigan) surrenders.

JUNE 15: Fort Presque Isle (Pennsylvania) lays down its arms.

JUNE 18: Fort Le Boeuf (Pennsylvania) is taken.

JUNE 20: Fort Venango (Pennsylvania) surrenders.

British North America is merely a seaboard strip about a thousand miles long and one or two hundred miles deep.

JUNE 21: Settlements of L'Arbre Croche (Michigan), Sault Ste. Marie (Michigan) and Sault Ste. Marie (Ontario) are attacked by Ota'wa-Anishinabe forces.

JUNE 24: The British fail in their surprise attack on Obwandiac's encampment.

SEPTEMBER 14: The British are soundly defeated at Devil's Hole (Fort Niagara, New York).

OCTOBER 7: King George III issues the Royal Proclamation.

OCTOBER 29: Obwandiac receives notice of France's surrender at the signing of the Treaty of Paris.

NOVEMBER: The siege at Fort Detroit ends.

1768 NOVEMBER 5: Treaty of Fort Stanwix (New York) signed.

1785 JANUARY 21: Treaty of Fort McIntosh (Pennsylvania) acknowledges American sovereignty.

1786 JANUARY 31: Treaty of Fort Finney (Ohio) cedes parts of Ohio.

1789 JANUARY 9: Treaty of Fort Harmar (Ohio) transfers most of Ohio.

1790 General Josiah Harmar (United States) suffers a major defeat.

1791 NOVEMBER 4: St. Clair defeated by Mi-chi-ki-ni-kwa (Miami-Anishinabe) and Ho-ko-les-kwa (Shawnee-Anishinabe).

1794 AUGUST 20: Tecumtha's brother Sau-wa-see-kau is killed at the Battle of Fallen Timbers (Ohio).

1795 AUGUST 3: Treaty of Greenville (Ohio), negotiated by Joseph Brant, William Johnson and George Croghan, recognizes the United States as a sovereign power.

1796 FEBRUARY 29: Jay Treaty establishes the international boundary between Canada and the United States.

British North America is merely a seaboard strip . . . .

Little Turtle's War

TECUMTHA

1774 OCTOBER 10: Tecumtha's father, Pu-ke-shin-wa n'wau, is killed while fighting with Ho-ko-les-kwa at the Battle of Point Pleasant (West Virginia).

1794 AUGUST 20: Battle of Fallen Timbers (Ohio).

1795 AUGUST 3: Tecumtha challenges the Greenville Treaty. The treaty established the Greenville Treaty Line, which would serve as the "middle ground" and boundary between Anishinabe territory and lands open for settlers. The treaty is unacceptable to Tecumtha because, in his opinion, no single village or nation leader can sign away sovereignty over lands that belong collectively to all Anishinabeg.

1802 Tecumtha begins to lobby other Anishinabe nations.

1809 SEPTEMBER 29: William Henry Harrison negotiates the Fort Wayne Treaty (Indiana and Illinois).

1810 AUGUST: Tecumtha meets with William Henry Harrison at Fort Vincennes (Indiana) to challenge the Fort Wayne Treaty.

1811 NOVEMBER 7: William Henry Harrison and Lau-lau-we-see-kau skirmish at the Battle of Tippecanoe (Indiana). Tecumtha is not present, as he is still organizing the nations of the N'swi-ish-ko-day-kawn Anishinabeg O'dish-ko-day-kawn.

1812 JUNE 18: The colonies declare war on the British.

JULY 17: Fort Michilimackinac surrenders, cementing Shingwauk's place as one of the greatest war leaders of the Anishinabeg, celebrated throughout Manitou Aki.

AUGUST 15: Mack-e-tay-be-nessy and his Ishkodawatomi-Anishinabe forces take Fort Dearborn (Illinois).

AUGUST 16: The Americans surrender Fort Detroit (Michigan) to N'swi-ish-ko-day-kawn Anishinabeg O'dish-ko-day-kawn and British forces led by Tecumtha, Shingwauk and General Isaac Brock.

OCTOBER 3: Battle of Queenston Heights (Ontario). General Brock is killed.

1813 MAY: A multi-nation conference takes place on the Mississinewa River.

JUNE 19: Fort Erie (Ontario) is recaptured by the British.

JUNE 24: The Americans surrender to the Ojibway and Haudenosaunee-Anishinabeg at the Battle of Beaver Dams (Ontario).

SEPTEMBER 26 AND 27: The British evacuate Fort Detroit (Michigan) and Fort Malden (Ontario).

OCTOBER 5: Tecumtha is killed in battle at Moraviantown (Ontario).

1814 JULY 14: Sault Ste. Marie (Ontario) is raided and burned by the Americans.

JULY 21: In retaliation, N'swi-ish-ko-day-kawn Anishinabeg O'dish-ko-day-kawn and British forces capture Fort Shelby and Prairie du Chien (Wisconsin).

JULY 23: Americans destroy what is left of Fort St. Joseph (Ontario).

AUGUST 4: N'swi-ish-ko-day-kawn Anishinabeg O'dish-ko-day-kawn and British forces successfully defend Fort Michilimackinac (Michigan).

DECEMBER 24: Treaty of Ghent signed, ending the War of 1812.

SHINGWAUK

1827 Kettle and Stoney Point, Walpole Island and Sarnia treaties signed.

1836 Bond Head Treaty signed.

1838 DECEMBER 15: Shingwauk petitions Lieutenant-Governor Archibald Acheson.

1849 MAY 9: Shingwauk, Na-bah-nay-go-jing, Ogista and Ka-bah-o-sa leave for Montreal.

SEPTEMBER 13: Shingwauk and Tah-gay-wi-ni-ni are presented with medals to honour their service during the War of 1812.

NOVEMBER 14: Shingwauk, Na-bah-nay-go-jing and Naw-qua-gah-bow take over the Mica Mine on Lake Superior.

DECEMBER 4: Shingwauk, Na-bah-nay-go-jing and Naw-qua-gah-bow turn themselves in to the British.

1850 SEPTEMBER 7 AND 9: Robinson-Superior and Robinson-Huron treaties signed.

Interpretation and Glossary

A

ah-di-so-kah-nahg: *sacred stories*

ah-di-so-kahn-i-ni-ni-wahg/kwe-wahg: *sacred storytellers* (men/women)

ah-do-win: *self-determination*

ah-ji-jahk: *crane*

ah-mahn-si-nahm: *I have a vision,* or *a spirit comes to me*

ah-ni-kay-o-gi-mah-kah-nah-wahd: *hereditary leaders*

ah-ni-kay-o-gi-mah-kah-ni-wid: *hereditary leader*

ah-se-ma-ke-wahd: *tobacco offering*

ah-way-chi-gay-win: *teaching by telling a story*

ah-way-chi-gay-wi-nan: *moral stories*

ah-zhi-di-bah-ji-mo-win: *tradition*

ah-zhi-di-bah-ji-mo-wi-nan: *traditions*

ah-zhi-kay-ni-mo-nahd-a-di-sid bay-mah-di-sid: *how we use our way of doing, thinking, ceremony and spirituality to find answers* (*methodology*)

A-nim-aki: *Thunder*

Anima-wi-ti-go-ing: *Cross Village* (*see also* Tchingabeng *and* Waw-gaw-naw-ke-zee) animiikiig: *the thunderers*

Anishinabe: *human being*

Anishinabewiwin: *the essence of the Ojibway-Anishinabe understanding of humanity – its heart and vision*

an-o-gon-sit: *war leader* (used in ceremony; *see also* ni-gahn-no-say-wi-ni-ni)

asemaa: *tobacco*

A-shig-a-ning: *Land That Has Everything: Rivers, Hills, Mountains, Swamps, Hardwoods;* present-day *Michigan*

asinii-wajiw: *rocky mountain*

B

bah-nah-ji-too-win: *genocide*

bah-wah-ji-gay-win: *dream*

bah-wah-ji-gay-wi-nan: *dreams*

Bawetigong: *Place of the Rapids; Where the Fish Were Good and Lived Well; Garden River* (*see also* Ba-wi-ti-gong *and* ba-wi-ti-gong)

Ba-wi-ti-gong: *Where the Fish Were Good and Lived Well; present-day Sault Ste. Marie* (*see also* ba-wi-ti-gong *and* Bawetigong)

ba-wi-ti-gong: *Where the Fish Were Good and Lived Well; Sault Ste. Marie* (Bawdwaywidun's spelling; *see also* Bawetigong *and* Ba-wi-ti-gong)

beedahbuhn: *the new dawn*

be-jig-wen-da-mo-win: *unity*

be-nays: *bird* (Bawdwaywidun's spelling; *see also* bineshi)

bezhig onaagan gaye bezhig emikwaan: *one dish with one spoon*

biin-di-go-dah-di-win: *to enter each other's lodges*

bi-mee-ku-mau-gay-win: *stewardship*

bineshi: *bird* (*see also* be-nays)

bi-sa-nii-we-win: *peace*

bish-kayn-di-ji-gay-win: *pedagogy*

bkejwanong: *Where the Waters Divide; Detroit River* (Bawdwaywidun's spelling)

C

chi-bi-mo-day-win: *migration*

D

de-bwe-mo-win: *speaking the truth*

de-bwe-win: *truth*

de-bwe-win-da-mo-win: *faith*

debweyendamowin: *belief*

de-we'i-gun: *the Big Drum*

di-bah-ji-mo-wi-nan: *stories of personal experience*

di-bah-ko-ni-gay-wi-ni-ni: *judge*

di-bayn-di-zi-win: *to own one's self; to be self-determining and self-governing*

di-bish-ko: *equality*

doodem: *clan (see also* ododem *and* ototeman*)*

duh-buh-say-ni-mo-win: *humility*

G

gah-gi-gi-do-win: *oral history*

gah-ki-gi-do-wi-ni-ni: *spokesperson*

gah-na-we-nin-di-zo-win: *self-sufficiency*

gah-sha: *mother*

gah-wi-zi-mah-ji-say-muh-guhk: *stories of origin*

Gai wiio: *Good Word*

g' doodemonaanik ki-nah-mah-gay-wi-nan: *teachings of our clan system*

gemaa zha-ga-wa-mi-kahg mooniyaang: *a turtle-shaped island*
   (Bawdwaywidun's spelling)

giigoo: *fish (see also* gi-goon*)*

gi-goon: *fish* (Bawdwaywidun's spelling; *see also* giigoo)

gii'i'go-shi-mo: *fast for a vision; vision quest*

gi-kayn-daw-so-win: *ways of knowing* (Bawdwaywidun's spelling and
   interpretation; *see also* kayn-dah-so-win *and* kayn-daw-so-win)

gi-ki-do-gah-gi-bi-i-zhi-say-ma-guhk: *written talks and pictographs that
   included the wampum belts and birchbark scrolls*

gi-ki-nah-mah-gay-wi-nan: *teachings (see also* ki-nah-mah-gay-wi-nan*)*

goos-ko-say aki: *earthquakes*

gwayakotam: *a way to find out the truth*

gwu-yu-kaw-ji-win: *honesty*

I

ikwewag: *women*

i-nah-bayn-dam: *dreaming in a certain way*

i-nah-di-zi-win: *our way of being and traditions* (*ontology*)

i-nah-ko-ni-gay-win: *social order; sovereignty* (*see also* sa-ga-katch)

i-nah-ko-ni-gay-wi-nan: *laws*

indian ways: *ceremony, spirituality and thought*

indianness/Anishinabeness: *humanity*

ish-payn-du-go-si-win: *honour*

i-zhi-chi-gay-win: *way of doing things; how we used this way of knowing,*
thinking, doing and ceremony to find answers (*methodology*)

i-zhi-tah-win: *customary; ways and customs*

J

jeeskahn: *shaking tent*

jeeskahn i-ni-ni: *shaking tent man*

jeeskahn i-ni-ni-wahg: *shaking tent men*

jěs´sakkid´: *revealer of hidden truths* and *shaking tent man* (very old term)

jiibayag: *spirits*

K

Karihwi: io: *Code of Handsome Lake*

kay-go-wah-ni-kayn andi-wayn-ji-ahn: *don't ever forget where you come from*

kayn-dah-so-win: *ways of knowing* (*see also* kayn-daw-so-win *and*
gi-kayn-daw-so-win)

kayn-daw-so-win: *ways of knowing* (Bawdwaywidun's spelling and
interpretation; *see also* kayn-dah-so-win *and* gi-kayn-daw-so-win)

Ke-tap-e-kon-nong: Ishkodawatomi-Anishinabe for *Town* or *Place;*
Tippecanoe

Ketegaunseebee: *Garden River*

Ki-chi-ka-be-kong: *Place Where the Water and Thunder Meet; Niagara Falls*
(*see also* wa-yaa-nag ga-kaa-ki-kaa)

ki-nah-mah-gay-wi-nan: *teachings* (*see also* gi-ki-nah-mah-gay-wi-nan)

kinoomage gamig: *teaching lodge*
kinozhe doodem: *Pike clan*
kitchi anishinabeg: *elders*
Kitchi Gumi: *the Great Lakes*
Kitchi Manitou: *Creator* or *Great Mystery*
kwe: *woman*

M

maada 'oo-ni-di-wahg: *sharing*
madoodiswan: *sweat lodge*
mae-mae-gway-suk: *little people*
mahng: *loon*
ma-kah-day-kay-win: *vision quest*
makwa: *bear* (*see also* mu-kwa)
Manitou Aki: *Creator's Land*
manitou kay-win: *ceremony*
manitou kay-wi-nan: *ceremonies*
Manitou Minising: *Manitoulin Island*
manitou na-ga-mo-nan: *sacred songs*
manitou wi-win: *coming to an understanding of the mystery*
mash-ka-wi-zii: *strength*
maw-naw-ji-win: *respect*
Metacom: *King Philip*
Midewigun: *Grand Medicine Lodge*
Midewiwin: *Grand Medicine Society*
mikinak: *turtle*
mi-ni-si: *turtle* (very old term)
mino bi-mah-di-zhi-win: *good life*
Mi-shi-ne-mack-i-naw-go: *Michilimackinac*
mi-shi-no-way-wahg: *economic assistants*
miskew ah-zha-way-chi-win: *the act of flowing; blood memory*
mizhibizhi doodem: *Black Panther clan*
mi-zhi-ni-way: *spirit messenger, dream helper*
mi-zhi-ni-way-wahg: *spirit messengers, dream helpers*

Mo-ning-wun-a-kawn-ning: *Turtle-Shaped Island; Madeline Island*
    (*see also* mo-ning-wun-a-kawn-ning gemaa zha-ga-wa-mi-kahg
    mooniyaang and Zha-ga-wa-mi-kahg)
mo-ning-wun-a-kawn-ning gemaa zha-ga-wa-mi-kahg mooniyaang:
    a turtle-shaped island (Bawdwaywidun's spelling and interpretation;
    see also Mo-ning-wun-a-kawn-ning *and* Zha-ga-wa-mi-kahg)
Mo-ni-yang: *Turtle Island* (very old term)
mu-kwa: *bear* (Bawdwaywidun's spelling; *see also* makwa)

N

naa'wi aki: *the middle ground*
nah-may doodem: *Sturgeon clan*
nah-nah-gah-dah-wayn-ji-gay-win: *how we came to think a certain way about
    our reality (epistemology)*
nah-nahn-dah-wi-i'we: *cure by sucking*
na-noo-kaa-siins: *hummingbird*
Nanticoke-Anishinabeg: *Tidewater People*
ni-gahn-nah-ji-mo-wi-nan: *prophecies*
ni-gahn-no-say-wi-ni-ni: *leader, military leader, war leader*
ni-gahn-no-say-wi-ni-ni-wahg: *leaders, military leaders, war leaders*
nigig: *otter*
N'swi-ish-ko-day-kawn Anishinabeg O'dish-ko-day-kawn: *Our Hearts
    Are as One Fire*
n' zhwa-sho o-nah-ki-ni-gay-wi-nan: *seven natural laws*
n' zhwa-sho-gi-ki-nah-mah-gay-wi-nan: *the seven teachings*

O

Obishikokaang: *Land of the White Pines; Lac Seul First Nation*
o-dah-bah-ji-gahn: *sacred bundle*
ode: *heart*
ododem: *clan* (Ota'wa-Anishinabe term; *see also* doodem *and* ototeman)
o-gi-chi-dah: *strong heart protector*
o-gi-chi-dahg: *strong heart protectors*
o-gi-ma-kahn: *Indian Act chief*
o-gi-ma-win: *governance*

o-gi-ma-wi-win: *to be esteemed*

O-ji-bion: *to write or draw on birch bark scrolls or pictographs*

Ojibwaymowin: *the Ojibway language*

o-nah-ko-ni-gay-win: *natural law*

onki-akeeng: *from the earth – our sustenance, our sovereignty*

oodena: *town* or *village*

opwaagan: *pipe*

opwaaganan gay-nay-wayn-ni-mahd: *pipe carriers*

oshkabewis: *ceremonial helper*

oshkabewisahg: *ceremonial helpers*

ototeman: *clan* (Ishkodawatomi-Anishinabe term; *see also* doodem *and* ododem)

o-zhi-bi-i-gay i-nah-ko-ni-gay-win: *jurisdiction*

S

sa-ga-katch: *social order* (*see also* i-nah-ko-ni-gay-win)

T

Tchingabeng: *Cross Village* (*see also* Anima-wi-ti-go-ing *and* Waw-gaw-naw-ke-zee)

W

waa-bi-zhe-shi: *marten* (*see also* wa-bi-zha-shi)

waa-wash-shke-shi: *deer* (*see also* wa-shesh-she)

Wabanowiwin: *initiate dreams and manipulate fire [in an] attempt [to reverse] an existing situation; Dawn Medicine Society, men/women who had the ability to manipulate fire and interpret dreams for healing, and who specialized in the natural order of the earth by studying the stars, the moon and the sun; People of the Dawn Sky*

wa-bi-zha-shi: *marten* (Bawdwaywidun's spelling; *see also* waa-bi-zhe-shi)

wah-wi-yah-kah-mig: *universe*

wa-shesh-she: *deer* (Bawdwaywidun's spelling; *see also* waa-wash-shke-shi)

Waw-gaw-naw-ke-zee: *Cross Village* (*see also* Tchingabeng *and* Anima-wi-ti-go-ing)

Wa-wii-a-ta-nong: *Where Two Bodies of Water Are Connected – connects Lake*

St. Clair and Lake Huron to Lake Erie; Detroit River

wa-yaa-nag ga-kaa-ki-kaa: *great falls, Niagara Falls* (Bawdwaywidun's spelling; *see also* Ki-chi-ka-be-kong)

weweni: *in a more truthful way*

Wi-kwe-dong: *Spirit Island* (*Duluth*)

wkamek: *leaders* (in Ishkodawatomi-Anishinabe dialect)

Z

zagaswe'i'di-win opwaagan: *pipe way*

zaw-gi-di-win: *love*

Zha-ga-wa-mi-kahg: *Turtle-Shaped Island; Madeline Island* (*see also* Mo-ning-wun-a-kawn-ning *and* mo-ning-wun-a-kawn-ning gemaa zha-ga-wa-mi-kahg mooniyaang)

Zhi-gahg-gong: *Chicago*

zoong-gi-day-win: *bravery*

NOTES

MAAITAA | PROLOGUE

1 Darrell Boissoneau, in ceremony and personal communication, June 15, 2011.

NITAM IGO | INTRODUCTION

1 William Johnson, curator at Ziibiwing Centre, Mount Pleasant, Michigan, told me that Isabel Ozawamik (language specialist) and Angus Pontiac (aged ninety-two) suggest that there are two interpretations to the name "Obwandiac," the first being *"The Man Who Travelled to Many Places"* and the second *"Man Stopping at Different Places."* Obwandiac was buried on *Apple Island*, Michigan. He was Ojibway-Ota'wa-Anishinabe of the nigig doodem (*Otter clan*).

2 Tecumtha (*He Walked Across*) was initially named Sha-Wa-Lung (*Southern Star Falling*) because of a star that fell across the southern sky when he was born. During the Treaty of Greenville negotiations in 1795, he was given the name *"He Walked Across"* after he "walked across" the line drawn in the sand by Anthony Wayne. It was during these negotiations that Tecumtha was raised to a leadership position within the Shawnee-Anishinabe nation. Tecumtha was Shawnee-Anishinabe of the mizhibizhi doodem (*Black Panther clan*). Tecumtha himself cannot be understood without specific reference to Obwandiac.

3 Shingwauk/Shingwaukonse (*The White Pine, Boss of All the Trees*) was also known as Sah-kah-odjew-wahg-sah (*Sun Rising over the Mountain*) to acknowledge his relationship with the sun, which conveyed the power of the sun and sunrise to him. As a Wabanowiwin medicine person, he

was able to regulate the natural order on earth, fertility and the reincarnation of souls by studying the stars, moon and sun. The names "Shingwauk" and "Shingwaukonse" were used interchangeably; he was called Shingwauk from noon to early evening and Shingwaukonse from early evening to sunset to acknowledge the sun's waning power. Shingwauk was Ojibway-Anishinabe of the ah-ji-jahk doodem (*Crane clan*).

4 *how we use our way of doing, thinking, ceremony and spirituality to find answers (methodology)*

5 John Borrows, "Ground Rules: Indigenous Treaties in Canada and New Zealand," *New Zealand Universities Law Review* 22, 2 (2006): 188–212.

6 Kaswentha (*Two Row Wampum*) is a Mohawk-Anishinabe term for the 1613 Tawagonshi Treaty between the Haudenosaunee-Anishinabe confederacy and the Dutch.

7 "Prayer Sticks ... a sacred place to the anishinabeg for many centuries and ... the historical gathering place for all the Grand Sacred Fire Councils." (Pine Shomin [Mack-a-day Ming-giss-was], *The Sacred Fire of the Odawa* [A-shig-a-ning Mi-shi-ka Mi-nis-sing: Odawa Anishinaaybeg Tchingabeng Min-is-sing, 1990], 7.)

8 "Land that has everything: rivers, hills, mountains, swamps, hardwoods." (Ibid., 7.)

9 *written talks and pictographs that included the wampum belts and birchbark scrolls*

10 Could be used and written on birchbark scrolls to help with memory, such as in the singing of Midewiwin songs, or as a heraldic device to help identify one's clan. It could also be shared in the renderings of a medicine person's visionary experiences.

11 *how we came to think a certain way about our reality (epistemology)*

12 *way of being and traditions (ontology)*

13 The o-dah-bah-ji-gahn explores the contemporary use of Ojibway-Anishinabe i-zhi-chi-gay-win (*way of doing things*) and the *indian ways* (*ceremony, spirituality and thought*) – thinking, knowing and doing to find answers.

14 Blood memory is the centre of Anishinabe strength. It is the thread that ties us to our families, the earth and our spirit.

15 Gerald Vizenor, *The Everlasting Sky: Voices of the Anishinabe People* (St. Paul, MN: Minnesota Historical Society Press, 2000), 10–13.

16 Ibid.

17 Mi-a-mi-Anishinabeg

18 Dakota, Lakota and Nakota-Anishinabeg

19 Shomin, *Sacred Fire* 56–57.

20 manitou gii-zhis (*moon of the spirits*) – *January*; na-may-bi-ni gii-zhis (*moon of the suckers*) – *February*; o-na-ba-ni gii-zhis – (*moon of the snow-*

crust – the sun covers the top of the snow with a firm crust, making it a good
time to travel) – *March*; boo-poo-ga-may gii-zhis (*moon for the breaking of*
snowshoes because the snow disappears and the snowshoes are often broken),
gemaa ish-ki-ga-mi-zi-ge-gii-zhis (*boiling sap moon*), mii o' a-pii ish-ki-ga-
mi-zi-ged aw Anishinabeg (*this is when the Anishinabeg boil maple syrup*) –
April; na-may-bi-nay gii-zhis (*sucker moon*), zaa-gi-bah-gah gii-zhis
(*flower budding moon*), mii o'apii zaa-gi-ba-gaa gii-zhis (*this is when the*
leaves begin to bud) – *May*; ode' mi-ni-gii-zhis (*strawberry moon*), mii o'apii
gii-zhi-ging ode'i-mi-nan (*this is when the strawberry begins to ripen*) –
June; aa-bi-ta-nii-bi-no-gii-zhis (*mid-summer moon* or *raspberry moon*),
mii o' a-pii-aa-bi-ta-wi-se-seg nii-bin (*the middle of summer*) – *July*; miin
gii-zhis (*moon of the bilberries or whortleberry*), gemaa a-noo-mi-ni-ke gii-
zhis (*ricing moon*), mii o'pii ma-noo-mi-ni-ked a'aw anishinabeg (*this is*
when we pick rice) – *August*; waa-te-ba-gaa gii-zhis (*leaves turning colour*
moon), mii o'pii waa-te-ba-gaag (*this is when the leaves start to turn colour*)
– *September*; b' naa-kwii gii-zhiz (*falling leaves moon*), mii o'pii bi-naa-
kwe-wad a-nii-bi-shan (*this is when the leaves fall*) – *October*; gash-ka-di-no
gii-zhis (*freezing moon*) – *November*; manitou gii-zhoonhs (*moon of the*
little spirits) – *December*.

21 Over the last several years, I've had the opportunity to speak to
Bawdwaywidun at ceremonial, political, spiritual and environmental
gatherings throughout Canada and the United States regarding
Obwandiac, Tecumtha, Shingwauk and the N'swi-ish-ko-day-kawn
Anishinabeg O'dish-ko-day-kawn, the American Indian Movement and
many other issues. I draw from these talks throughout *Our Hearts Are as*
One Fire.

22 Joseph Couture, "The Role of Elders: Emergent Issues," in *Visions of the*
Heart: Canadian Aboriginal Issues, ed. Olive Dickason and David Long
(Toronto: Harcourt Brace, 1996), 12–16.

23 Ibid.

24 Shomin, *Sacred Fire*, 56–57.

CHAPTER 1 | GAH-O-MAH-MAH-WAHN-DAH-WI-ZID GAH-KI-NAH-GAY-GOO JI-GI-KAYN-DAH-SO AKI

1 My mom and dad took pride in being born in Sagkeeng territory.
My dad would often tell me that he was not *Canadian* and was darned
proud of this. To some extent he was right; indians were not given the
right to vote until 1961.

2 Anishinabeg generally don't make the distinction between generations
of grandparents and grandchildren. Great-grandchildren are recognized
simply as grandchildren, great-grandfathers as mishomis (*grandfather*),
and great-grandmothers as kokomis (*grandmother*).

3 ah-ji-jahk (*crane*), mahng (*loon*), gi-goon (*fish*), mu-kwa (*bear*), wa-bi-zha-shi (*marten*), wa-wa-shesh-she (*deer*) *and* be-nays (*bird*) (Bawdwaywidun Banaise)

4 *Land That Has Everything: Rivers, Hills, Mountains, Swamps, Hardwoods; present-day Michigan*

5 Shomin, *Sacred Fire*, 51.

6 The first time I heard this term was during a lecture by Dr. Rose Cameron, an Ojibway-Anishinabe kwe (*woman*) from Treaty 3 territory.

7 Darrell, along with members of the Shingwauk/Pine family, were leading advocates for the creation of Shingwauk Kinoomage Gamig, an Ojibway-Anishinabe–focused post-secondary institution in the ancestral territory of Shingwauk at Ketegaunseebee. Despite institutional, government and bureaucratic challenges, Darrell and the Shingwauk/Pine family held firm to the vision of Shingwauk and the kinoomage gamig (*teaching lodge*). Shingwauk's fire still burns brightly in their being, and I respect them for this. Obviously, there have been detractors of Shingwauk Kinoomage Gamig, who've sought to undermine the message with meaningless terms like "indigenization," "diversity" and all those other catchwords that seek to minimize the Ojibway-Anishinabe vision and narrative and imply that non-indians and wannabes, with no roots in or connection with Ojibway, Ota'wa and Ishkodawatomi-Anishinabe communities, somehow know better than us. Meegwetch to Darrell, Doreen, Betty Lou, Morley, Dan Jr., Willard and Lana for holding firm to Shingwauk's vision.

8 Our sacred stories and scrolls describe how the Anishinabeg migrated westward from the great sea and eventually settled around Kitchi Gumi (*Great Lakes*). The James Redsky scroll showed an otter breaking through a sandbar, depicting the start of the migration. There is a spiritual meaning to the journey, which is told to us in the creation of the N'swi-ish-ko-day-kawn Anishinabeg O'dish-ko-day-kawn and the seven stopping places: mo-ning-wun-a-kawn-ning gemaa zha-ga-wa-mi-kahg mooniyaang (*a turtle-shaped island*), wa-yaa-nag ga-kaa-ki-kaa (*great falls/Niagara Falls*), bkejwanong (*Where the Waters Divide; Detroit River*), Manitou Minising (*Manitoulin Island*), ba-wi-ti-gong (*Where the Fish Were Good and Lived Well; Sault Ste. Marie*), Wi-kwe-dong (*Spirit Island; Duluth*) and moningwunaekauning (*Place of the Golden-Breasted Woodpecker; Madeline Island*). (Migration story and spelling of the stopping places as shared by Bawdwaywidun Banaise.)

9 Antonio Gramsci argues that hegemony in postcolonial thought is domination by consent, "the active participation of a dominated group in its own subjugation." I found this most helpful in coming to some understanding of a peoples' acceptance of domination and subjugation. "In

some cases, the dominated group's desire for self-determination will have been replaced by a discursively inculcated notion of a greater good, couched in such terms as 'social stability' and 'economic and cultural achievement.'" (S.D. Moore, *Empire and the Apocalypse: Post-Colonialism and the New Testament* [Sheffield, UK: Sheffield Phoenix Press, 2006], 101.)

10 Nemattenow was a noted spiritual advisor to Opechancanough, one of the main leaders of the Powhatan-Anishinabe Confederacy during the period 1611–22, who came to prominence in the first Anglo-Powhatan-Anishinabe war in 1611.

11 In 1805, Lau-lau-we-see-kau described a vision in which he was on a journey on a path taken by the souls of the dead. He described coming to a fork in the path, where one branched left and the other right. Three houses stood along the wayside of the path he chose. The first two houses had sidetracks that led back to the other path, offering travellers an opportunity to make amends. However, at the most travelled-to third house (eternity), he heard cries of suffering and agony. He decided to go no farther and quickly returned to the fork and took the other path. It was on this path that he foresaw whites being removed spiritually.

12 The question of land was always central to the conflicts between the Anishinabe nations and the state and federal governments.

13 Issued by Pope Alexander VI on May 4, 1493, Inter Caetera divided the world into "*north and west,*" granting sovereignty or a feudal investiture to Portugal and Spain.

14 Surveyor and frontiersman from *Virginia,* whose youngest brother, William, would be leader of the Lewis and Clark expedition.

15 Virginian physician and lawyer.

16 Continental Army officer and frontiersman from Pennsylvania.

17 Wi-a-an-dot (*Somebody Lives There*)

18 Lawyer and general from *Connecticut.*

19 Near present-day Cincinnati, Ohio.

20 Americanism as an ideology is founded on the idea of liberty, egalitarianism, individualism, republicanism democracy and laissez-faire principles.

21 Alexis de Tocqueville, *Democracy in America* (New York: Bantam Classics, 2000).

22 Mi-a-mi (*Downstream People*)

23 St. Clair wanted clear title to the territory, which is why our people suggest that the terms were imposed rather than negotiated. Again, the "chiefs" who signed the treaty had no authority to do so.

24 Benjamin Drake, *Life of Tecumseh and of His Brother the Prophet: With a Historical Sketch of the Shawanoe Indians* (Cincinnati, OH: Anderson, Gates & Wright, 1999), 279.

25 Joel Martin, *Sacred Revolt: The Muskogees' Struggle for a New World* (Boston, MA: Beacon Press, 1993), 8.

CHAPTER 2 | OBWANDIAC

1 Willie Dunn, "Pontiac," *The Pacific*, Trinkont, 1980.
2 *the essence of the Ojibway-Anishinabe understanding of humanity – its heart and vision*
3 Anishinabeg see this misrepresentation of history as gwayakotam (*a way to find out the truth*).
4 On May 7, 1763, the siege of Fort Detroit began; on May 16, Fort Sandusky (Ohio) fell; on May 25, Fort St. Joseph (Ontario) was taken; on May 27, Fort Miami (Michigan) surrendered; on June 1, Fort Ouatanon (Indiana) was captured; on June 4, Fort Michilimackinac (Michigan) raised the white flag; on June 15, Fort Presque Isle (Pennsylvania) laid down its arms; on June 18, Fort Le Boeuf (Pennsylvania) gave way to Anishinabe forces; on June 20, Fort Venango surrendered; on June 21, L'Arbre Croche (Michigan) and Sault Ste. Marie (Michigan and Ontario) were attacked by Ota'wa-Anishinabe forces; on June 24, the British failed in their attack on Obwandiac's encampment; and on September 14, the British were soundly defeated at Devil's Hole (Fort Niagara).
5 Randolph G. Adams, *Dictionary of American Biography* (New York: Charles Scribner's Sons, 1935).
6 Richard Middleton, *Pontiac's War: Its Causes, Course, and Consequences* (London: Routledge Taylor and Francis Group, 2007).
7 Middleton, *Pontiac's War*, 5.
8 All of humankind were entitled to the same rights of survival, which were acknowledged in ceremony, in the memory of the peoples and in history (What happened in the past? What would be the future relationship and behaviour to each other?). It was also acknowledged that each would refer to the other as family, that the uncle was not a dominating figure and that the brother was obligated to help the other. And that social unity was acknowledged during the practice of gift-giving.
9 Anishinabe speakers rarely spoke without lengths of wampum, either strings or belts or both. Speakers would sometimes open councils by offering wampum strings to quiet anger and open the hearts of the listeners.
10 *from the earth – our sustenance, our sovereignty*
11 A memorial and monument to those former allies of the Ojibway, Ota'wa and Ishkodawatomi-Anishinabeg who once occupied the lands along the straits that connect Lake Huron and Lake Michigan.

12 John Borrows sees this as one of the more important elements of middle ground diplomacy where political, economic and military alliances are established using Ojibway, Ota'wa and Ishkodawatomi-Anishinabe ideas, protocols and ceremonies.

13 Neolin promised to do as he was told and returned silently to his village, speaking to no one until he had presented to *"the chief"* the prayer and the laws that had been entrusted to his care by the *Master of Life* (Gitchi Manitou). In response to a subsequent vision, Neolin drew on a piece of deerskin parchment, about fifteen or eighteen inches square, a map of the soul's progress in this world and the next. This map he called *The Great Book of Writing.* (Anthony F.C. Wallace, *Death and Rebirth of the Seneca* [New York: Alfred A. Knopf, 1970].)

14 All remaining French holdings, including Detroit, would be transferred to British possession, completing Britain's conquest of New France.

15 The Lunaapewa-Anishinabe delegation who brought a war belt asking for support to avenge their defeat at Kittaning (Pennsylvania) in 1756.

16 George Copway, *The Traditional History and Character Sketches of the Ojibway Nation* (Boston: Benjamin B. Mussy and Co., 1851; Honolulu, HI: University Press of the Pacific, 2002), 135: "These beads and shells were colored, and each had a meaning, according to its place on the string. Black indicated war or death – White, peace and prosperity – Red, the heart of the enemy would represent – Partial white or red, or both intermixed, the beginning of peace or the commencement of war."

17 This included Ojibway, Ota'wa, Ishkodawatomi, Wendat-Anishinabe forces led by Ninivois (Ishkodawatomi-Anishinabe) and Takay (Wendat-Anishinabe).

18 Men-neh-weh-na was an influential Ojibway-Anishinabe leader (1710–1770) from Mackinac Island who was an ardent supporter of Obwandiac during the resistance.

19 Henri Bouquet (June 25, 1763).

20 Jeffery Amherst to William Johnson, (July 9, 1763).

21 Henri Bouquet to Jeffery Amherst (June 29, 1763; July 13, 1763); Jeffery Amherst to Henri Bouquet (July 16, 1763).

22 Middleton, *Pontiac's War*, 30.

23 This is my personal understanding and translation of the term "Royal Proclamation."

24 Michael Angel, *Preserving the Sacred: Historical Perspectives on the Ojibwa Midewiwin* (Winnipeg, MB: University of Manitoba Press, 2002), 31–32.

25 Alexander Henry, *Alexander Henry's Travels and Adventures (1760–1776)* (Chicago: R.R. Donnelley & Sons, 1921).

26 Ibid., 31–32.

27 Ibid., 163.

28 Ibid., 164.

29 George Croghan to William Johnson (October 1765).

30 A twenty-four nations wampum belt was made, showing twenty-four people (British, Wendat, Menominee, Algonquin, Nippising, Ojibway, Mississauga and Haudenosaunee-Anishinabeg) holding hands from a rock to a ship.

31 This would see the Iroquois-Anishinabeg surrender land between the Appalachian Divide and the Ohio River.

CHAPTER 3 | TECUMTHA

1 In the events leading up to and during the War of 1812, Me-ne-wau-laa-koo-see's husband, Wah-si-ke-ga-bow (*Stands Firm*), would be a leading supporter of her brothers.

2 Sau-coth-caw was one of the signatories to the treaty with the Shawnees in 1831 at Wapaghkonnetta (Ohio).

3 Patricia and Norman shared a story of Tecumtha reprimanding a Shawnee-Anishinabe man for beating his wife because his mother and sister taught him that Shawnee-Anishinabe men were expected to treat their wives and partners like they would their mothers and sisters.

4 Colonel William Stanley Hatch, *A Chapter of the History of the War of 1812 in the Northwest* (1872), chapter 10.

5 Rachel Buff, "Tecumseh and Tenskwatawa: Myth, Historiography and Popular Memory," *Historical Reflections* 21, 2 (1995): 289.

6 Thomas Heuglin, *Exploring Concepts of Treaty Federalism: A Comparative Perspective* (Don Mills, ON: Oxford University Press, 1993), 19.

7 Lord Dunmore (born John Murray) was the last colonial governor of Virginia.

8 St. Clair suffered a loss of more than six hundred soldiers.

9 Buff, "Tecumseh and Tenskwatawa," 289.

10 The Northwest Territory (Ohio, Indiana, Illinois, Michigan, Wisconsin, *Minnesota*) was created on July 13, 1787, by the Congress of the Confederation of the United States through the Northwest Ordinance.

11 Three million acres in Indiana and Illinois were transferred to American control.

12 "*You must treaty with the whole, not with just part of the anishinaaybeg.*" (Shomin, *Sacred Fire*, 69.)

13 Ishkodawatomi-Anishinabe: Ke-tap-e-kon-nong (*Town* or *Place*)

14 People try to make sense of a leader's style and impact, and whether he/she transcends expectations and results. But leadership and the responsibilities that go with it are filled with ambiguity, because leadership means so many different things to different people.

15 This was in contrast to the "begging bowl" that the United States was intent on sharing with the Anishinabe nations through treaties that served a portion of limited independence.

16 "Gah-ween o-ni-zhi-shi-toon mazina'igan, ga-shi-to-what kitchi moo-ka-mahn a-nin ... " (Patricia and Norman Shawnoo in conversation, 2012.)

17 Patricia and Norman Shawnoo, 2012. If the Twelve Fires present were not the whole (there should have been sixteen Anishinabe fires), how can any alleged treaty made with only Two Fires (Ojibway and Ota'wa-anishinabeg) constitute a whole and be valid?

18 Kin-na gi mood-na-wa-ada akim-na. "*They stole our land. And they shake your hand, and pat you on the back and say you are a good man.*" (Little Elk; Headman, Isabella Reservation, Mount Pleasant)

19 Patricia and Norman Shawnoo, 2012.

20 Schoolcraft was an American geographer and ethnologist, husband of Jane Johnston Schoolcraft, the first known Ojibway-Anishinabe literary writer, and granddaughter of Waubojeeg, an Ojibway-Anishinabe civil leader.

21 Shoman, *Sacred Fire,* 69.

22 Buff, "Tecumseh and Tenskwatawa," 297.

23 "You wish to prevent the Indians to do as we wish them to unite and let them consider their land as the common property of the whole and we do not accept your invitation to visit the President." (Tecumtha, August 20, 1807, as related by Patricia and Norman Shawnoo, 2012.)

24 The United States has a specific world mission of spreading liberty and democracy. This mission has its roots in the American Revolution, from which America emerged as the first new nation other than Iceland to become independent.

25 The Treaty of Fort Wayne was signed on September 30, 1809, surrendering 3 million acres of southern Indiana.

26 William H. Bergmann, *Commerce and Arms: The Federal Government, Native Americans, and the Economy of the Old Northwest, 1783–1807* (Cincinnati, OH: University of Cincinnati Press, 2005), 234.

27 Buff, "Tecumseh and Tenskwatawa."

28 Ibid., 289.

29 The Treaty of Paris (February 10, 1763), for example, promised the British the right to retain territory at Oswego (New York), Niagara (New York), Detroit (Michigan) and Michilimackinac (Michigan) for approximately thirteen years.

30 It's estimated that thirteen thousand men fought on the side of the British.

31 *Code of Handsome Lake*

32 Neal Salisbury describes Anishinabe nations as using "wampum words to cement social and political relations both among the First Nations and with outside allies." (Neal Salisbury, "Toward the Covenant Chain: Iroquois and Southern New England Algonquins, 1637–1684," in Daniel K. Richter and James H. Merrell, eds., *Beyond the Covenant Chain: The Iroquois and Their Neighbors in Indian North America, 1600–1800*, University Park: Pensylvania State University Press, 1987), chapter 4.

33 *Good Word*

34 Anishinabeg understood that colonization and the inherent racism that it engendered would lead to poverty and hopelessness. Obwandiac, Tecumtha, Shingwauk and like-minded leaders wanted to make certain that Anishinabe societies would avoid becoming the roadkill of American policy.

35 Mack-e-tay-be-nessy Chief, *History of the Ottawa and Chippewa Indians of Michigan: A Grammar of Their Language and Personal and Family History of the Author* (Ypsilanti, MI: Ypsilantian Job Printing House, 1887; Cambridge, MA: Harvard University Press, 2007), 29.

36 The War of 1812 officially ended with the Treaty of Ghent in 1814. Although the war itself was an important event in the history of Canada, I have made a conscious effort to avoid discussing it directly because my purpose is to share an Anishinabe-focused narrative. Historians and academics alike often misinterpret Anishinabe participation in the War of 1812; many believe that Tecumtha and Shingwauk intervened in this war simply to support the British and abide by their wishes.

CHAPTER 4 | SHINGWAUK

1 The British and Anishinabe joint forces experienced serious casualties during this period in the war, beginning with the death of General Isaac Brock, who was killed on October 13, 1812, at the Battle of Queenston Heights (Ontario).

2 Thor and Julie Conway, *Spirits on Stone: The Agawa Pictographs* (San Luis Obispo, CA: Heritage Discoveries, 1990), 73.

3 Willie Ermine, "Aboriginal Epistemology," in *First Nations Education in Canada: The Circle Unfolds*, ed. Marie Battiste and Jean Barmann (Vancouver: UBC Press, 1995), 89.

4 What a young man sees and experiences during these dreams and fasts is accepted by him as a truth, and it becomes a principle to guide his life. He relies on these dreams and visions. If he has been gifted during his fasts, the people will come to believe that he has the ability to look into the future. The young person will often try his or her power in secret, with only one oshkabewis, who is there to help and bear witness. As he/she continues, he/she will describe and record the dreams by

symbols on birchbark or other material until an entire winter passes as he/she explores the nature of dreams and revelations.

5 The 1850 Robinson Huron and Superior treaties established a new template for treaty negotiations, which included an obligation on the part of the Crown to provide for education, health and shelter in exchange for the sharing of land and allowing for settlement. The previous agreements had included only one-time payments and few lasting obligations. Shingwauk was successful in changing this.

6 Henry R. Schoolcraft, *The American Indians, Their History, Condition and Prospects from Original Notes and Manuscripts* (Rochester, NY: Wanzer, Foot and Co., 1851; Project Gutenberg Ebook of the American Indians, Ebook 39607, 2012), 86.

7 Johann Georg Kohl, *Kitchi-Gami: Life among the Lake Superior Ojibway* (St. Paul, MN: Minnesota Historical Society Press, 1985), 378.

8 The British had fewer than five thousand soldiers in British North America.

9 Robinson-Huron Treaty, 1850.

10 Walter James Hoffman, *The Midē'wiwin or "Grand Medicine Society" of the Ojibwa: Seventh Annual Report of the Bureau of Ethnology to the Secretary of the Smithsonian Institution, 1885–1886* (Washington, DC: Government Printing Office, 1891; Project Gutenberg Ebook, 2006).

11 *Creator* or *Great Mystery*

12 *"As the seasons change, give food to the water spirit; this must be done," the turtle said. "After this, bring your people together and speak to things the community wants to do. These meetings will last for four days, and following this feast and dance," the bear said. "The people will tell you what needs to be done. They will be the stars that guide you," the little people said.*

13 Schoolcraft, *The American Indians*, 36.

14 Ibid.

15 Rainey Gaywish, retired University of Manitoba and Algoma University professor and the recorder of history for the Midewiwin, points out that this is different from the teachings about zeegwun, which brings spring and life to the land. (Rainey Gaywish, *Neegawn I-naw-buh-tay Ayn-nayn-duhmuhn: My Thoughts Flow Forward to the Future* [dissertation, Trent University, 2008], 82.)

16 Conway, *Spirits on Stone*.

17 Leroy Little Bear, "Jagged Worlds Colliding," in *Reclaiming Indigenous Voice and Vision*, ed. Marie Battiste (Vancouver: UBC Press, 2000), 77–85.

18 Waynaboozho is the name used when Nanabush (or Nanabozho, the Anishinabe hero and trickster) is speaking with human relations. Wiiskay-jahk is used when Nanabush is talking with animals, and may-mi' i-nah-ko-ni-gay is used when Nanabush is making spiritual laws.

19 Bacqueville de Potherie describes this battle, in which a force of only fifty Ojibway-Anishinabe men using arrows and tomahawks against muskets easily defeated an armed force of approximately one hundred Iroquois-Anishinabeg who had travelled to Ketegaunseebee. (From Peter S. Schmalz, *The Ojibway of Southern Ontario* [Toronto: University of Toronto Press, 1991] 18–19.)

CHAPTER 5 | N'SWI-ISH-KO-DAY-KAWN ANISHINABEG O'DISH-KO-DAY-KAWN

1 Shomin, *Sacred Fire*, 18–19.
2 Adapted from Harry H. Anderson, ed., "Myths and Legends of Wisconsin Indians," *Milwaukee History* 15, 1 (1992): 2–36.
3 Conquest renders people subject to the legislative powers of the ruling body and terminates the external powers of the sovereignty of that nation.
4 Anthony J. Hall, *The American Empire and the Fourth World: The Bowl with One Spoon* (Montreal and Kingston: McGill-Queen's University Press, 2003), 90.
5 A forty-by-twenty-mile area.
6 Bah-wah-ji-gay-win is a very powerful element in Anishinabe spirituality, as is a-mahn-si-nahm (*I have a vision* or *a spirit comes to me*), which is another level of the dream experience.
7 James A.Clifton, George L. Cornell, and James M. McClurken, *People of the Three Fires: The Ottawa, Potawatomi and Ojibway of Michigan* (Kalamazoo, MI: West Michigan Printing, 1986), 17.
8 Richard White, *The Middle Ground: Indians, Empires and Republics in the Great Lakes Region, 1650–1815* (Cambridge, UK: Cambridge University Press, 1991), 6.
9 Massachusetts, New Hampshire, Delaware, Maryland, Georgia, Connecticut, North and South Carolina, Pennsylvania, Virginia, New Jersey and Connecticut.
10 The French signed the Treaty of Alliance with the colonies in 1778 in case of attack by Britain.
11 John O'Sullivan (columnist and editor), 1845: "Checking the fulfillment of our manifest destiny to overspread the continent allotted by Providence for the free development of our yearly multiplying millions."
12 In Canada, Section 91(24) of the *Constitution Act, 1867* also assigned this responsibility to the Canadian federal government rather than to the provinces.
13 Their territory consisted of present-day northwest and eastern portions of the Lower and Upper Peninsula in Michigan and northwest Minnesota.

14 Shomin, *Sacred Fire*, 19–20

15 George Copway, *The Traditional History and Characteristic Sketches of the Ojibway Nation* (Boston: Benjamin B. Mussy & Co., 1851; Honolulu, HI: University Press of the Pacific, 2002), 21–22.

16 Peter S. Schmalz, *The Ojibway of Southern Ontario* (Toronto: University of Toronto Press, 1991).

17 In 1750, the population of Britain was estimated at 1 million. Despite this relatively large population, the British had a relatively small land base, which made the negotiation of peace treaties and agreements to share the land and resources in North America all the more important.

18 The Foot of the Rapids and SaginawTreaties (Ohio) signed in 1817, the Sault Ste. Marie and L'Arbre Croche (Michigan) treaties signed in 1820 and the Treaty of Chicago signed in 1821.

19 Shomin, *Sacred Fire*, 59–60.

20 Rupert's Land was territory in British North America that was owned by the Hudson's Bay Company (1670–1870).

21 In 1670, King Charles II gave the Hudson's Bay Company the "trading rights" to 7.7 million acres of land draining into Hudson Bay. The Hudson's Bay Company then sold the land to Canada for $1.5 million, and in the spring of 1870, the Canadian Parliament passed the *Manitoba Act*.

22 This legislation appointed indian agents as chairmen of the chief and council, who in turn were authorized to remove (*Indian Act*) chiefs considered unfit to discharge their duties effectively.

CHAPTER 6 | MEEGWETCH BI-ZHIN-DAH-WI-YEG

1 Our beliefs are assumptions that we make about ourselves and others, about how things really are and what we think is true. What is being Ojibway-Anishinabe all about?

2 Values that are about honesty, integrity and transparency.

3 *Johnston v. McIntosh* (1823), *Cherokee Nation v. Georgia* (1831) and *Worcester v. Georgia* (1832).

4 Section 16, *Constitution Act, 1982*. The Assembly of Manitoba Chiefs argued in 1990 and 1992 that the notwithstanding clause gave the provinces too much power and was a threat to our collective treaty rights. We also argued in 1990 and 1992 for inclusion of a non-derogation clause to protect these collective rights, because the notwithstanding clause essentially allows provinces to override sections of the Charter of Rights and make laws that conflict with treaty rights. We argued further that what's good for the goose is good for the gander – that a non-derogation clause be entrenched and that we should also have the power to invoke a notwithstanding clause should our rights be threatened.

5 John Kenneth Galbraith, *The Voice of the Poor: Essays in Economic and Political Persuasion* (Cambridge, MA: Harvard University Press, 1983), 17–18.
6 Demeny voting provides a political voice for children by allowing parents or guardians to vote on their behalf.

WAYEKWAASE | IT IS FINISHED

1 "*looking back to tomorrow through Ojibway eyes with our hearts as one fire was the way forward*"
2 "*Tell these important personal and sacred stories of long-ago. This is important, so don't have doubts, stand strong and remember these leaders well.*"

INDEX

Note: Following usage in this book, Ojibwaymowin terms are used as main headings when possible, with cross-references from the English.

Printed and bound in Canada by Friesens

Set in Eames, Sero, and Baskerville by Artegraphica Design Co.

Copy editor: Merrie-Ellen Wilcox

Proofreader: Kristy Lynn Hankewitz

Indexer: Stephen Ullstrom

Cover designer: George Kirkpatrick